THE TASTE OF AMERICA

THE Taste of AMERICA

COLMAN
ANDREWS

INTRODUCTION

What does America taste like? Like hot dogs, Cincinnati chili, and grass-fed beef. Like Maine lobster, Hawaiian tuna, and soft-shell crab. It has the tang of Ruby Red grapefruit, Chimayo chiles, and pickled okra; the lure of Hershey's Bars, New York cheesecake, and key lime pie; the reassuring starch of granola, grits, and sourdough bread. It shines through even in our staples, in our flour, honey, coffee, and salt.

The flavor of this abundant nation resides in its homegrown specialties and its factory-made treats alike, and in the many foods that we've adopted and adapted from the tables of the world. It's found in pimento cheese and bandage-wrapped Cheddar, apple cider and ginger ale, miso and tortillas and knishes, Coca-Cola and peppermint stick ice cream and whoopie pie. America has not one taste but a panoply of them, an immense multicultural sensory anthology of good things to eat and drink, commercial and artisanal, decadent and virtuous, silly and sublime.

To begin with, America produces some of the finest culinary raw materials imaginable, from fish to fowl to meats both fresh and cured, from fruit to nuts, with glorious grains and vegetables in between. Our craftsmen and -women make sausages, pickles, cheeses, and preserves as good as anybody's; we can justly brag about our homey baked goods and our commercial confectionery alike. Our vivid condiments (ketchup, Tabasco sauce, ranch dressing) have gone international. We invented barbecue potato chips.

The pioneering "New American" chef Larry Forgione once said that when he was a commis in Michel Bourdin's classical French kitchen at the Connaught Hotel in London, he'd watch the wealth of perfect fruits and vegetables arriving every day from France and beyond, and find himself thinking that in a land as vast as ours, with its boundless geographical and climatic diversity, we simply *must* be able to produce a similar range of great ingredients. And of course—as Forgione was one of the first

to demonstrate when he came back to this country and opened his seminal Manhattan restaurant, An American Place—we were, and are.

It isn't that we had never before known, as a nation, how wonderful our provender was; it's that somehow, somewhere along the way, we had unaccountably forgotten what a wealth we had in that regard. Some hint of the richness and diversity of the American table more than a century ago, is suggested by Charles Ranhofer's classic cookbook *The Epicurean*, published in 1894. The longtime chef at the celebrated Delmonico's in Manhattan (and the creator of lobster Newberg), Ranhofer listed as available products in New York City some forty-six varieties of fish, including both Kennebec and Oregon salmon and the jauntily named lafayette, also known as chub; forty-one kinds of hooved and feathered game, from antelope to woodcock; and more than fifty different vegetables, among them cardoons, celeriac, hops, oyster plant (salsify), girolle and morel mushrooms, and corn salad (mâche).

Fifteen years before *The Epicurean* appeared, that most American of writers (and one of Ranhofer's regular customers), Samuel Langhorne Clemens, better known as Mark Twain, undertook a journey through parts of Germany, Switzerland, France, and Italy. Twain was serious about the pleasures of gastronomy ("I have a neat talent in matters pertaining to nourishment"), but judging from his account of the trip, published a year later as *A Tramp Abroad*, he was not impressed by what the European larder had to offer. "A man accustomed to American food and American domestic cookery," Twain proposed, "would not starve to death suddenly in Europe; but I think he would gradually waste away, and eventually die." The typical *table d'hôte* menu, he said, was apt to include soup without character, roast mutton or beef without flavor, "insipid lentils, or string-beans, or indifferent asparagus," roast chicken "as tasteless as paper," and "decayed" strawberries or cherries.

What Twain pined for instead was a fantastical groaning board laden with, well, the taste of America—with the simple foods he'd enjoyed throughout his life, in his peregrinations across the country from Missouri to Louisiana, California to New England. He'd gone so many months in Europe without a decent meal, he claimed, that he planned to send the menu for what he called "a modest, private affair … [with] a few dishes" back to the States on the steamer before his, so that his dream meal would be awaiting him when he returned. Then he proceeded to list more than eighty specific foods, both finished dishes and raw materials, often with their place of origin attached.

This bill of fare is a fascinating compendium of American foodstuffs and prepared dishes. (Journalist and novelist Andrew Beahrs has written a terrific book inspired by the list, *Twain's Feast: Searching for America's Lost Foods in the Footsteps of Samuel Clemens*.) It starts with radishes and ends with "All sorts of American pastry." In between are soups and breads, fish from both fresh water and the sea (mostly the former), birds both wild and raised, a bit of meat (not very much), a cornucopia of vegetables (boiled onions, turnips, squash, sweet potatoes, lettuce, succotash, celery, and more), and five kinds of pie—as well as "American coffee, with real cream."

Twain qualifies many of his choices with a place of origin: Philadelphia terrapin soup, Connecticut shad, black bass from the Mississippi, prairie hens from Illinois, bacon and beans from Boston. Although the conceit of appending the name of a farm or artisanal producer to menu offerings is a comparatively recent one, we have long identified certain foodstuffs with specific places of origin ourselves. In the restaurants of my childhood, the duckling was always from Long Island, the whitefish from Lake Superior, the lamb from Colorado. A menu from Charlie's Cafe Exceptionale in Minneapolis, from about 1958, specifies Wisconsin baby frog legs, Minnesota walleyed pike, Florida pompano *en papillote*, jumbo Gulf of California shrimp, genuine Cape (as in Cape Cod) scallops, and jumbo Louisiana frog legs. That kind of thing was once typical.

In assembling the present catalogue of American foods (and a few drinks), I have sometimes identified their home state or city in the heading, when that term is essential to their identity (Cincinnati chili, Florida stone crabs). In other cases, the source may not be specified initially, but there is no question what it is: Turkey Joints are made in Rome, New York, and nowhere else; ponce comes from Cajun country. For some foods, though, I've strayed across a state border or two (or more), following my palate. I found my favorite Mexican-style chorizo, for instance, not in Texas or California, but in Chicago; the barbecue sauce I ended up preferring doesn't hail from Kansas City or the Deep South, but rather from Wyoming. For the purposes of this book, at least, I'm not a locavore—or rather I *am* a locavore, but one whose locus stretches from Alaska to Florida, Washington to Maine. When appropriate, in other words, I let flavor trump geography.

Speaking of geography: whenever possible, I've supplied mail-order sources for the foods and drinks included here (see pages 274–281). In some cases, these aren't necessary—the items in question (Coca-Cola and Snickers, for instance) are sold everywhere. In other cases, they are perishable and/or hyper-local, and so best purchased at seasonal farmers' markets (or grown at home).

Unlike Mark Twain, in choosing foods to include on my own roster of edible Americana, I haven't thought in terms of an imagined meal. My guiding principle wasn't so much "What do I want to eat?" as "What would I want *you* to eat?"—whether you are a visitor with an appetite for real American grub, or a citizen or resident of these United States interested in expanding your culinary horizons without crossing our frontiers.

It is hardly necessary to say, I hope, that this selection of comestibles is a highly personal one, no doubt erratic and illogical if not sometimes downright eccentric. I have included many emblematic American foodstuffs, the kinds of thing that, regardless of their origins, no book purporting to represent the best of what we eat could possibly ignore (the aforementioned Maine lobster, for instance, but also bratwurst and bialys). Also included on the list, though, are products that are hardly ours exclusively but that figure in our diet (at least some of our diets), and that we grow or raise or make very well here—

among them mozzarella and chèvre, canned tuna, free-range chicken, asparagus, bacon, peaches, tea, mayonnaise, and mustard.

I've identified local bakery specialties, but also commercial snack foods and condiments; I've put handmade chocolates in the inventory, and machine-made candy bars as well. If there are good and easily obtainable foods raised in an organic and sustainable way by small producers, I've often favored those, but I'm not an organic-and-artisanal snob, and if I were, and let my feelings guide my choices, I'd be presenting a skewed picture of the way we really eat.

Some readers may quarrel with my inclusion of "junk food" and sugary soft drinks, but I have chosen a few of these that are so clearly representative of the way we eat and drink as to be almost heraldic. Others may note that I have elected certain canned goods (tomatoes, collard greens, chili); these have a story, and represent aspects of our regimen, for better or for worse. Preserved products (mostly smoked or pickled) aside, I have included very few finished foods, but there are certainly some, mostly baked goods such as (frozen) biscuits and red velvet cake. Here is where my illogicality shows itself most plainly. Why red velvet cake and not, say, pecan pie? Why pasties and not empanadas? I have no good answer, except to say that I chose whatever I thought most vividly expressed the essence of the way we eat.

Inevitably, I suppose, I've included several foods that Mark Twain put on his all-American menu, among them maple syrup, Blue Point oysters, hominy, "catsup," soft-shell crabs, and wild turkey. I have also, of course, included a good many other things that Twain likely wouldn't recognize, and might well dismiss with the same scorn he heaped upon European strawberries and soup. What would this man of neat gastronomic talent have made of Fritos, Snickers, or Grape-Nuts?

One very heartening phenomenon I encountered in choosing entries for this book was that of continuity: I was frankly surprised, pleasantly, by how many of the farms or other producers whose products I identify are family operations, going back three or four generations and occasionally more. In some cases, older enterprises have changed hands, but their original proprietors have sold them not to big corporations but to other farmers or businessmen with compatible philosophies. (A proviso: small and/or family-owned companies do sometimes go out of business quietly and quickly; the sources given in these pages are up-to-date at the time of publication, but their longevity is not guaranteed.) Of course, there are cases of companies that started small and are now owned by multinational concerns—not too many of those in these pages, but a few. This isn't necessarily a bad thing: Laura Chenel's goat cheese is still superb, even though she sold her original operation to a big French dairy producer; Hidden Valley Ranch Dressing, now owned by a branch of the Clorox Company, contains ingredients that the man who invented it wouldn't recognize, but it has become an American classic anyway.

This brings me neatly back to my original question: What does America taste like? It tastes like all the foods and drinks I've found a place for in this book, and many, many more besides. It tastes like whatever we want it to taste like. That's why it's America.

SNACKS

BARBECUE POTATO CHIPS

Potato chips (their British name, crisps, is more apposite) were probably first made by French or English chefs in the early nineteenth century. The commonly told story, though, attributes their invention to one George Crum, a chef of American Indian and African-American descent, who worked at Moon's Lake House in Saratoga Springs, New York. According to the tale, in 1853, when a customer (some say it was railroad tycoon Cornelius Vanderbilt) complained that his fried potatoes were too thick and soggy, Crum—either trying to satisfy the patron or teach him a lesson—sliced the next batch extra-thin. They turned out to be delicious, and Crum capitalized on his success, opening his own place at which the potatoes, dubbed Saratoga chips, were featured. Commercial potato chips, sold in barrels or tins, first reached the marketplace around 1910 (several companies claim to have pioneered them). In 1926, a California attorney turned entrepreneur named Laura Scudder started a food company to produce the chips, and was the first to package them in waxed bags (she was also, incidentally, the first food purveyor of any kind to put freshness dates on her products).

The idea of adding flavorings other than salt to potato chips comes from Ireland, where, in the 1950s, one Joe "Spud" Murphy developed methods for flavoring his Tayto brand chips with cheese and onion and with vinegar. Other potato chip makers followed suit, and chips are sold today all over the world in a bewildering variety of flavors—among them paprika, mint, coriander, Caesar salad, ranch dressing, dill pickle, fruit chutney, various kinds of cheese, beer, roast chicken, doner kebab, shashlik, crab, caviar, sauce Bolognese, and such fanciful elaborations as meat pie and ketchup, turkey and bacon, Stilton and cranberry, and roast beef with Yorkshire pudding.

I've tasted a lot of these, and while they can occasionally be quite pleasant (Cheddar flavoring, for instance, works nicely), many of them taste unsurprisingly artificial, with only the faintest resemblance to whatever they're supposed to evoke. I have a serious weakness, though, for "barbecue" flavored potato chips. Of course, barbecue isn't a flavor, it's a cooking technique—but the term obviously refers to the spicy tomato-based sauces often slathered on barbecued meats (see page 234). There are dozens of brands of barbecue chips on the market today—including some under the Laura Scudder label—and I've probably tasted most of them. The best of the bunch, to me, are Kettle Backyard Barbeque chips. They're comparatively thick, peppery, not too salty, and a little sweet, with a good balance of spices (the chile burn is slight but noticeable); best of all, they actually taste like potatoes.

BLACK WALNUTS

I lived for several years in a rented house in Venice, California—the part of Venice that looks more like middle-class suburbia than boardwalk circus, where lawn mowers are more prevalent than rollerblades—and in the backyard was a magnificent old tree with gnarled limbs and dense green foliage. I had no idea what it was until an English friend came over for an al fresco dinner one summer evening and exclaimed, "What a beautiful walnut!" Much of the rest of our conversation consisted of him describing to me various methods of pickling the walnuts while they were still green, making walnut wine, and even distilling walnut ratafia.

I never got around to doing any of that, but I did enjoy eating the walnuts when they started dropping from the tree, and I learned that this part of Venice had once been a sprawl of walnut groves. The trees in question were the native American black walnut (*Juglans nigra*), which hails from the Eastern Seaboard, where it grows wild from southern Ontario down to northern Florida and west as far as the middle of Texas. (My English friend knew so much about it because the tree was recognized as beautiful and fecund and was transplanted across the Atlantic to Britain and Europe as early as the mid-seventeenth century.)

About two-thirds of the wild black walnut harvest today comes from Missouri, and the folks who virtually own the walnut trade there are the proprietors of Hammons Products, from Stockton, in the southwestern part of the state. The company got its start in 1946, when grocer Ralph Hammons noticed how fast sacks of black walnuts were selling. He bought himself a cracking machine and began contracting with locals to gather the nuts. Today, Brian Hammons, Ralph's grandson, collects nuts from hulling stations in sixteen states and supervises their cracking, sorting, packaging, and shipping.

The meat of black walnuts has a rich flavor, much more vivid than that of English walnuts, and is firm and toothsome. It's pretty much the nut you want in fudge, chocolate cake, ice cream, and other confections, but it's also good in salads and not at all bad as a simple snack, lightly salted. Hammons doesn't sell by mail order, but their black walnuts are widely available—for instance, at that little neighborhood grocery store called Walmart.

BOILED PEANUTS

Boiled peanuts are one of those traditional foods from the American South—pimento cheese (see page 65) is another—that Northerners usually just don't understand. Ballpark peanuts in the shell, yes; salted peanuts out of the shell, sure. But why would anybody boil the things? Well, because they get soft and savory (and incidentally their antioxidant properties increase). And because it's tradition.

The practice seems to have started in states like North and South Carolina, Georgia, and Mississippi in the late eighteenth or early nineteenth century. Peanuts, known locally as "goober peas" (they are in fact legumes, more closely related to peas than to tree nuts), were an important food crop, originally from South America but grown in Africa since the 1500s and almost certainly brought to North America by slaves. After the peanut harvest in those Southern states, field workers—possibly adapting an African tradition—would boil in salty water, still in the shell, any that weren't fully ripened, then sit around and eat them. A peanut boil was thus a social occasion, as much about the chance to relax and talk as it was about eating.

In fact, fully ripened peanuts don't boil well. The raw, or green, ones—which are full-sized but haven't yet dehydrated into that familiar peanut-beige hue—are essential for the process, and Valencia peanuts, smaller than the plump Virginias most often packed in shelled, salted form, are best. Some boiled peanut lovers these days like to season the water not just with salt but with cayenne, black pepper, beer, and even salt pork or ham hocks.

Matt and Ted Lee, brothers from Charleston, South Carolina, loved boiled peanuts so much that when they left home to go to college in the Northeast, they'd have them shipped up—and then eventually had the idea of publishing a catalogue offering them, along with other Southern delicacies hard to locate in Yankee country. The original Lee Bros. Boiled Peanuts Catalogue, as it was called—now a collector's item—was a surprise hit, and the Lees parlayed that early success into what has become a stellar career as food writers in New York City, complete with cookbooks, articles in the *New York Times* and elsewhere, and programs of lectures and demonstrations throughout the country. They still sell boiled peanuts, though, made in small batches to their specifications, and, as the brothers like to say, they are "guaranteed to turn any party into a cultural event."

CHEESE CRACKERS

The Center Serving Persons with Mental Retardation doesn't exactly sound like a place that would produce delicious specialty food products, but the Center's Willow River Farms, on the Brazos River in San Felipe, Texas, just west of Houston, does exactly that. A 300-acre (120-hectare) property with a 50-acre (20-hectare) organic farm, Willow River offers "rural, family style" living "for adults with developmental disabilities and related conditions." It also hosts a thriving bakery and a community of artisans drawn from its population.

To raise money, residents of the farm started baking holiday fruitcakes for local sale under the direction of Alicia Lee, a volunteer whose son lives at the facility. Lee had worked for Barbara Bush when she was First Lady, and Bush apparently suggested that Willow River add gingersnaps to their portfolio. The first ones were produced in 1998, and were a great success. They're very good gingersnaps, with a real bite, unlike many commercial versions of the cookie. Even better, though, are a newer addition to the line, "cheesesnaps." These are small, buttery, irregularly shaped bites with a nice sharp Cheddar flavor, a bit of spice, and—this is Texas, after all—flecks of pecan throughout. Cheesesnaps, like the farm's gingersnaps and fruitcakes, come in tins decorated with handmade paper ornaments, with all work done by Willow River residents. The cheesesnaps are delicious; the circumstances under which they are produced make buying them more satisfying still.

CHEESE STRAWS

Hosting a gathering without their cheese straws, the folks at McEntyre's Bakery of Smyrna, Georgia, like to say, "is considered a social faux pas in some parts of the Deep South." Well, maybe so. And even if that's an exaggeration, it can't be denied that these crunchy, tangy, Cheddary, cayenne-kissed batons of dough would add a lot to the party. Cheese straws are often made from puff pastry dough, which is fine, but these are solid and dense, more like shortbread than flaky pastry in texture. They also have what wine-tasters call a long finish: Their savory cheese flavor lingers glowingly, at least until it's washed down by another swig of Jack and Coke.

The roots of McEntyre's Bakery date back to the late 1940s, when Howard McEntyre, Sr., his wife, and their three sons opened the Smyrna Bakery in the town of the same name, just northwest of Atlanta. It closed in 1954, but five years later, one son, Howard Jr., opened McEntyre's Bakery in the same town. Howard Jr.'s son, Steve, now runs the operation with his two sons, Ryan and Brandon. In addition to cheese straws, a traditional Southern snack, the bakery also makes a wide assortment of pies, cakes, pastries, and breads, sometimes using equipment dating back to the 1950s on the "if it ain't broke, don't fix it" principle. The key to great baking, says Steve McEntyre, isn't so much advanced equipment as it is good ingredients and a high degree of care put into "making a product as if it were for your own family."

CORN CHIPS

Yes, they're "junk food," salty and high in calories, and there probably aren't any good excuses for eating a whole lot of them at one sitting, but Fritos are an American original (however Mexican-inspired they may be), and—almost alone among such products— they contain no preservatives other than that salt. In fact, their ingredient list is a marvel among packaged food products in general: whole corn, corn oil, salt. And that corn, incidentally, does not include anything genetically modified.

Fritos were the invention of Elmer Doolin, who ran the Highland Park Confectionery in San Antonio in the 1930s. The creation myth has it that one day, either at a lunch counter or in a gas station shop, he encountered bags of little chips made from fried extruded masa (dough made from hominy, see page 196, the basis for corn tortillas). He liked them so much that he tracked down their maker, a local Mexican man, who described them as *fritos*, meaning little fried things. For some $100 (about $1,300, or £800, in today's money), Doolin bought the recipe, the machinery (such as it was), and a small customer list from the man, and began making the chips in his kitchen. He soon set up business as The Frito Company, tinkered with the formula, and

slowly but steadily expanded production. By 1934, he had plants in Dallas and Houston making the chips, and in the following years, he began developing other products. (Cheetos were another of Doolin's inventions.) An enthusiastic self-marketer, he made an arrangement to install a restaurant, called Casa de Frito, in the much anticipated original Disneyland when it opened in Southern California in 1955.

In 1945, Doolin had signed a distribution deal with Herman Lay's potato chip business, based in Atlanta. In 1961, two years after Doolin's death, The Frito Company and the H. W. Lay Company merged, forming Frito-Lay. Four years later, that firm merged with the Pepsi-Cola Company, and the conglomerate became PepsiCo, Inc., which continues to make Fritos, among many other Frito-Lay brands, to this day. I've written elsewhere of my affection for potato chips flavored like barbecue sauce (see page 12), and I'm very fond of flavored Fritos, too—not just barbecue, but also Sabrositas (with chile and lime, found mostly in Hispanic neighborhoods), and above all the fairly fiery "Flamin' Hot" variety. That said, the familiar unmistakable corn flavor and serious crunch of the original kind make them my favorite of all.

CRACKLINGS (FRIED PORK RINDS)

Fried pork rinds are exactly what they sound like: bits of pig skin deep-fried in lard or oil until they turn dark brown, crunchy, and irresistible. They've probably been made in some form or another for as long as people have raised pigs for food, on the principle that nothing edible should be thrown away ("We eat every part of the animal except the squeal," as the saying goes). Called "cracklings" and even "cracklins" in the American South (and known as "scratchings" in parts of the United Kingdom), fried pork rinds are made by salting and scoring small, thick pieces of the animal's skin, usually with a layer of fat attached and sometimes with bits of meat still clinging, then

submerging them in a cauldron of boiling fat. Originally, though, they were probably an unintended by-product of the process of rendering lard; when all of the pork fat had melted off the skin, what was left crisped up in the pot.

Cracklings are hardly healthy fare, it should be stressed—though a Chicago nutritionist once computed that, ounce for ounce, fried pork rinds have about the same calories and fat content as potato chips. They are also high in protein and low in carbohydrates, so they enjoyed a vogue in the early 2000s when the Atkins Diet and other low-carbohydrate regimes first gained popularity. Bill Clinton was a big fan, regularly consuming them by the bagful until he started watching his weight, eventually becoming a vegan.

Though Clinton was from Arkansas, it has been rumored that his favorite cracklings came from the other side of the Mississippi River, in Clarksdale, Mississippi, where the Wong family produces some of the best under the name Kim's Pork Rinds. Kim Wong came to America from China's Guangdong Province in 1949, and in the 1960s moved to Clarksdale, where he and his family opened a restaurant and grocery store. Though he served a few Chinese-style dishes, the cooking was mostly Southern, and Wong's wife would render her own lard to make her famous biscuits, throwing away the bits of fried pork that remained. Wong noticed that stores in the area sometimes stocked a few bags of fried pork rinds near the cash register, and asked his wife to save the cracklings she produced. They sold so well that before long, the Wongs gave up the restaurant and made the rinds full-time. Crackling-crisp, faintly spicy, nicely salted, and thoroughly addictive, Kim's Pork Rinds have become a Southern classic.

MACADAMIA NUTS

I used to savor a fact that an early teacher had passed along—that a particularly rich and delicious variety of tree fruit and a utilitarian kind of road paving were named for the same man—until I learned that this wasn't true. The road paving, called macadam and consisting of small stones bound in tar or asphalt, was developed by John Loudon McAdam, a Scots surveyor born in 1756. Macadamia nuts borrow their name from a Scots-born Australian chemist and politician, John Macadam, born some seventy-one years later. His colleague Ferdinand von Mueller, who was official government botanist for the state of Victoria, christened the nut-bearing tree in Macadam's honor in 1857. The first cultivated macadamias were grown as ornamentals, and because related nuts of different species are toxic, nobody ate macadamias for some years. One Walter Hill, superintendent of the Brisbane City Botanical Gardens, is said to have been the first non-native Australian to sample the nuts, and he discovered what we all know now: that they are particularly delicious, tasting like a creamy, buttery cousin to blanched almonds, though with a softer, oilier feeling in the mouth.

More or less round and slightly bumpy (from a distance, shelled, they might be mistaken for overgrown chickpeas), macadamia nuts thrive in their native country, but are now grown in several parts of Africa and South America, New Zealand, Israel, California, and mostly notably Hawaii—where the trees were first planted as a windbreak for the cane fields in the 1880s. Though Australia produces more macadamias today than any other place, the ones from Hawaii are particularly famous. Just as California almonds are mostly grown on small independent farms under contract to one massive packer (Blue Diamond), a large portion of Hawaii's macadamias are primarily produced on a small scale and then sold to the big boys—in this case Hershey's, the chocolate people (see page 210). Chocolate and macadamias go very well together, as it happens, but The Hershey Company also markets excellent plain salted macadamias under the Mauna Loa label.

OLIVES

The first olive trees in California were planted in 1769 by Franciscan priests at the Mission of San Diego de Alcalá, in what is now San Diego. They turned out to be very well suited to the local climate, and quickly spread north. By 1892, when the entrepreneurially minded C. C. Graber headed west from Clay City, Indiana, to Ontario, due east of Los Angeles, they were thriving in much of Southern California. Graber may have had thoughts of farming citrus, but he sampled cured olives made by his neighbors and liked them well enough to try to figure out how to make his own, and make them better.

He planted olive trees and went into business in 1894, and his family still farms and packs olives today. In 1963, the Graber olive groves were moved north to Lindsay, in the San Joaquin Valley, but the olives are still packed in Graber's original home town. The Grabers grow two of the earliest California varieties, Manzanillos and Missions. Hand-picked, they are cured and packed without artificial treatment. California black olives are oxidized to that color; Grabers retain their natural hue, a color that must be described as, well, olive—sort of a yellowish-brownish green. They are rich in flavor, with a silky texture and a nutty flavor that seems purely, elementally *olive*. They're quite possibly the tastiest of all California olives—and the surprising thing is that they're sold not in bulk or in glass jars, but in cans.

PECANS

According to an old joke, a proper Bostonian once asked a Texan if he called these native American nuts "PEE-kans" or "puh-KAWNS." "Well, ma'am," the Texan replied, "where I come from, puh-KAWNS grow in the front yard, and the PEE-kan's out back." Ba-dum-dum.

The pecan tree is a native of North America, growing wild particularly in the southern Midwest, the South, and parts of Mexico. Related to the hickory, it takes its English name from the term *pacane*, an interpretation by French explorers of the Cree word *pakan*, meaning a hard-shelled nut. Though Americans have enjoyed the fruit of the pecan tree for centuries (and Thomas Jefferson propagated pecans at Monticello), it wasn't cultivated commercially until around 1880. The nut is grown today in parts of South America, South Africa, Australia, and China, but most of those eaten in the U.S. come from Georgia or Texas.

Pecans are unique in appearance when shelled, rectangular with rounded corners and two furrows running down their center (I've always thought they looked a little like miniature loaves of artisanal bread). They have

a buttery, slightly woody flavor, often tinged with bitterness—which may explain why they are so often encased in caramelized sugar for pralines (see page 227) or drowned in corn syrup for pecan pie.

Pearson Farm in Crawford County, in west-central Georgia, is a fifth-generation family-run enterprise best known for its peaches and its pecans. Al Pearson and his sisters, Ann and Peggy, took over the farm from their parents in 1973. In 2008, the sisters retired and Al's son, Lawton, came into the business. The Pearsons grow two varieties of pecans, Desirable and Elliott. I actually find the latter more, well, desirable; they're a little smaller, though still meaty, and may be slightly sweeter than the Desirables.

Just as an aside, since it's a different kind of product altogether, I'm also very fond of Oren's Kitchen Smoked Paprika Pecans, made in El Cerrito, California, just north of Berkeley. I don't know where proprietor Arnon Oren gets his nuts, or what variety they are, but he slow-roasts them with sea salt and Spanish *pimentón* (paprika), and they are mighty good.

PISTACHIOS

Pistachios are a relative newcomer to the agricultural treasure-trove that is central California. Originally from Persia, they are now grown throughout the Middle East and Central Asia, as well as in Sicily and, to a lesser extent, Australia. The pistachio first reached the Golden State as an ornamental in the 1850s, but it wasn't grown commercially for its nuts until the early twentieth century, and serious plantings didn't take place until the 1960s. Today, there are about 100,000 acres (about 40,000 hectares) of the trees in California.

David Fiddyment began growing the nuts in 1968 at his farm in Roseville, just northeast of Sacramento. Not content with merely growing them, he invented a new machine that hulls and dries the nuts in the field immediately after harvest. This is important, because pistachios are high in oil content, and can start to go rancid quickly. In 2004, Fiddyment expanded, purchasing a second farm east of Delano, near Bakersfield in south-central California. The packing plant is still near Sacramento, in Lincoln, and there the company bags perfect, mildly earthy, faintly sweet, lightly salted pistachios, both in and out of the shell (shelling them is easy—they're sold partially cracked open—and part of the experience, in my opinion). There is also a range of flavored nuts, for those who enjoy that sort of thing, and the chile-lime version is pretty irresistible.

POPCORN

In 1893, a Decatur, Illinois-based confectioner named Charles Cretors, who had devised an automated steam-powered machine that could pop corn uniformly in oil, demonstrated his invention at the Columbian Exposition in Chicago—thus introducing Americans to what was to become one of our nation's most popular snacks. Modern-day Americans, that is. Fossil evidence suggests that Native Americans in New Mexico were eating popped corn as early as 3600 BC, and it may have been known in Peru a thousand years before that. Spaniards found and described it in Mexico in the sixteenth century, and French explorers around the Great Lakes encountered it in the 1600s. Some culinary historians have speculated that popcorn might have been one of the indigenous foods introduced to the Pilgrims at the first Thanksgiving.

Popcorn is made from a specific variety of corn that produces hard-shelled, teardrop-shaped kernels. In the simplest terms, it "pops," blossoming into that familiar puffy shape, because each kernel's exterior forms an impervious seal trapping the corn's natural moisture within until it is heated so much (to about 347°F, or 175°C) that tremendous pressure builds up and the starch and protein at the kernel's core explode into a kind of foam, which instantly cools and crisps upon exposure to air.

Popcorn has of course come a long way since 1893, and has even gained a reputation as a healthy snack—among other things, a recent University of Scranton study has shown that it contains about twice the antioxidants called polyphenols that fresh fruit does—but the family of Charles Cretors is still in the popcorn machine business. A manufacturer

in Algona, Washington, called Tim's Cascade Snacks—started in 1986 by Tim Kennedy and his family—uses a small Cretors popper to produce a brand called Erin's All Natural Original Popcorn that is quite possibly the best packaged popcorn on the market. The corn is based on a special variety of white corn grown on a family farm in Nebraska, and is popped in corn oil in small batches. The result is faintly sweet and nicely crisp, not at all like the cottony stuff some of the larger producers sell. It's better than homemade, and you won't get any "old maids" (correctly called pericarp)—the unpopped kernels that can wreak havoc on your dental work.

BAKED GOODS

BIALYS

Bialys look sort of like flattened-out bagels, except that they have rounded rims and there's a soft, indented center filled with chopped onions where the hole in the bagel would be. Though bialys have an obvious kinship with bagels, and are similarly chewy, bagel dough is boiled before baking, while bialys are simply baked. Their name is shorthand for the Yiddish term *Bialystoker kuchen*, or Białystok cake—Białystok being a city on the White River in northeastern Poland. The kuchen was a daily staple of the Ashkenazi Jewish population there until the Holocaust, and might well have disappeared had it not immigrated as early as 1920 to New York City, where it was preserved under a shortened version of its name.

Though other bakers have produced bialys over the years—some bake them today on a major commercial scale—Kossar's, on Manhattan's Lower East Side, has been Bialy Central since the 1930s. Unlike its counterparts, Kossar's has so far resisted mechanization. Its bialys are formed by hand, made with just high-gluten flour, brewer's yeast, New York City tap water, fresh onions, and salt, then baked for about seven minutes in brick ovens (the exact timing depends on the humidity in the atmosphere). There is one other important part of the process: Kossar's bialys are kosher, which means, among other things, that the bakery must observe the ritual of intentionally burning a small percentage of the dough every morning as the Talmudic "priest's portion."

Some bialy producers add preservatives, use freeze-dried onions, and bake in automated tunnel ovens, practices which add up to bland, overly dense bialys. A freshly made Kossar's bialy, on the other hand, is simply great bread—toothsome and yeasty, with the pleasant crunch and mild bite of onions to offset its doughy richness. It's delicious with cream cheese spread across the top (some people split their bialys open like bagels, but connoisseurs frown on the practice), but so good that it doesn't really need any condiments at all.

BISCUITS

I know folks who would rather eat Wonder Bread than a store-bought biscuit. Biscuits, especially in the South and Midwest, are an iconic foodstuff, as emblematic of home baking (and thus of wholesome family values) as apple pie. Anyone who can't bake biscuits is considered, in some circles, to be somehow suspect. For those of us who lack the baker's touch, however, or who simply don't have the time or the inclination to make biscuits, there are commercial offerings that are very good—as good, if I dare say it, as a lot of the kitchen-counter ones I've tasted over the years.

The word "biscuit" derives from the Latin words *bis* and *coctus*—meaning twice and cooked, respectively—and a biscuit was originally a small, flat cake that had been baked and then rebaked into hardness or crispness. That sense is preserved in British English, in which a biscuit is what Americans call a cookie or cracker. Over here, a biscuit is more like what the British call a scone: a soft, often fluffy or flaky little bread roll.

Fluffy and flaky are the operative terms for Callie's Charleston Biscuits, from Charleston, South Carolina, which prove just how good commercial biscuits—and sold frozen, at that—can be. Callie White was a popular caterer in the Lowcountry capital, but in the mid-2000s she began thinking about retiring. One of her most popular creations had been her interpretation of that savory Southern standby, the country ham biscuit, which she made with Virginia ham and Dijon mustard butter sandwiched inside plump, light buttermilk biscuits flavored with sharp Cheddar and fresh chives. White's daughter, Carrie Morey, thought they deserved a wider audience, and in 2005 she convinced her mother to postpone retirement and go into the biscuit business.

Today, Callie's also makes biscuits flavored with cinnamon, and black pepper and bacon, and sells the Cheddar-chive biscuits by themselves as well as in ham-sandwich form. Purists will appreciate, most of all, her "plain" buttermilk biscuits, which pretty much define what a great Southern biscuit can be: many-layered, airy but filling, slightly salty, slightly sour ... and frankly almost certainly better than most people can make themselves.

COMMON CRACKERS

Vermont is known as a no-nonsense, hard-working state, "green" before being so was fashionable, and unimpressed by the fancy and the faddish. It is fitting, then, that one of its more celebrated foodstuffs is called the common cracker. Common crackers are basically what, in other times and places, would be called hardtack or ship's biscuits: they're round and smallish, about the size of an old-fashioned pocketwatch, and very dry (the point of ship's biscuits was that they wouldn't grow moldy on long sea voyages). They taste of not much more than baked flour.

Vermont common crackers were first made in Montpelier, in the northwestern quarter of the state, by the brothers Cross in 1828. It is said that their processing equipment was run by horsepower—literally: They owned one

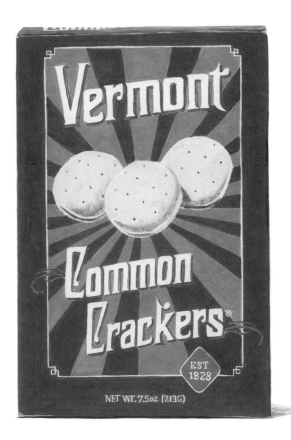

trusty steed who walked a treadmill three days a week while the crackers were being made, then spent three more days a week pulling a delivery wagon to disseminate them, often packed in wooden barrels, to shops around the region and to the railway depot for delivery further afield.

Locals used to sit around the cracker barrel at their town store and chew common crackers while they talked about whatever locals talked about. Supposedly they also sometimes played a game: Each one would eat a cracker, then see which of them could whistle first through his dried-out, crumb-dusted mouth.

The Crosses and their successors continued making the crackers the same way, on more or less the same equipment, until 1980, when the Orton family—who ran the Vermont Country Store in Weston, southwest of Montpelier—bought the concern. They have continued making common crackers in the same way under their Vermont Common Foods label, but have refined the recipe to remove any trans fats or hydrogenated oils that have crept into the formula over the years.

Vermont common crackers are austere but (or perhaps thus) highly versatile. They are a perfect foil for cheese, especially firmer varieties (for instance, some of Vermont's famous Cheddar). Crumbled, they add texture to clam chowder and other hearty soups, and work well in stuffings for turkey and other birds. Ground to powder in a food processor, they make great breadcrumbs and a fine coating for fried chicken. Purists, though—and Vermonters are nothing if not purists—like to eat them plain, either split (they're formed into two halves, rather like macarons, and can be pulled apart with a little effort) or whole. Common crackers are a simple pleasure.

CORN TORTILLAS

Almost twenty years ago, when I first moved to southwestern Connecticut from Southern California—with its large Hispanic population and its integration of Mexican culture into many aspects of daily life—I went looking for tortillas one day at the local supermarket. They had them, all right, rather pallid-looking and sealed in plastic; the brand name was El Gringo. I almost booked the next flight west.

The word tortilla means "little cake" in Spanish. While the term is used in Spain to mean frittata-style omelettes, in the Americas, it is of course a flat savory pancake sort of thing. Flour tortillas (see page 31) are more popular in America today, but the original ones—eaten in Central and South America since pre-Columbian times—were based on corn, or maize. They were not made from ordinary cornmeal, however. The Mayans, Aztecs, and other early cultures in the region discovered that corn was not in itself a complete nutrient, but that treating it with ash or lime (the mineral, not the fruit), which were high in alkalines, rendered it more nourishing. This process, which produces what we know as hominy (see page 196), is called nixtamalization, after the native Nahuatl words for ashes and corn dough.

The dried, nixtamalized (treated with alkali) corn is ground into flour called masa harina, which in turn is made into tortilla dough. Preparation of the corn aside, making tortillas is a very simple process: pieces of dough are pinched off a larger ball of it, flattened by hand (or, these days, with a tortilla press), and cooked on a griddle—traditionally the kind called a *comal*. Once cooked, tortillas have scores of uses: by themselves or used to scoop up food; for enchiladas; fried in the form of chips or the bases for tostadas; torn and stirred into soups or chilaquiles; and so on.

In an ideal world, all tortilla-lovers would make their own, or at least buy them freshly made from a nearby Hispanic market. If that's not possible, there are high-quality mass-production tortillerias that will ship freshly made tortillas around the country. One good one is Luna's Tortillas in Dallas, founded in 1924 by María Luna, a recent immigrant from San Luis Potosí, who started by making tortillas in her home kitchen. Her son, Francisco "Pancho" Luna, took over the operation—which had grown steadily and moved into a small factory building—in 1939. His sons run the business today, and while it supplies restaurants all over the Dallas-Fort Worth area, and has a restaurant of its own, it remains a small operation, turning out no more than 1,500 tortillas a day.

DOUGHNUTS

One good way to start a foodie fight is to announce that such-and-such a place makes the best doughnuts in America. The fact is that there are still a surprisingly large number of independent doughnut shops and small regional chains around, making doughnuts in all kinds of styles and variations, and even if you were to filter out the ones that get too fancy (if you have to eat it with a fork, it ain't a doughnut), naming just one source for the "best" would be impossible. How could any reasonable person choose between the output of, say, Primo's or Randy's in Los Angeles, the Coffee An' Donut Shop in Westport (Connecticut), Dat Donuts in Chicago, the Doughnut Plant in New York City, Kane's (just outside of Boston), and on and on? (We will leave discussion of the overrated Krispy Kreme for another time.)

One way to narrow the field down a little, though, is to consider doughnut shops that ship, and ship fast, so that their wares are available to almost anyone. With that criterion in mind, and realizing that almost nobody will be likely to agree with me, I'm going to single out Congdon's Doughnuts, headquartered in Wells, Maine, just southwest of the coastal town of Kennebunkport. The Congdon's story

starts in 1945, when a couple of émigrés from Colebrook, New Hampshire, Clint and Dot Congdon, opened a restaurant in Kennebunk. It did well overall, but Dot's doughnuts were particularly popular, so the Congdons sold the restaurant and went into the baking business full-time. In 1955, Dot, known as "Nana," went back into the restaurant business, in partnership with her son-in-law, Herb Brooks, opening Congdon's Doughnuts Family Restaurant in Wells. Brooks and his wife, Nana's daughter, Bev, expanded the business, opening branches back in Kennebunk and in Old Orchard Beach and Ogunquit, but they were killed in a plane crash in 1965. Brooks's sister, Eleanor, and her husband took over the business, and it is now managed by their son and his wife and children.

Congdon's doughnuts have a handmade look—they're always a little irregular in shape—and taste old-fashioned and straightforward. The sugared and raised varieties are classics; the chocolate is frosted with something that tastes like a good milk chocolate bar; the maple crème has a caramelized flavor—and a plain Congdon's dipped in coffee is an elemental treat, a taste of old diners and simpler times.

FLOUR TORTILLAS

Until the coming of the Spanish in the sixteenth century, there were no flour tortillas in Mexico because there was no wheat—and thus no flour. Corn was the staple grain crop in the country, and still is (it is planted on about a third of the cultivated farmland), but wheat thrived in its new home, especially in northern Mexico, and Mexico is today one of the major wheat-producing countries in the Western Hemisphere.

Though nobody knows who first made flour tortillas or when, the idea of them must have appealed to the Spanish: unlike corn, wheat needed no special processing before being turned into flour and then dough, and flatbreads not unlike flour tortillas had been prepared in parts of northwestern Spain for centuries before the European discovery of the Americas. Flour tortillas are still comparatively uncommon in southern and southeastern Mexico, but are an integral part of the cuisines of Chihuahua, Sonora, and Baja California; on the other side of the border, they are an essential ingredient in Tex-Mex cooking and in the Mexican-inflected and Native American culinary idioms of California, Arizona, and New Mexico.

Flour tortillas are folded around various ingredients as burritos (or chimichangas, which are fried burritos) and found almost everywhere in America in the form of quesadillas, but they're also widely used, as corn tortillas are, to scoop up or simply accompany various other foods. In the Tex-Mex food capital of San Antonio, it's hard to imagine a meal without them, even breakfast. Crispy bacon wrapped in a warm steamed flour tortilla, for instance, is a real treat.

Something approximating the flour tortilla is now ubiquitous in America in the form of the sandwich variation called the "wrap"— basically a tortilla rolled around cold (usually) sandwich ingredients. Wraps were apparently invented in Southern California in the early 1980s (though a sports bar in Stamford, Connecticut, also claims to have first come up with them). Tortilla-like flatbreads flavored with everything from spinach to sun-dried tomatoes are now sold specifically for the purpose. Most of them don't taste like much on their own, unlike good flour tortillas. Freshly made examples of the latter from smaller tortillerias are always better than the mass-produced kind made by big companies. The best mail-order source I've found is La Abucla Mexican Foods in Weslaco, Texas, which ships raw 6.5-inch (16-centimeter), 8-inch (20-centimeter), and 9-inch (23-centimeter) flour tortillas (for making real Mexican quesadillas, though they only take a few seconds to cook for other uses) around the U.S. daily. They come frozen, and in cases of ten to twenty packages, depending on the size; each package contains up to twenty tortillas (and don't worry about having too many; keep them frozen and they'll last for at least six months).

FRY BREAD

If you buy fry bread mix from Redcorn.com, which isn't a bad idea, you might be interested to know that the "red corn" in question isn't just a variety of grain—it's a name. In 1932, an Osage Indian named Raymond W. Red Corn, Jr., of Pawhuska, Oklahoma, married a local woman named Waltena C. Myers. An Osage woman, Mary McFall, taught Myers how to cook traditional Osage dishes, including fry bread.

Fry bread in various forms is common to Indian cooking in many parts of America, but seems particularly popular in the Midwest and Southwest. (It is the official "state bread" of South Dakota.) It's a slightly puffy flatbread leavened with lard and, not surprisingly, fried. It functions as a kind of tortilla, eaten with beans and other basics of the Native American diet. It is also the base of so-called Navajo or Indian tacos, typically made with ground beef, onions, tomatoes, and cheese (Pawhuska hosts an annual National Indian Taco Championship).

It is said that fry bread was invented by Navajos who were given U.S. government rations of flour, sugar, salt, and lard when they were relocated from Arizona to New Mexico in the mid-nineteenth century. Like the tortilla, it is made from scratch in many households, even today, but dry fry bread mix has become increasingly popular. Some of the best is sold by Raymond and Waltena's grandson, Ryan Red Corn, from Redcorn.com headquarters on the Osage Nation Reservation. It takes a bit of practice to get the kneading and rolling down right, as it does with any bread, but fry bread isn't particularly difficult to make. And eaten still warm, out of fresh, neutral-tasting oil at the proper temperature, it is pretty nice—a little chewy, a little salty, with a bit of a yeasty flavor and a solidity that is positively grounding.

GRAHAM CRACKERS

Reverend Sylvester Graham, the nineteenth-century Presbyterian minister who invented the graham cracker, was ahead of his time. He thought that chemical additives in bread and other processed foods were unhealthy, he advocated vegetarianism and a high-fiber diet, and he helped introduce Americans to the once-radical notions that they should bathe and brush their teeth daily. His famous crackers, originally called Dr. Graham's Honey Biscuits and probably based on the so-called digestive biscuits popular in Britain, appeared in 1829, and were made with a combination of white and coarse-ground wheat flour and wheat germ, sweetened with honey. They were intentionally bland because Graham believed that spicy and strong-flavored foods stimulated illicit sexual appetites; he promoted his crackers, in fact, as a means of preventing or discouraging "self-abuse"— i.e., masturbation.

Nobody owns the patent on graham crackers today, and they are made by numerous bakeries large and small (Nabisco's Honey Maid brand seems to be the main grocery store interpretation). Some are made entirely of white flour, and most commercial versions include precisely the kinds of additives their inventor would have abhorred. Nonetheless, graham crackers have become an American staple, eaten plain (or spread with butter), but also as part of the campfire "sandwiches" called s'mores (apparently invented by a Girl Scout in 1927) and as the basis of crusts for pies and cheesecakes.

If Reverend Graham were around today— and if he had loosened up a little—he might well admire the graham crackers made by Potter's in Madison, Wisconsin. Peter Potter Weber studied food science at the University of Wisconsin in Madison; his mother, Nancy Potter, was a successful bakery owner in New Glarus, just southwest of the city. When the two noticed that the specialty (as opposed to bulk) cheese industry in their state was taking off, they thought there might be a market for specialty crackers to go with the new high-quality offerings, and in 2006 formed Potters Fine Foods LLC to supply them. They now produce specialty crackers with a number of flavorings, including caraway rye, rosemary, toasted sesame, and Washington Island flax. Their real prize, however, is a unique graham cracker enlivened with crushed organic hazelnuts. Made with organic stone-ground wheat flour, cracked wheat, butter, sugar, and milk, these crackers have a toasty, nutty character with plenty of that familiar graham flavor. They're an improvement on a classic.

KOLACHES

The true sound of the Texas Hill Country isn't cowboy ballads or Willie Nelson songs; it's polka—German-, Polish-, Czech-, and Slovak-born music, accordions in the forefront, woven into the jazzy lilt of Western swing. (If you want a taste, look for music by Adolph Hofner and the Pearl Wranglers.) By extension, it could well be said that the true flavor of that wonderful part of the Lone Star State—other than the barbecue which perfumes the air and fills so many tables in those parts—is the kolache. Kolaches were originally a wedding confection back in Central Europe: round or square pastries with a center of fruit preserves or of poppyseeds or sweetened cream cheese (see page 54). Other variations involve something savory—cheese, sausage, even (in Texas at least) barbecue brisket or Cajun boudin or andouille (see pages 126 and 121). (Purists point out that true kolaches are always sweet, and that savory pastries of this type should be called *klobasnek*—but don't waste time arguing this point with your average denizen of the Hill Country.)

Weikel's Bakery in La Grange, between Houston and Austin, isn't technically in the Hill Country—it's just a little too far east—but it has a large population of German and Czech descent, and is the home of the Texas Czech Heritage and Cultural Center. (It was also,

incidentally, the nearest town to a different kind of cultural institution: the infamous Chicken Ranch brothel, inspiration for the hit musical and movie *The Best Little Whorehouse in Texas*.) Weikel's—whose slogan, I regret to report, is "We Gotcha Kolache"—traces its origins to the Bon Ton Café, opened in La Grange by brothers Alvin and L.D. "Pop" Weikel in 1929. La Grange was a convenient place for travelers to stop along State Highway 71, and there wasn't much competition in town, so the café thrived. Alvin's son, Jim, took over the business in 1969, and ran it for the next sixteen years, before he and his wife, Jo Ann, decided to sell the place and downsize to a small bakery and convenience store. It was the Bon Ton Store & Bakery at first, but soon became Weikel's Store & Bakery. Jo Ann's mother, Nolie, was the kolache expert in the family, having learned the secrets of perfect dough from her mother, Annie Kulhanek, who had moved to Texas from her native Czechoslovakia as a child. Today, Philip Weikel, son of Jim and Jo Ann, helps run the business, along with three or four other family members.

Weikel kolaches are dense but moist, sugary, full of fruit—no savory varieties here, unless you count cottage cheese, cream cheese, and poppyseeds—and delicious.

MATZO

Matzo is the original "Mediterranean flatbread," dating back to Biblical times. Made with nothing more than water and, at least in its purest form, milled grain (usually wheat today, though five different grains are permitted), matzo has great symbolic significance in Judaism. It is one of the foods widely eaten during Passover (when eating leavened bread is forbidden), and is essential for the Passover seder.

Matzo is typically rectangular in shape (homemade versions are usually round), and about the thickness of shirt cardboard. It's crisp and dappled, with dark spots from the baking process. Some people think it *tastes* like shirt cardboard, but in fact it typically has a mild flavor, a bit like undersalted, lightly flame-touched saltines (see page 41). To be non-traditional, and, I'm sure, religiously incorrect, I'd say that with a little soft butter and sea salt on top, matzo is pretty good.

The best commercial brand I've found is Streit's Passover Matzo, made with unbleached wholewheat flour by a New York-based factory originally founded in 1916. The company had its origins in a matzo-making business that was started earlier in the century by Rabbi Moshe Weinberger. Forced out of his synagogue in part because his congregation took exception to his commercial activities (heckling during his Passover sermon in 1906 led to a full-scale riot and his eventual resignation), Weinberger turned to his baking business full-time, forming a partnership with one Aron Streit to produce handmade matzos. In 1925, Streit and his son opened an automated bakery on Rivington Street, where it still stands. Little by little, the factory grew, and today, as the only family-owned and -operated matzo producer in America, it does close to $17 million (about £11 million) in business annually, supplying about 20 percent of the matzo eaten in America.

The process of making matzo is closely regulated by religious mandate. The workers who bake it don't have to be Jewish, but they have to observe certain essential conditions. The water to be used must sit overnight before being added to the flour; once the dough is made, the matzos have to be in the oven within eighteen minutes (to avoid any possible promiscuous leavening from airborne yeasts). No preservatives may be used. It's the most basic bread imaginable—and to more than thirteen million Jews worldwide, the most important.

MEAT PIE

A runza is a meat pie, made with seasoned ground pork or beef, shredded cabbage (sauerkraut in earlier days), and onions, enclosed in a casing of bread dough, more or less square, with rounded edges. It is of Russian (some say Ukrainian) origin, and became particularly popular with the Volga Germans, ethnic Germans living in southern Russia. They apparently brought it to the American Midwest some time in the late nineteenth or early twentieth century. An alternate name for this savory pastry is bierock, probably a corruption of the Russian pierogi, though bierocks are usually rounded, looking more or less like a tall hamburger bun with sealed edges.

Runzas entered the American consciousness—and may well have been given their name—in 1949, when Sarah "Sally" Everett and her brother, Alex Brening, who were of Volga German descent, opened the Runza Drive Inn in Lincoln, Nebraska, serving runzas based on a family recipe. Sally's son, Donald, went to work at the place as a young man in 1964. Locals responded favorably to this easy-to-eat savory hamburger substitute, and two years later a second location was opened in Lincoln. At the same time, Donald and a partner, Rod Beckman, bought the Runza trade name and incorporated the company. In 1979, they began franchising the operation, and today Runza has more than eighty locations in Nebraska, South Dakota, Kansas, Iowa, and Colorado.

There are plenty of recipes available for runzas or bierocks, but the original, which is salty and moist and quite delicious, is definitely worth trying. (For legal reasons, the company will not ship runzas, but if you can get to one of their outposts, they'll sell them to you frozen and offer shipping instructions so you can get them home safely.)

NEW ORLEANS BEIGNETS

Do not visit Café du Monde, in the French Quarter of New Orleans, wearing black—not, that is, if you're planning on eating something. The menu at this 150-plus-year-old institution (now with eight much younger branches elsewhere in New Orleans and in nearby communities) offers nothing but coffee with chicory, fresh-squeezed orange juice, milk and chocolate milk, a few other beverages, and, for solid fare, beignets. That word, which might be translated as "fritter," is used in France to describe several kinds of fried pastry and also vegetables and other foods fried in batter, but in New Orleans it means exactly what you'll get at Café du Monde: airy square pillows of fried dough beneath a blanket of powdered sugar. And there is no way to eat one (or two, or three—they're pretty addictive, and anyway come three to an order) without spilling some of the sugar on yourself. Trust me.

Beignets were brought to Louisiana by the Acadians of eastern Canada — who became the Cajuns—in the mid-eighteenth century. More elaborate versions, filled with different types of fruit, were common in the nineteenth century, and are occasionally still found on the dessert menus of old-line New Orleans restaurants. The simpler, sugar-showered kind, though, established itself as a local tradition—and, in fact, the beignet has been named the official Louisiana state doughnut. It would be impossible to ship beignets—they'd collapse and harden—but Café du Monde does sell its beignet mix online. You'll need water, frying oil (the café uses cottonseed oil), and of course plenty of powdered sugar.

PASTIES

The pasty is a member of the vast meat-and-vegetable-pie family that seems to span almost every culture. It is related to the runza (see page 36), the pierogi, the empanada, and more—but in this case is particularly associated with the British region of Cornwall, so much so that it is considered the region's national dish and the term "Cornish pasty" has been given Protected Geographical Indication (PGI) status by the European Union. The traditional version is shaped like a half-moon (or like an empanada), and made with beef, onions, rutabagas, and potatoes, none of it too finely minced.

The Cornish pasty made its way to America, and particularly to Michigan's Upper Peninsula (U. P.), with an influx of Cornish coal miners to the area in the mid-1800s. Because the pasties were easily portable, they became a favored lunch for miners to take with them when they descended underground. At about the same time that the Cornish were baking them in Michigan, a group of miners from Finland came to the U. P., and, perhaps because the pasty reminded them of a Finnish meat and rice pie called *lihapiirakka*, they quickly adopted it as their own—to the extent that, today, pasties are often considered a Finnish specialty in that part of the country.

Pasties also became popular with miners in Wisconsin and Pennsylvania, but the U. P. remains the hotbed of pasty culture. There's even an annual PastyFest in Calumet, Michigan, and Calumet is the home of one of the best purveyors of the pies. For years, residents of the city's Still Waters Assisted Living Community in Calumet had peeled vegetables and helped assemble pasties to sell for fundraising purposes. Charlie Hopper, a retired vice-president of National Software Systems, had become active in several local nonprofit organizations in the U. P., including Still Waters. In 1994, he was asked to become the home's full-time administrator, and one of his first projects was to establish Pasty Central and several attendant Web sites, through which the homemade pasties could be sold to a larger customer base. Pasty Central grew, and in 2001, its employees bought the concern from Still Waters. Still Waters closed in 2006, but Pastry Central, which now operates a pasty kitchen in Kearsarge, near Calumet, continues to support assistance programs for the elderly throughout the U. P.

The company's traditional Michigan-style pasties are made with ground beef and pork in a three-to-one ratio, plus potatoes, carrots, rutabagas, onions, and assorted spices, baked in a flaky pastry crust made with vegetable shortening. Pasty Central also offers a Cornish-style pasty, however. The difference? "No carrots."

POTATO KNISHES

Almost every culture seems to have some version of the turnover or filled bun, including runzas, pasties (see pages 36 and 38), pierogi, and empanadas, but also the samosas of India, the baos of China … and, as anyone who has ever strolled the streets of New York City will know, the knishes of Eastern European Jewish cooking. The knish (the "k" is not silent, though I did once hear a well-dressed preppie ask a knish-and-pretzel vendor in midtown Manhattan for a "nish") takes its name from a Ukrainian or Russian word for cake or bun, and it may have first been brought to American shores by Ukrainian immigrants in the late nineteenth century.

Yonah Schimmel, the name with which the knish is most associated in this country, was Romanian, not Ukrainian, and he started selling potato knishes, made by his wife, from a pushcart on New York's Lower East Side (or, some say, at Coney Island) some time around 1890. The business expanded to a small storefront bakery, and then, in 1910, in partnership with his cousin, Schimmel moved to a site on Houston Street, where the bakery remains to this day. Schimmel's cousin married his daughter, and their descendants run the operation today—the sixth generation of the family. The original recipes are still used, though the classic potato knish and another traditional variety, filled with *kasha* (buckwheat groats), have been joined by versions made with spinach, red cabbage, broccoli, and mushrooms, among other ingredients.

The knish, at least according to this pioneering knishery (yes, they use that term), is always round—many street vendors sell square versions—and always baked, not fried. It is not a light, flaky treat: knish dough is substantial, and gives the traditional potato version most of its flavor (the filling is not heavily seasoned). Knishes are almost always eaten dipped in mustard, preferably the spicy brown variety. It has been said that no politician has ever been elected in New York City without having first been photographed eating a knish.

PRETZELS

Pretzels are made from boiled and baked dough traditionally formed into a knot-like shape, and are associated above all with Germany—the pretzel is a common emblem for bakers in that country—but they may have originated in ancient Rome or elsewhere in Italy, or even in the south of France. Their unique shape may have been meant to suggest crossed or folded arms, and their German name, *Brezel*, may be related to the Latin *bracchium*, arm.

The Pennsylvania Dutch—who of course aren't Dutch, but "Deutsch," German and German-Swiss—are commonly credited with having introduced the pretzel to America in the nineteenth century, quite possibly in Lancaster County, Pennsylvania. It's not surprising, then, that the best classic pretzels are made there—specifically in the borough of Akron, outside the city of Lancaster, by Martin's Pretzel Bakery. Here, the Martin family, conservative Mennonites with a long history in the county, have been hand-fashioning pretzels for more than sixty years.

In Germany, pretzels are typically soft, a freshly baked product with a consistency like that of chewy dinner rolls. The frugal Pennsylvania Dutch realized that drying out the pretzels would give them a longer shelf life, and Martin's Special Hard Pretzels are pretty much the ideal interpretation of this style. They begin with a sourdough made with only unbleached flour (from the acclaimed Snavely's Mill in Lititz, Pennsylvania), water, yeast, and salt—no preservatives or shortening. After rising, the dough is cut into pieces, hand-kneaded, shaped, and twisted. Each employee can produce ten or twelve pretzels a minute this way. The pretzels are next boiled in water with baking soda, then salted by hand with coarse salt (a no-salt version is also available) and baked for fifteen minutes in a 500°F (260°C) stone-lined oven. Finally, they are dried at 180°F (82°C) so that they are crunchy throughout.

The resulting pretzels are fun to eat, breaking into shards as you bite into them, and filling your mouth with a salty, sourish baked flavor that can only be described as, well, pretzel-like. Mass-produced pretzels pale by comparison.

SALTINES

One of the first cooking tricks I learned when I was getting to know my way around a kitchen was the old wet-saltine routine: dip saltine crackers into ice water, brush them with melted butter, then bake them, and they'll turn into little squares of golden-brown flaky pastry that the non-wet-saltine-savvy will probably think you made yourself from scratch. These can be utilized to make all kinds of hors d'oeuvres: melt cheese on top, spread with cream cheese and jalapeño jelly (see pages 54 and 244) or herb butter, top with seafood salad or deviled ham, and so on. Of course, plain saltines work pretty well for those purposes, too. They're great little crackers, crisp and lightly crumbly, with a distinctive flavor of their own that's mild enough not to conflict with whatever you put on them.

They're also simple crackers, made of flour, yeast, baking soda (hence their other name, soda crackers), a little shortening, and salt,

with a dimpled surface and baked in sheets. Credit for inventing the saltine is usually given to one Joseph Garneau of the Joseph Garneau Company, inevitably described as a "manufacturer of biscuits and crackers," who reportedly came up with it as early as the mid-1800s. On the other hand, a man named Frank Sommer, who had a small cracker factory in St. Joseph, Missouri, won a blue ribbon for his soda crackers at the 1876 Buchanan County Fair, and at the time, similar crackers were already known as Premium Flakes or Saltinas. In 1898, Sommer's company merged with another cracker maker to form the National Biscuit Company—which grew into the worldwide brand now known as Nabisco. Though "saltine" isn't a brand name, and there are numerous manufacturers of the crackers, Nabisco is the largest by far, baking more than 35 *billion* saltines annually.

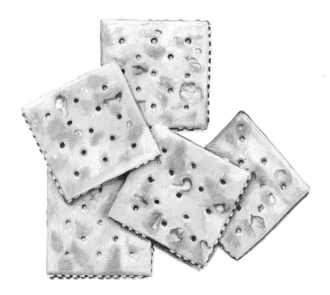

SAN FRANCISCO SOURDOUGH BREAD

San Francisco sourdough bread is arguably the foodstuff most closely associated, at least traditionally, with the City by the Bay. Dense, crusty, pleasantly chewy, and indisputably sourish, slices of sourdough may be enjoyed plain, toasted, and grilled, slathered with butter or drizzled with olive oil, and are considered an indispensable accompaniment to such San Francisco specialties as *cioppino* (the Ligurian-influenced seafood stew) and Dungeness crab cocktail.

Sourdough is simply unbaked bread dough that contains a combination of various yeasts and a bacterium called *Lactobacillus* (other forms of which are involved in the fermentation of wine, beer, cider, kimchi, and yogurt, among other substances). From at least the time of the ancient Egyptians through the Middle Ages, this bacterium was the principal means of leavening bread. While it was eventually supplanted in much of the world by cultivated yeasts for most breads, it remained popular in Europe, especially for use with rye flour, with which it reacted particularly well. Basque immigrants to Northern California probably brought it to the San Francisco area in the early nineteenth century, and it became popular with gold miners because sourdough starter, unlike live yeast, was easy to transport and store in the wilds of Gold Rush country. It became so identified with these treasure-seekers, in fact, that they were popularly known as "sourdoughs"—and today, the mascot of the San Francisco 49ers football team is a character called Sourdough Sam. Sourdough-lovers maintain that only bread made in the Bay Area has the unique flavor they crave, and indeed the locally used strain of *Lactobacillus*, apparently unique, has been dubbed *sanfranciscensis*.

One big commercial baker of San Francisco sourdough, Boudin, dates its origins from 1849. Others, including San Francisco French Bread and Colombo (under the same corporate umbrella, but run separately), are more recent. All make a good standard product, as does SoCal Bakeries (formerly Pioneer Bakery) in Southern California. The sourdough rounds produced by the Acme Bread Company in Berkeley, however, though they're not labeled as "San Francisco," are on another level: the sourness is pronounced but moderated, allowing good wheaty flavor to shine through. It is somehow light but chewy at the same time, with a crisp, very faintly caramelized-tasting crust. It would be great bread even if you called it "Peoria" or "Miami Beach."

SAVORY PALMIERS

A palmier is a palm tree to the French, but it is a popular form of pastry, too. Also known as an elephant ear or pig's ear in English, the palmier is sugar-glazed puff pastry rolled into a shape thought to resemble a palm frond (or the ear of certain beasts)—or, some say, a butterfly. Tiny palmiers are sometimes served with coffee after meals in fancy French restaurants, and larger ones are an essential at pastry shops all over France—though virtually identical confections are found in bakeries in Germany, Italy, and Spain, as well, and they have became fairly common in the United States.

What are not common here (though they are sometimes seen in France) are palmiers that are savory rather than sweet. Savory palmiers are a specialty at La Tulipe Desserts, a mom-and-pop bakery in the suburban community of Mount Kisco, about 30 miles (48 kilometers) northeast of Manhattan in New York State's Westchester County. La Tulipe's proprietors, Maarten and Frances Steenman, met while working in another Mount Kisco bakery. Dutch-born Maarten is a second-generation pastry chef who plied his trade in his homeland and in Belgium, France, and Norway before immigrating to New York in the late 1980s. The couple set up shop for themselves in 1999, and while they did very well selling custom cakes, chocolate truffles, French-style tarts, and such, they also wanted to offer something different, a signature item.

Maarten had made savory palmiers at Fauchon in Paris, and thought he might be able to adapt successfully the idea to American tastes. He starts by making delicate puff pastry with top-quality flour, rich European-style butter, and purified water, then rolls it out and puts an all-American melting-pot spin on it by scattering it with polyglot flavorings—Cheddar, Parmesan, pesto, curry, or "Mexican." Then he rolls the dough by hand from both ends toward the center to form long tubes, slices it into frond-shaped pieces, and bakes the pieces twice so that they're perfectly crisp. The palmiers crackle and dissolve into buttery goodness in the mouth, leaving a glow of true (not artificial-tasting) flavor on the palate. All La Tulipe savory palmiers are good, but the Cheddar and Parmesan varieties are particularly hard to resist.

SCHNECKEN

Schnecken are coiled, buttery cinnamon rolls with raisins (*Schnecken* is German for "snails"), especially popular in German and Jewish households. They taste like a cross between ordinary cinnamon rolls and the small, dense pastries called rugelach. Schnecken are said to be particularly popular in Baltimore and Philadelphia, but I first encountered them in Cincinnati, where the venerable Busken Bakery sells excellent examples every year for a month or so before Passover and Easter.

Busken's schnecken, they proudly advertise, are made according to the Virginia Bakery recipe. This requires some background: a German immigrant baker named Wilhelm Thie opened the Wm. Thie Baking Co. in Cincinnati in 1906. His oldest son, Bill, struck out on his own and bought the Virginia Bakery not far away. Bill's son, Howard, and his wife, Cindy, took over management of the bakery, and it passed in turn to their son, Tom, and his wife, Maureen. Along the way, the bakery became known for many varieties of bread,

cake, and cookies, but it became especially famous for its schnecken, and even had a "Schnecken Club," offering customers one free for every dozen bought. Much to the dismay of locals, Virginia Bakery closed in 2005 after Tom was hurt in an accident.

Joe and Daisie Busken, meanwhile, had started a small bakery of their own in 1928, earning renown for breads and apple pies. Joe Jr. eventually took over the business and expanded the bakery and its offerings, among other things developing a reputation for elaborate wedding and birthday cakes. Joe's younger brother, Page, is now in charge. When Virginia Bakery went out of business, Busken inherited the recipe, the success of which is due largely to the immense amount of butter it calls for: half a pound (250 grams) for every loaf. When it mixes and melts with the generously applied cinnamon sugar, the resulting "goo" is memorably decadent. For years, Cincinnatians who strayed from home could order schnecken shipped from Virginia Bakery, and they can now turn to Busken.

DAIRY PRODUCTS

ASH-COATED SOFT-RIPENED CHEESE

Korean-born Soyoung Scanlan is a serious concert pianist who holds degrees in life science and dairy science and has worked as a biochemist and dairy scientist, but her passion is cheesemaking. She embraced this métier as a new career in 1999, taking over Laura Chenel's original cheese factory in Santa Rosa, California (see page 70), and dubbing her enterprise Andante Dairy. *Andante*, she explains, is the tempo mark in some musical movements that indicates the "moderate rate of speed of a strolling walk." She chose the term to symbolize her longing for a slower pace of life, and what she calls "the proper speed of traditional cheesemaking."

Her Nocturne is a good example of what she's talking about. Scanlan produces about ten cheeses in all, some from Jersey cow's milk (she now makes cheese in Petaluma, on the farm where the cows graze), some from goat's milk, and three from a mixture of the two; all have musical names such as Rondo, Acapella,

Legato, and Pianoforte. Nocturne, which was the first cheese Scanlan made and for me remains her definitive one, is all cow's milk, but it looks like a goat cheese from the Loire and it is made with the long, slow method that produces many chèvres. This involves using a culture that acidifies the milk gradually so that coagulation takes as long as eighteen hours, compared with an hour or so for many other cow's milk cheeses. The result is a block of cheese shaped like a pyramid with its top lopped off, coated with vegetable ash and a soft white mold; it is tart and a little chalky when it's very young, growing softer and creamier and developing an earthy flavor as it matures. Scanlan says that she called it Nocturne both because the slow pace of its manufacture suggests to her the tempo of Chopin's nocturnes, or short piano solos, which she loves to play, and because the color of the exterior reminds her of James Abbott McNeill Whistler's Nocturne paintings.

BANDAGE-WRAPPED FIRM CHEESE

The Fiscalini family traces its origins to the tiny village of Lionza, about 10 miles (16 kilometers) west of Locarno in Ticino, the Italian-speaking portion of Switzerland. It was a desperately poor region, and in 1890, like many of his countrymen, Mateo Fiscalini immigrated to America in search of work. He made his way across the country as a railway hand, ending up in Cambria, on California's Central Coast, where many other Italian-Swiss immigrants had gathered—among them relatives of his who ran a dairy farm. Matteo's son, John Battista, wanted to go off on his own, and in 1914, hearing of cheap land that had become available, moved north to Modesto, in the Central Valley—a town perhaps best-known as the home base of the massive Gallo wine empire (and as the locale of the hit film *American Graffiti*, directed by Modesto native George Lucas). There, the younger Fiscalini bought 160 acres (65 hectares) of pasture and twenty cows, and went into the dairy business for himself.

Today, under the direction of John Battista's grandson, John, Fiscalini Farms sprawls over 530 acres (214 hectares). It has become known for its innovative dairy practices (among other things, electricity to run the operation is generated with the help of an anaerobic digester that produces methane fuel from cow manure and other waste products) and for being one of California's top cheese producers—above all for an extraordinary product called 30-Month Bandage-Wrapped Cheddar.

Two cheesemakers produce about 900 pounds (400 kilograms) of the cheese per batch, working by hand in open vats. The cheese is made with raw milk set with microbial rennet. Where does the bandage come in? Many cheeses are wrapped in something to protect them as they age. Some traditional varieties are enclosed in leaves of various kinds (grape, fig, walnut, even sycamore leaves); blue cheese is usually protected with foil, which helps keep it moist; wax is used to form an airtight seal on cheeses, like Edam and many commercial Cheddars, that are meant to be eaten fresh or aged very slowly. Sometimes wax-wrapped cheeses are first swathed in cheesecloth to help the wax adhere. Some rare cheeses are only protected by the cloth, which has the effect of protecting them but allowing them to "breathe" and form a natural rind. These cheeses are sometimes described as "bandage-wrapped," because the gauzy cheesecloth resembles bandages.

It is an assertive cheese, sharp but not mouth-burning, with an earthy, Cheddary flavor and a faint bitter tang at the end—memorable.

BREAD CHEESE

I vividly remember sitting in the cafeteria at Stockmann, the massive department store in Helsinki, late one morning years ago, and watching a nicely dressed middle-aged woman at a nearby table casually dunking a brown-splotched slab of something off-white into her coffee, then taking a bite. It didn't look like bread or pastry, but I couldn't imagine what else it could be. "Ha!" my Finnish friend Leena laughed later that day when I described this strange breakfast treat to her. "That's real Finnish food. It's *leipäjuusto*—bread cheese." This unique specialty, I later learned, is basically just baked cheese curd, formed into flat loaves (its name is also sometimes inverted as *juustoleipä*, cheese bread), then baked and slightly caramelized. It's salty and rich, with a texture suggesting that of firm mozzarella (see page 59); it has a creamy flavor, and is best eaten slightly warm—hence the tradition of immersing it briefly in coffee. (It doesn't melt, just softens slightly. Oh, and it squeaks a little when you bite into it.)

The technique for making bread cheese came to America with Finnish immigrants to Michigan and Wisconsin in the nineteenth century, but commercial production had pretty much died out until the middle of the last decade. That's when a big cheese producer in central Wisconsin, Carr Valley Cheese Company (founded 1902), developed a recipe for it and put it into regular distribution, turning it from a Scandinavian curiosity into an American one. At least two other Wisconsin dairies make a version of bread cheese, but their best efforts are flavored with jalapeños or chipotles, which seem to me to turn them into something else entirely. I like the purity of Carr Valley's version—a bite of Finland transported to America.

BUTTER

I remember once, probably twenty-five years ago, having lunch in a restaurant in Brussels and noticing an immense solid mound of butter, irregularly shaped but roughly the size of a squared-off soccer ball, sitting on the counter by the kitchen. Servers would come by periodically and cut off a piece whenever somebody needed butter at their table. What engaged my interest wasn't just the size of this buttery monolith (I'd never seen butter in more than 1-pound, or 450-gram, slabs) but the fact that, apart from what was carved off by the servers, it maintained its definition throughout the lunch rush, neither visibly softening around the edges nor melting into liquid at its base. I suspected, in fact, that what gave this butter its solidity was a low water content, and I remember thinking: you can't get butter like this in America.

Today, you can. Imported brands like the dense, luscious Kerrygold from Ireland, the leaner but pleasantly cheesy Delitia made from Parmigiano-Reggiano whey in Italy, the classic *beurre d'Échiré* from France, and the American-made "European style" Plugrá, all with higher butterfat (and lower water) content than the usual domestic kind, are readily available in supermarkets all over the country. And then there's Five Star Butter.

Five Star was developed for Clint Arthur, a Wharton Business School graduate who runs the Metro-Luxe Real Estate Development company. The way he tells the story, in 1999, his doctor suggested that he go on a dairy-rich raw-foods diet to help ameloriate his chronic knee injuries. He discovered that raw-milk (unpasteurized) butter didn't exist. He called 158 small family dairy farmers around the nation looking for somebody who made it or was willing to try, he says, and they all thought he was crazy. Finally, he found a couple in Kansas who had a herd of Certified Organic Guernsey cows and agreed to produce high butterfat butter for him from their unpasteurized cream. They shipped him a quantity of the butter, which he loved. He sold what he didn't need to friends, and found a few more farmers who could supply something similar. One day he got a call from a famous chef (unnamed) who'd heard about the butter and wanted some, too. Shortly thereafter, Arthur realized that he was onto something and launched the Five Star Butter Co. Today, many noted chefs use it (especially in Las Vegas, where Arthur is now based).

Arthur's operation has evolved over the years. To serve a large commercial base, Five Star is now produced from pasteurized milk, and that milk comes exclusively from Northern California, from grass-fed, organically raised cattle. It is still very high in butterfat, as much as 85 percent, compared with around 80 percent for most commercial butters (82 percent for Plugrá). It is golden in color and has a dense, creamy flavor and a fresh finish. Above all, it is rich, rich, rich, and I'll bet a block of it could stand the heat in a Brussels kitchen.

CANNED CHEESE

Cougar Gold is cheese in a can—which sounds immediately suspicious. Is this some kind of over-processed pseudo-cheese? Some marketing gimmick? Not at all. In 1926, the dairy sciences department of Washington State University, in eastern Washington, moved into a new building on campus, sharing space with a commercial dairy, Milk House. Working together, the university and the dairy began producing various products, including a number of cheeses. In the 1940s, with support from the American Can Company and the U.S. government, the two began experimenting with canning as a way to preserve cheese for storage and shipment. (Plastic packaging was not yet commercially available, and the wax seals that had been traditionally used for firm cheeses sometimes cracked, leading to spoilage.)

The university's most successful cheese was widely considered to be a variety of white Cheddar, which they began packing in 30-ounce (851-gram) cans. The school's athletic mascot is the cougar, and the man who refined the vacuum-packing process for the cans was a Dr. N. S. Golding, so the cheese was dubbed Cougar Gold.

Washington State took over full responsibility for the cheese in the late 1940s, and the commercial dairy moved out. The university also opened an ice cream shop, Ferdinand's, which to this day sells excellent frozen desserts to students and townspeople alike. By the early 1990s, the school's dairy operation had outgrown its original home, and in 1992 it had moved into the new Food Quality Building—an edifice whose construction had been largely funded by cheese and ice cream sales. Today, the school produces about 250,000 cans of cheese annually, with Cougar Gold, now available in several flavors, accounting for roughly 80 percent of that.

The original version remains the most popular, for good reason. While it has the sharp, aromatic character of any good white Cheddar, it has a slightly nutty overtone, too, reminiscent of the flavor of aged Gouda. It can be stored almost indefinitely in an unopened can in a cool place, and the cheese changes character with age, becoming slightly grainy (in an attractive way) and crumbly. The regular Cougar Gold is canned at the age of about a year; a special three-year-old version, with a sharper, more robust flavor, is even better.

CHEESE CURDS

Cheese curds are an acquired taste. Or maybe I should say an acquired texture, or even an acquired sound. Cheese curds aren't exactly cheese; they're more irregularly shaped lumps of soured milk on their way to becoming cheese—typically pieces of just-made Cheddar before it's processed and formed into blocks for aging. They are firm and rubbery in texture, and when they're fresh, they squeak when chewed (an effect caused by the release of air pockets trapped inside them).

In Canada, and especially Quebec, cheese curds are typically eaten partly melted as part of a fearsome local specialty called *poutine*, which consists of French-fried potatoes strewn with the curds, the whole then drenched in thick brown gravy. (Upscale variations add ingredients like foie gras or truffles to the mix.) In Wisconsin, where they might have been invented—or at least first identified as something comestible—and in parts of New York State and upper New England, they are eaten plain or seasoned with various herbs and/or spices, or even the American way: battered and deep-fried.

Many dairy operations large and small, above all in Wisconsin, produce cheese curds. Because they quickly lose their trademark squeak after they're made, cheese-curd fanatics tend to automatically prefer whichever ones are produced closest to where they live. For those beyond the cheese-curd belt, operations with efficient mail-order programs can supply the curds quickly. One of the best of these is the Ellsworth Cooperative Creamery, in the Wisconsin town of the same name—which was once proclaimed the state's Cheese Curd Capital by a former Wisconsin governor. The cooperative, whose roots date back to 1908, sources rBST-free milk (milk free of the hormone recombinant bovine somatotropin) from more than 400 independent dairy farmers all over Wisconsin and Minnesota. Some 1,700,000 pounds (77,000 kilograms) of milk are processed daily, twenty-four hours a day, five days a week. Ellsworth makes forty or so varieties of cheese in all, and since 1968 has produced particularly flavorful cheese curds, with a faintly sour, mild-Cheddar flavor and all the toothsome chewiness and squeak that connoisseurs demand.

CREAM CHEESE

In 1872, a dairyman named William Lawrence of Chester, in New York State's Orange County, decided to try to reproduce a French cheese called Neufchâtel, a soft, mold-ripened offering from Normandy, formed into the shape of a heart and believed to have been first made as early as the sixth century. He failed, and instead came up with something smoother and a little sourer than its French model, firm but still spreadable. He called it "cream cheese," and began marketing it in 1880, in blocks wrapped in foil, under the Empire label. He soon added the name "Philadelphia," not because it had anything to do with that city, but because, in late nineteenth-century America, the name had implications of quality and refinement. It did well until the Empire factory was destroyed by fire in 1900. Local businessmen and farmers rallied to build a new factory, called the Phenix [sic] Cheese Company, and Phenix bought the rights to Lawrence's recipe and the name Philadelphia. In 1928, the Kraft Cheese Company (which grew into Kraft Foods), then in the midst of an aggressive expansion campaign, purchased the operation, and Kraft continues to manufacture Philadelphia Cream Cheese to this day.

Cream cheese is rich (by law, it must contain at least 33 percent fat, though there are low-fat versions available) and mild in flavor, with a lively edge of tangy sweetness. It is an essential ingredient in New York-style cheesecake (see page 240), and it is pretty well impossible to imagine bagels without it. The Kraft plant that produces Philadelphia is now in Lowville, New York, north of Utica, near the Canadian border. Lowville holds an annual Cream Cheese Festival, featuring not just a recipe contest and concerts by local bands, but also a display of "the nation's largest cheesecake" (and the world's, too, I'd bet), as well as a cream cheese toss and cream cheese bingo. You have been warned.

CRÈME FRAÎCHE

Not long after Laura Chenel began producing her iconic goat cheese (see page 70) in Sebastopol, California, another young woman, Sadie Kendall, began doing the same some distance to the south, in Atascadero, on California's Central Coast. Kendall, who planned to go to law school, tried making some simple cheese at home just for fun in the meantime and found that she was so fascinated by the process that she changed her career plans and enrolled in the dairy science program at California Polytechnic Institute instead. When she completed her studies in 1981, she launched the Kendall Cheese Company, making delicious French-style chèvre. As a side project, she also began producing crème fraîche.

Its name is French for "fresh cream," but crème fraîche is actually intentionally soured, with a bacterial culture, and thus not strictly fresh at all. Probably originating in the Calvados region of Normandy (though similar products exist in Scandinavia, Eastern Europe,

and Mexico), crème fraîche is not as sour as conventional sour cream, and, unlike that substance, it won't break or curdle when cooked. It is also carbohydrate-free and lower in calories than butter or oil. These qualities, along with the fact that nobody else on the West Coast was making it, turned Kendall's crème fraîche into her best-selling product, eclipsing her cheese. It was so successful, in fact, that she gave up the goat cheese business and converted Kendall Cheese Company into Kendall Farms, selling crème fraîche and nothing but.

Kendall's product is very similar to the best French versions, based on cultured milk (she buys the raw material from a small local dairy whose cows are free of synthetic growth hormones), with no thickeners or other additives. It is thick and creamy but not gooey, and has a faintly nutty flavor, with mild acidity and just a trace of sour bite. Thomas Keller calls it "the paradigm of crème fraîche," and he should know.

CREOLE CREAM CHEESE

This traditional New Orleans specialty, a kind of farmer's cheese or clabber made from skim and half-and-half milk solids that have turned and separated, almost disappeared from the American larder. The theory is that the idea for this cream cheese—which is nothing like the Philadelphia kind (see page 54)—was brought to the Louisiana territory in the late eighteenth or early nineteenth century from Brittany. It was taken up by local food-lovers, remaining extremely popular in and around New Orleans for 150 years or so. Serious cream cheese lovers ate it for breakfast, seasoned with salt and pepper or sugar; it was also widely employed in cheesecake and other pastries, and in savory pies. For whatever reasons (perhaps wartime dairy shortages, or the sudden availability of new convenience foods), its popularity started waning after World War II. By 1980, there was only one concern still making it commercially.

The revival of interest in indigenous Southern foods, spurred by the Southern Foodways Alliance, among other groups, has encouraged at least one producer—Mauthe's Progress Milk Barn, not quite in Louisiana, but in Progress, Mississippi, a few miles from the Louisiana border—to start making this specialty again. Mauthe's, which describes the product as "a wet skim milk cheese curd surrounded in a heavy cream bath," supplies it to the restaurants run by New Orleans celebrity chef John Besh and to other Crescent City establishments. It's tart and ever so slightly floral, and tastes like something from the good old days.

DOUBLE-CREAM SOFT-RIPENED CHEESE

Al Wehner grew up on a dairy farm in western New York State, but headed down to the University of Georgia to attend agricultural school. There he met his future wife, Desiree, and after a freezing winter back home, he moved permanently to the South. In the early 1980s, the couple set up their Green Hill Dairy farm in Thomasville, Georgia, just north of the Florida state line. For two decades, they raised and milked their thousand-plus cows in the conventional way. Then, at a dairy seminar in Wisconsin, they learned about New Zealand-style rotational grazing, by which herds are moved from one small pasture to another, allowing forage growth to regenerate, and they converted their operation to adopt the practice. Their new philosophy, Al says, was to "let cows be cows."

Along the way, Desiree became interested in cheesemaking, and flew across the country to Cal Poly University in San Luis Obispo, prime Central California dairy country. There,

she fell in love with goat cheese, and she returned to Georgia determined to produce her own. For a year, she made it herself for family and friends. Then, in 2000, the Wehners set up Sweet Grass Dairy, near their farm, using milk from a small herd of dairy goats and their own cows at Green Hill. The Wehners' daughter, Jessica, had ambitions to leave farm life and launch a career in marketing; her husband, Jeremy Little, was an aspiring chef from Toledo, Ohio. Somehow, the elder Wehners talked them into revising their life plans and taking over Sweet Grass, and in 2005, they sold the operation to the Littles.

Green Hill was the first cheese Sweet Grass produced, and it remains the star of their line. It is simply world-class cheese, a Camembert-inspired double-cream, soft-ripe wheel with an ivory-hued interior and a fine white rind; it is buttery and salty-sweet, with a faint foresty aftertaste, and I'd put it up against almost anything from France.

EXTRA-AGED FIRM CHEESE

Pleasant Ridge, near Dodgeville (home of the Land's End mail-order operation), is in southwestern Wisconsin, in a portion of what is called the Driftless Area—so named because it's a region that wasn't flattened by receding glaciers at the end of the Ice Age, and so lacks residual drift, the name given collectively to rocks and soil left behind by glacial retreat. But the region's gently rolling hills and aeolian silt, or loess, on which flourish a variety of grasses, legumes, and wildflowers, make it very good dairy country.

In the early 1980s, local dairy farmers Dan and Jeanne Patenaude had helped pioneer rotational grazing (see page 57), then virtually unknown in America. In 1994, they and their neighbors, Mike and Carol Gingrich, went into partnership to buy a 300-acre (120-hectare) property nearby, where they divided the pasture into small paddocks. Cows graze in a different one each day, and are milked only seasonally, with a few months off every winter. This results, the Patenaudes and Gingriches believe, in unusually rich and flavorful milk. That milk is at the heart of the extraordinary Pleasant Ridge Reserve, made by Uplands Cheese, which the partners founded in 2000.

Pleasant Ridge is a Gruyère-style raw-milk cheese, produced in 10-pound (4.5 kilogram) wheels only from May through October. The cheese is ripened at the creamery, its rind washed several times a week with brine to promote the growth of bacteria beneficial to the aging process. Each year a small batch of the cheese is aged for twelve months or so, and this is sold as "Extra Aged." This is a rich, firm, nutty cheese with some of those wonderful, crunchy little crystals of lactic acid throughout.

FRESH CHEESE

Unless you lived in New York City's Little Italy or another predominantly Italian neighborhood around the country, "mozzarella" used to mean a firm, rubbery orb that squeaked when you cut it and was useful mostly for melting on pizza and in lasagna. Then, before the real thing was being widely imported from Italy, as it is today, California-born Paula Lambert started making her own version of the cheese in her adopted home of Dallas, Texas, and our perception of the cheese changed for the better.

The only thing more unusual than Texas mozzarella might be the conditions under which Lambert fell in love with it and learned how to make it for herself. A one-time first-grade teacher, she went to Italy after college to study art history and learn Italian. It was in her temporary home in Perugia, Umbria, in central Italy, that mozzarella first captivated her—and it was in nearby Assisi, at the Caseificio (cheese factory) Brufani, that she learned how it was produced. This is surprising only because the traditional home of mozzarella, and especially of *mozzarella di bufala* (the most prized variety, made from the milk of the water buffalo), is the region of Campania, 175 miles (280 kilometers) or so and a vast cultural and culinary distance to the southeast. Learning to make mozzarella in Umbria, it might be said, is a bit like learning how to make tortillas in Montana. Nonetheless, Brufani makes excellent cheese, mozzarella and otherwise, and Lambert obviously learned her lessons well.

Back in the States, Lambert took various jobs as a community volunteer—experience she later said taught her how to run a business—and then, in 1982, launched the Mozzarella Company. Today, she produces a range of mozzarella relatives including a smoked version, a Mexican-style mozzarella, burratas filled with butter or crème fraîche, and a goat's milk mozzarella, but her classic cow's milk cheese remains her signature. (She made *mozzarella di bufala* for a short time, but had problems finding a consistent source of good milk, and so gave it up.) It is a moist, luxuriously soft cheese, mild but with a definite fresh-milk flavor. It melts just fine on pizza, but is good enough to eat alone, with just a little sea salt sprinkled over it.

MILD BLUE CHEESE

Michael Miller was the publisher of the Pulitzer Prize-winning *Berkshire Eagle*, out of Pittsfield in Berkshire County, Massachusetts, a newspaper his grandfather had founded, until the family sold it to a big Colorado-based media company in 1995. Miller was a cheese-lover who once said that he had a hard time finding a good blue cheese to go with his nightly martini, so he decided to devote his new-found free time to making one himself. He liked an English cheese called Exmoor Blue, made in Somerset by Dr. Alan Duffield, so he contacted Duffield and asked if he could come visit. Duffield taught Miller how to make blue cheese, and even licensed to him the bacteria he used so that he could try producing his own version back in Massachusetts. In 1999, Miller set up Berkshire Cheese, LLC in the town of Dalton and commenced making what has turned out to be quite possibly the premier blue cheese in America, based on raw Jersey cow's milk and inoculated with two blue molds and one white one.

About half a dozen years ago, Ira Grable, a New York businessman looking for a career change, ended up in the Berkshires and took a job assisting Miller and helping to expand the market for Berkshire Blue. When Miller mentioned that he was getting ready to close down the cheese factory to retire, Grable bought it from him, and he continues operating it as Miller did.

Berkshire Blue might remind you of Stilton, but it's creamier and milder, low in acidity and not too salty, with a texture that can be as soft as young Brie but also firms up nicely with a bit of age. Unlike some small-batch cheeses, it seems very consistent in quality; I have yet to try a disappointing sample. Now, hand me my martini.

MILD FIRM CHEESE

Dairy farming has been a major industry in the Azores since cattle, goats, and sheep were first imported to the islands from the Iberian Peninsula in the fifteenth century. A Portuguese-owned archipelago in the North Atlantic, roughly a third of the way across the ocean from Portugal to America's East Coast, the Azores have sent many émigrés to this country, many of them settling in Rhode Island and parts of Massachusetts, most notably New Bedford and Fall River. (Celebrity chef Emeril Lagasse's family are among the Fall River Azoreans.) Some, though, continued on across the nation to Northern California, where many of them became fishermen or farmers.

Joe and Mary Matos are more recently imported from the Azores than many of their compatriots, having left the island of São Jorge, or St. George, only in the 1970s. Like many Azoreans before them, though, they also made their way to California, where they bought a dairy farm in Santa Rosa, in Sonoma County. Of all the Azores, São Jorge was particularly famous for its cheese, and the Matos family had been making it there for generations. Joe Matos brought the formula and the know-how with him, and started producing a version of the cheese, named after his native island, in his new home. It is the only cheese Matos produces, using unpasteurized milk from his own cows, and he has been doing it now for more than three decades. It's hardly surprising, then, that he has it down right. Aged for at least two months and for as long as seven, St. George is quite firm in texture, with small, irregularly sized holes—more like Havarti, say, than Swiss. It is richly flavored, a bit buttery in taste though not in texture, and finishes with a trace of Cheddar-like pungency.

MILD GOAT CHEESE

Like so many goat cheese producers, in America and elsewhere, Mary Keehn started with just one goat. A single mom living in Sonoma County, she decided that she wanted to feed her young children healthy foods, and goat's milk was near the top of the list. There was a cow dairy nearby that used goats for brush control, and she asked them if she could buy one. "If you can catch one," she was told, "you can have it for free." She managed to do just that, and discovered that she loved these bearded little animals. Before long, she had fifty goats, and of course with fifty goats came more milk than she and her four children could drink, so Keehn started teaching herself how to turn it into cheese for family and friends.

Her efforts got better and better, and by 1983, when she moved her children and her goats to Arcata, in Northern California's Humboldt County, she was ready to go into cheesemaking professionally, setting up a small cheese factory that she dubbed Cypress Grove Chevre. Today, Cypress Grove offers a line of thirteen cheeses, the best-known of which is Humboldt Fog, a creamy, faintly citrusy chèvre bisected and lightly coated with a thin layer of edible vegetable ash (like that in the noted French cheese Morbier). In 2010, Keehn sold the company to Roth Käse USA, a division of Emmi, the largest processor of fresh milk in Switzerland, but she and her staff remain in place and the cheese hasn't changed.

MILD SEMI-FIRM CHEESE

Meadow Creek Appalachian is what Brie might look and taste like if it had been invented in the mountains of rural Virginia instead of the flat farmland of the Seine-et-Marne. It is thicker than Brie and square rather than round, with a soft white rind dotted with flecks of brown and a rich yellow interior that grows increasingly unctuous with age. It has a grassy freshness with a hint of citrus up front, and finishes with a foresty mushroom flavor that intensifies as the cheese grows older. It melts superbly (making a great grilled cheese sandwich, among other things), but is also a first-rate cheese-and-crackers cheese.

All good cheese depends on good milk, of course, and Meadow Creek proprietors Helen and Rick Feete (she is also the cheesemaker) have been raising Jersey dairy cows since 1981 on their farm in Galax, in southwestern Virginia. For years they sold their raw milk to local dairies for pasteurization, but in 1998 they decided to try making cheese, diverting about 20 percent of their herd's yield for that purpose. They make cheese only from milk produced in seasons when the Jerseys can graze in open pastures, but varying aging periods for different types of cheese mean that they can sell at least one product at any given time all year round. Their Swiss-style Mountaineer is available from November through July each year; their Grayson, reminiscent of Italy's Taleggio, and Appalachian are usually on the market from June through March. The Feetes cite their "elevation, pure water, clean air, and deep soils" as contributing to the quality of the milk they use, and they note proudly that they put great emphasis, in general, on their cows' "quality of life."

MILD SEMI-SOFT CHEESE

Many foods have creation myths, which are often tales of accidental discovery. In the case of Teleme cheese, it is said that some time in the early twentieth century, a Greek cheesemaker named Serafino Iacono, in Pleasanton, California, southeast of Oakland, was trying to make feta, and somehow ended up with a creamier cheese that ripened into buttery softness instead of drying into a crumbly state as feta does. (Iacono is an Italian name, usually associated with Sicily and the island of Ischia, off the coast of Naples.) He knew a good thing when he tasted it, and set up a dairy facility in Tomales, on the Sonoma coast, to manufacture what he dubbed Tomales Bay Teleme Cheese. Just to add to the Greek-Italian confusion, *teleme* is the Turkish word for "curd."

Iacono's cheese, in any case, was similar in consistency to Italian cheeses like Crescenza and other members of the Stracchino family, and Italian cheesemakers in California were soon making Teleme as well. Among these were the Peluso family, who set up shop in Los Banos, in California's Central Valley, in 1925. They added the refinement of coating the finished cheese in a dusting of rice flour.

As the cheese ages, this forms a thin crust that helps keep the interior moist.

Teleme is a truly luscious cheese: smooth and rich, lightly salty, and a little tart in a lemony sort of way, with a delicious flavor that its fans say is the pure taste of the best California cow's milk. At the age of six or eight weeks, it develops a nicely sour aroma and becomes so soft that you can almost eat it with a spoon (one promoter of Teleme used to describe it as "the poor man's Brie," though the similarity is slight in my opinion). Teleme is excellent when spread on grilled country bread and scattered with sea salt; it also melts wonderfully into sauces, is perfect pizza cheese, and makes a superlative grilled cheese sandwich.

Franklin Peluso, whose grandfather Giovanni started the Los Banos facility, sold his cheese company in 2006 and moved to Maine to try to make cheese there. The cold weather defeated him and his family, and he returned to California the following year. He no longer had rights to the Peluso name commercially, though, so he now makes the same Teleme his family has long produced under the name Franklin's Cheese. I think it's the best of the genre.

PIMENTO CHEESE

It's the pâté de foie gras, the hummus, and the blue cheese dip of the American South—the ubiquitous condiment, traditionally served in tea sandwiches on crustless white bread but also spread on crackers, piped into celery sticks (or in fancy households, spears of Belgian endive), used in place of mayonnaise in deviled eggs (another favorite Southern specialty), even spread onto hamburgers or hot dogs (see page 134), or used in grilled cheese sandwiches. In tea-sandwich form, it is pretty much the official food of the Masters golf tournament held annually in Augusta, Georgia.

Pimento cheese is simply a seasoned spread of Cheddar cheese, mayonnaise (some recipes substitute or add cream cheese), and finely chopped pimentos, a variety of sweet red pepper usually out of a jar. Some recipes spice it up with hot sauce, chopped chiles, or cayenne pepper. Because it is easy to make, almost everybody mixes up their own, but there are also ready-made versions available, and quite possibly the best of these comes from Blackberry Farm in Walland, Tennessee.

The property supposedly got its name when Florida Laiser—passing through Tennessee with her husband, Dave, in 1930, on the way from Chicago to the Georgia coast—stopped on the site and snagged her stockings on the thorns of a blackberry bush. The Laisers, deciding that the location would be a perfect place to build their dream home, bought the land and constructed a farmhouse-style residence there. Another couple, Kreis and Sandy Beall, bought the place in 1976, and opened part of it as a six-room country inn. Today, Blackberry Farm is a rustic-elegant resort property, part of the Relais & Châteaux group, and run by the Bealls' son, Sam.

The cuisine at Blackberry Farm is one of its great attractions. Chef Joseph Lenn uses regional ingredients skillfully, serving elderflower-scented pear and farmstead duck salad, seared North Carolina trout in ham hock broth, and other sophisticated treats—but he also makes an irresistible pimento cheese. Good Cheddar is mixed with mayonnaise and with butter, which adds a note of richness, and the pimentos are roasted in-house, giving the blend a faintly smoky sweetness.

SHEEP'S MILK YOGURT

The first time I visited the Old Chatham Sheepherding Company—in Columbia County, New York, southeast of Albany, between the Hudson River and the Berkshire Mountains—it was a tiny country inn with an excellent restaurant and a barn full of sheep on the side. The owners of the bucolic 600-acre (240-hectare) property, Tom and Nancy Clark, closed the inn and restaurant in 1999 to concentrate on the sheep and specifically on making cheese and yogurt from their milk. They now tend more than a thousand East Friesian purebred and crossbred ewes, and claim to have the largest sheep dairy farm in America.

Sheep have fascinated Tom Clark ever since he won a blue ribbon for his Hampshire sheep at the Dutchess County Fair as a ten-year-old rural New York farmboy. He and Nancy are directly involved in every aspect of their operation. Their fields are organically managed, and their animals are raised without growth hormones and receive antibiotics only if they're ill. The Old Chatham staff of five employees and one border collie (Reggie) work seven days a week; between three and four hundred ewes are milked twice daily, and the milk is processed in state-of-the-art facilities. Sheep's milk is higher in calcium, protein, vitamins, and zinc than cow's milk, and it is more easily digested as well. It also converts splendidly into more complex products.

Old Chatham's cheeses are excellent (their Camembert is particularly good), but their yogurt is unparalleled. It is made solely from pasteurized sheep's milk and active cultures, with no stabilizers or thickeners added. There are several flavored varieties, including one with pure maple syrup added and another accented with crystallized ginger. The plain version, though, is so full of flavor, with an appealing creamy richness and a tangy sour bite, that variations, however good, seem beside the point.

STRONG BLUE CHEESE

Maytag Blue—yes, that Maytag. The washing machine folks. At least, the same family. In 1941, in Newton, Iowa, the original home of the Maytag Corporation, two young men named Fred and Robert Maytag—grandsons of the appliance company's founder, Frederick Louis Maytag I—began producing this cheese, using milk from a herd of award-winning dairy cows kept by their father, E. H. Maytag. (They later inherited the dairy from him.) The Maytag brothers were inspired to undertake their project when they learned that, several years earlier, a couple of microbiologists at Iowa State University had developed a new technique for making blue cheese. The researchers had long been attempting to make an American version of France's esteemed Roquefort—one of the world's great blue cheeses, based on sheep's milk—and had developed a way to produce what they believed was a similar product from homogenized cow's milk. (Among other things, they added an increased amount of rennet—the coagulating agent in most cheese—and ramped up the temperature at which the milk was allowed to set.) Maytag Blue turned out to be very different in flavor, consistency, and even color from Roquefort, but it became an American classic—and while there is plenty of competition these days (see, for example, page 60), it is certainly a blue cheese worth mentioning alongside just about anything in that category made anywhere else in the world.

As with Roquefort, Maytag Blue—before it becomes blue cheese—is inoculated with *Penicillium* mold, then aged in cool, damp chambers, where the mold spreads throughout the cheese, giving it its blue-green veins. Though the Maytag dairy no longer maintains its own milk cows, it does buy fresh milk from farmers in the surrounding area, and the cheese is still made the way it was at first: by hand, in small batches. It is a creamy rather than crumbly blue, and has a forthright, tangy flavor, though it is not as mouth-puckeringly intense as some blue cheeses. It goes very nicely with, among other things, full-flavored beer—for instance, Liberty Ale, from San Francisco-based Anchor Brewing, headed until his recent retirement by Maytag Blue co-founder Fred Maytag's son, Fritz.

STRONG FIRM CHEESE

To the unsuspecting pedestrian strolling past the corner of 20th Street and Broadway in Manhattan's Flatiron District, the view into Beecher's inevitably comes as a surprise. There, instead of the array of sporty clothing or sleek electronics that many vitrines in the neighborhood display, stands an immense arrangement of stainless steel vats and pipes, the former often filled with large blocks of something white sitting in what looks like milky water, while white-garbed workers manipulate it this way and that. This is cheesemaking, on a commercial scale, going on in the middle of the city. This is Beecher's.

After college, Kurt Dammeier helped run the family printing business, an international corporation with offices in Boston and San Jose, California, as well as in Germany and Scotland. He became CEO at thirty-two, and sold the company at thirty-eight. He'd always loved food, and, by then living in Seattle, he decided to set up a business that would allow him to pursue his passion. He named it Sugar Mountain, after the Neil Young song. Following a brief stint in the brewery business, he launched a "deli/bakery/pantry" called Pasta & Co., later adding Bennett's Pure Food Bistro and a food truck called Maximus/Minimus to his small culinary empire.

In the back of his mind, Dammeier also thought it might be a good idea to, as he once put it, "make cheese where people could see it and eat it." Walking through Seattle's celebrated Pike Place Market one day in late 2002, he saw a space for lease and thought it would be perfect for his purposes. His grandfather's name was Beecher, and he had a vivid memory of seeing him once buy a wheel of Stilton, so he decided to name the new enterprise in his honor. Taking a cheesemaking course at Washington State University (see page 52) convinced Dammeier that he shouldn't try to make cheese himself, so he hired Brad Sinko, former cheesemaker at the family-owned Bandon Cheese Factory in Oregon, and made an agreement to source milk for him to work with from a farm just northeast of Seattle. Beecher's opened its doors in Pike Place Market in November 2003, while the Manhattan outpost appeared in the summer of 2011. Sinko's triumph is Beecher's Flagship Reserve, a semi-firm Cheddar-like cow's milk cheese, aged for at least fifteen months, that is both smooth and a little crumbly, with a nice tang of salt, a nutty flavor, and a long finish. There is no scientific evidence that watching it being produced makes it taste better, but it doesn't hurt.

STRONG FIRM SHEEP'S CHEESE

In 1917, Buzzell Sankow, who had immigrated to Connecticut in 1903 from what later became Yugoslavia, bought a 175-acre (70-hectare) dairy farm in Lyme—called Beaver Brook after the stream that runs through the property—for $2,000 ($36,000, or £22,000, in today's money). After World War II, with the New England dairy industry in the doldrums, the Sankow family began raising beef cattle. Buzzell's grandson, Stan, and Stan's wife, Suzanne, took over the farm in 1984; because Suzanne was an avid spinner and weaver, Stan bought her a couple of sheep, named Ding and Sherry, to add to the livestock mix. Today, the Sankows have only about a dozen Jersey cows but more than 600 sheep, mostly Frislands and Romneys.

I first met the couple at the weekly spring-to-autumn Greenwich farmers' market, 70 miles (112 kilometers) or so down the coast from their farm. There, the Beaver Brook stand sells lamb and a little veal, some prepared dishes like lamb stew, some yogurt and milk, Suzanne's handspun woolen accessories (in cooler weather), and best of all a very nice array of cheeses, based on both sheep's and cow's milk.

Suzanne started making cheese in 1984, apprenticing with a Belgian cheesemaker and initially using only the surplus sheep's milk they had during lambing season each year. In 2002, they added cow's milk cheese, which can be made year-round, and today they produce more than 15,000 pounds (6,800 kilograms) of cheese in all each year. I'd have a hard time picking a favorite from among the half-dozen or so examples they produce, but if pressed, I'd probably have to choose the one they call simply Farmstead (meaning that it's made from the milk of animals raised on their property). Based on raw sheep's milk and aged to an old-ivory hue, it is tangy, a little grassy, and full of flavor, a bit reminiscent of an old Gouda.

STRONG GOAT CHEESE

Laura Chenel gave America the gift of goat cheese. Growing up in Sonoma County, in a family that had dabbled in poultry farming, Chenel found herself, as a young woman, raising goats, for goat's milk, with some friends. The milk soon outpaced their thirst, and Chenel tried making cheese with some of it—a disaster, she later reported. But she kept at it, eventually traveling to France to apprentice with cheesemakers there, and in 1979 began producing a rich, silky, tangy fresh chèvre in the Sonoma County town of Sebastopol. In 1981, Alice Waters, who had started Chez Panisse a decade earlier and was passionately dedicated to local food products long before "locavore" became a word, happened to taste the cheese, and liked it well enough to place a standing order for the restaurant. There, she breaded and baked whole small Laura Chenel chèvres and nestled them in beds of mesclun greens, thus creating the warm goat cheese salad that became one

of the first clichés of the New American Cuisine.

By the 1990s, Chenel's company was selling more than two million pounds (about nine hundred thousand kilograms) of cheese a year—and in 2006, she sold it to Rians, a family-owned French producer of cheeses and desserts. Chenel remains in charge of her own herd of about 500 goats, each of which she has named personally, and their milk goes into the chèvre that bears her name, along with that supplied by some thirteen other farmers in California and Nevada. Cheeses under the Chenel label are now available in several sizes, shapes, and ages, some flavored with pepper or herbs. The definitive version, to me, is the Crottin (the word, traditionally used for a small, rounded chèvre in France, literally means "dung"— presumably for its shape). This is a slightly firm 3-ounce (85-gram) cheese with a snowy exterior and a lingering earthy flavor.

STRONG SEMI-SOFT CHEESE

Its name is German and its pungent aroma might be considered by some to be downright alien, but Liederkranz as such exists only in America. The story of its creation begins with a German immigrant cheese factory owner named Adolphe Tode, who ran the Monroe Cheese Company in Monroe, in New York's Hudson Valley. Tode had customers who wanted a locally produced version of a smelly German cheese called Bismarck Schlosskäse. In 1891, one of his cheesemakers, Emil Frey—who also invented Velveeta—eventually came up with a good reproduction. (Liederkranz is also closely related to another strong-smelling cheese, Limburger.) Members of a famous New York City singing society, the Liederkranz Club (the word means "wreath of song"), were among the first to sample the new cheese, and Tode named it in their honor.

The saga of Liederkranz since its early days is a complicated one. Tode sold his company to new owners, and the operation was moved to Van Wert, Ohio, in 1926, with Frey in tow. In 1929, it was bought by the Borden Company, which ran the plant and produced Liederkranz and other cheeses for more than fifty years. Despite a fire that damaged the facility in 1973, manufacturing continued until Borden sold the

operation to the Fisher Cheese Company in 1981. Four years later, bacterial contamination was discovered in a batch of Liederkranz and several other Fisher cheeses, and production of Liederkranz was halted. The name and culture were sold to Beatrice Foods, which was in turn subsumed by the agribusiness giant ConAgra, and Liederkranz disappeared from the marketplace. ConAgra sold off their cheese holdings to Wisconsin-based DCI Cheese Company—makers of Black Diamond Cheddar and other popular brands—in the mid-2000s.

DCI thought that renewed interest in traditional and regional American products, and our increased exposure as a nation to varied cheeses from around the world, might mean that there could be a revived market for Liederkranz. In 2010—based on Emil Frey's original recipe, and new cultures developed by the University of Wisconsin Center for Dairy Research—they released the first Liederkranz seen in a quarter-century. And it has lost none of its power. If you can get past its ammoniated (some would say acrid) odor, it is pretty good—creamy, sharp, a little sweet, and very, very strong. Take a few bites of Liederkranz, and you'll know that you've been eating cheese. So will everyone around you.

STRONG SOFT-RIPENED CHEESE

When I was a young magazine editor and aspiring food and wine writer back in the 1970s, I had the very good fortune to fall in with a group of wine people—distributors, retailers, and serious collectors—who met every Saturday at a modest restaurant in Beverly Hills (this was back when there *were* modest restaurants in Beverly Hills) and tasted a heroic number of bottles of wine that could be anything from great to undrinkable. The final course of our weekly repast, which we brought ourselves from a nearby cheese shop, was always Brie—often the original French article, but sometimes an example from the Marin French Cheese Co., which was commonly agreed to be the equal of anything imported. I acquired a taste for this delicious and (compared to its French cousins) affordable luxury, and for a year or so ate it almost constantly. Then I branched out: I discovered Marin French Cheese Camembert (previously called Rouge et Noir Camembert).

Marin French Cheese was founded in 1865, and thus lays fair claim to being the oldest continuously operating cheese factory in America. The man behind it was one Jefferson A. Thompson, who owned a dairy farm in Petaluma, California, the Sonoma County community now best known as the state's poultry capital. He began making what he described as "California granular cheese," which he first sold to San Francisco saloons as a snack to replace pickled eggs during an egg shortage. The cheese was hauled by wagon to the Petaluma River, whence a steamer transported it to the Bay Area. In the early 1900s, Thompson turned his attention to French- and Italian-style cheeses. Until the 1930s, the operation used only milk from its own herds, but in an effort to help farmers in the area during the Depression, Marin French Cheese began buying milk from them. This was not only neighborly, but allowed them to expand their production. The company was sold to Rians (see page 70) in 2011.

A triple crème Brie, Marin French Cheese Brie is still as luscious as I remember it being many years ago. It is unfailingly creamy, with a hint of sweetness. On two occasions, in 2005 and 2010, it has taken first prize in an international blind tasting of Bries from around the world, edging out several prime examples from France, among other cheeses. This, of course, has been no surprise to me.

TRIPLE-CREAM SOFT-RIPENED CHEESE

Cowgirl Creamery's Sue Conley and Peggy Smith are veterans of the San Francisco Bay Area restaurant scene (Conley was co-proprietor of Bette's Oceanview Diner in Berkeley, while Smith worked nearby for seventeen years at Chez Panisse) who fell in love with cheese and decided to make it their business. Conley had become friendly with the Straus family, proprietors of the Straus Family Creamery in Point Reyes Station, which was in the process of becoming the first certified organic dairy west of the Mississippi, and moved to Point Reyes herself. Smith was inspired by the highly regarded Bordeaux-based *affineur*, or cheese merchant, Jean d'Alos, whose wares were featured at Chez Panisse, and by Randolph Hodgson, who helped revive the British artisanal cheese movement at his Neal's Yard Dairy in London. In 1994, Conley and Smith decided to go into business together, both making their own cheese and selling a selection of domestic and imported offerings from producers they respected. Today

they produce cheese in both Point Reyes Station and Petaluma, and have shops at their original creamery at the Ferry Plaza complex in San Francisco, and in the Penn Quarter in Washington, D.C. (Conley is from the D.C. area and Smith was raised nearby in northern Virginia).

Cowgirl Creamery produces seven different cheeses, most of them named for local landmarks, as well as crème fraîche, clabbered cottage cheese, and fromage blanc, all based on organic milk from the Straus family. Everything is first-rate, but the creamery's signature creation is Mt Tam, which borrows its moniker from Mount Tamalpais, the tallest peak in the Marin Hills, roughly equidistant from Mill Valley in one direction and Stinson Beach in the other. It is a plump round of cheese, a soft-ripened triple-cream (like Brillat-Savarin or St. André), dense and rich and creamy, with a flavor that is mild but pronounced, and a suggestion of wild mushrooms in the finish.

FISH & SHELLFISH

ABALONE

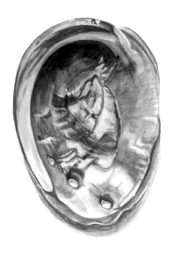 

In the 1950s and 1960s, when I used to stroll the beaches of Santa Monica and Malibu, there were abalone shells everywhere—big, concave affairs, typically 7 or 8 inches (about 18–20 centimeters) across, lined with iridescent mother-of-pearl. Almost everybody who lived on or near the beach had at least a few of them at home, probably used as ashtrays. In the same era, the meat—botanically the foot—that had come out of those shells was a staple on the menus at all the best restaurants in Southern California, always served the same way: pounded into an immense, irregularly shaped disk 10 or 12 inches (about 25–30 centimeters) in diameter, dredged in flour and cracker meal, fried in butter, and served with lemon wedges to be squeezed over the top. It was magnificent, mild and sweet. Long since disappeared from our tables, it is a dish that I mourn, and I'm sure I'm not alone.

Abalone is technically an overgrown sea snail, a marine gastropod mollusk. There are a number of varieties, and it is eaten all over the world, from Japan to South Africa, Chile to Australia. While it is still fished commercially in some places, it started becoming rarer and rarer in this country in the 1970s, and by the '80s, it had all but disappeared. Environmental protection measures had increased the population of sea otters, people said, and sea otters liked nothing better than to float on their backs eating abalone. So, more sea otters,

fewer of these delicious sea snails. In 1957, the commercial abalone harvest in California reached 5.4 million pounds (2.44 million kilograms); by the mid-1990s, it had dropped to about 300,000 pounds (136,000 kilograms). The commercial abalone fishery was officially closed in 1997.

The only way any of us are ever likely to be able to enjoy abalone in the old style is to know a licensed abalone sport-fisher and to cook it ourselves. With a permit, sportsmen may harvest—through shoreline scavenging or non-scuba-assisted diving in certain defined areas—up to three 7-inch (18-centimeter) or larger red abalone, up to a maximum of twenty-four a year, and only from April through June and August through November. Get to know one of those guys. It's worth it.

Failing that, the best alternatives are small farm-raised abalone, which measure 2–3 inches (about 5–7 centimeters) across and come five or six to the pound. These may be prepared the same way, but somehow they're not the same. If you want to try them, though, Dave Rudie, a one-time professional sea urchin and seaweed diver, supplies some of the best farm-raised abalone through his San Diego-based company Catalina Offshore Products. They have some of the sweetness of the wild abalone of old but just aren't as flavorful, and of course there's not as much of them.

BLUE POINT OYSTERS

Oysters were being harvested commercially in the Great South Bay, between Fire Island and the town of Blue Point on Long Island's Suffolk County coastline, as long ago as the early 1800s, and so-called Blue Point oysters became famous in the finest restaurants of New York City and beyond—they were even said to have found their way to London, where Queen Victoria pronounced them her favorite. They were so much in demand, in fact, that counterfeits started showing up— or at least the Blue Point name started getting applied to similar-looking oysters from other parts of the Eastern Seaboard. The situation got so bad that the New York State Legislature passed a law in 1908 restricting use of the name to oysters that had been cultivated in the Great South Bay. Of course, New York State law didn't much bother entrepreneurs from New Jersey, Connecticut, and elsewhere, so non-Blue Point versions continued to proliferate—all the more so after the original Great South Bay beds became depleted.

For generations, the Blue Points that showed up on restaurant menus all over America were actually harvested from the Long Island Sound off Bridgeport, Norwalk, and other Connecticut cities. These could be very good oysters, and in fact Connecticut Blue Points are still, to my taste, one of the better oysters coming out of the thriving New England oyster industry. In 1995, though, an oysterman named Chris Quartuccio revived the oyster beds off Blue Point itself, and today the only supplier of what I suppose must be called original Blue Points is his Blue Island Shellfish Farms. (He also developed and whimsically named the delicious oysters called Naked Cowboys.) Quartuccio's Blue Points stand out. They're a kind of classic oyster, medium in size, firm in texture, just briny enough, with a clean, lightly metallic aftertaste. Queen Victoria obviously knew her bivalves.

CALIFORNIA LOBSTER

In the 1970s, my friends and I sometimes used to drive down from Los Angeles into Baja California for lunch. It took about three hours to go south to Tijuana, and longer coming back, but it was worth it for the food—real tacos, not the Taco Bell variety(!)—and the exotic, seedy atmosphere of some of the bars we'd happen into. Then we discovered Puerto Nuevo, another forty minutes or so down the coast, and, for a few years at least, we forgot about tacos altogether.

Puerto Nuevo was a 1950s-era ticky-tacky fishing village, and what was mostly fished was *langosta roja*, otherwise known as California spiny lobster. A relative of the Caribbean lobster and other spiny species, this is a big, meaty creature with two spine-barbed antennae but no claws. Although these crustaceans become legal to catch when their carapace reaches 3 inches (about 7 centimeters) in length, a typical specimen is at least a foot (about 30 centimeters) long, and examples as long as 2 feet (61 centimeters) have been recorded. This lobster may bear California's name, but it's range reaches from San Luis Obispo Bay in Central California, and occasionally as far north as Monterey, all the way down the Mexican coast to the Gulf of Tehuantepec, almost to the Guatemalan border. Most of what's sold commercially in the U.S. and northern Mexico, though, comes from the waters of Baja California.

Puerto Nuevo in the 1970s didn't have restaurants per se, but a number of houses had rooms repurposed to serve food. The menu was always the same: spiny lobster, fresh in season (roughly October through March) and otherwise frozen, halved and cooked in lard on a griddle, then served with rice, beans, and homemade flour tortillas. There was usually a cooler in one corner with Mexican sodas and beer, but we figured out early on that nobody minded if you brought your own wine (and corkscrew). If I'm remembering correctly, this repast cost $2 per person (about $10, or £6, today), but at any rate it was cheap enough that on more than one occasion we ordered second helpings.

Puerto Nuevo is now a thriving tourist attraction, with more than thirty restaurants and acres of neon signs. I haven't eaten there for years, but I've never forgotten the sweet, full flavor of the lobsters I ate there—they feed on sea urchins, clams, and mussels, lending them a complex character—and I always order California lobster if I find it fresh someplace else. That's not always easy, as a good many restaurants, even in the Golden State itself, seem to believe that Maine lobster (see page 91) is superior to the local variety. Even the annual Port of Los Angeles Lobster Festival in the fishing town of San Pedro serves only Maine lobster! In my opinion, while the claw meat of good Maine lobster is unbeatable, I'd put the body meat of its California cousin up against the Maine equivalent any day.

Catalina Offshore Products (see page 76) ships live California lobster in season. A good year-round source for frozen ones is Anaheim-based Anderson Seafoods, founded by seafood business veterans Dennis and Leean Anderson in 1979 and still very much a family operation.

CALIFORNIA SPOT PRAWNS

Prawns aren't shrimp, at least not exactly. This gets a little complicated, because we sometimes describe very large shrimp as prawns—and in Great Britain, the term is commonly used for shrimp of all kinds. Marine biologists, however, will tell you that the two creatures come from different families and have slight differences in exterior anatomy (not that anybody pays marine biologists much mind in the matter). The rare, delicious little crustaceans called ridgeback shrimp, for instance, are in fact prawns, and the formidable California spot prawns fished off the Pacific Coast of Alaska, British Columbia, the U.S., and Baja California are—you guessed it—actually shrimp.

The prime waters for California spot prawns flow around the Channel Islands in the Santa Barbara Channel, and for that reason they are also sometimes called Santa Barbara spot prawns. (In sushi bars, under the name *amaebi*, they are frequently served as "sweet shrimp.") Spot prawns are in season in some part of their range from approximately March through October, but because they're hand-harvested and shipped live (at least the best ones are), they tend to be pretty pricey, up to $35 (£23) or more a pound ($70, or £47, or more per kilogram). Are they worth it? I think so. To begin with, fresh (live) shrimp in general tend to have a more vivid flavor than their frozen counterparts and are tender, not rubbery, in texture. Spot prawns are unusually savory, though, with a lightly salty sweetness and a rich flavor that reminds some people of lobster. They're also nice and big, usually measuring eight or nine to the pound (half-kilogram). The only problem is that they'll pretty much spoil you for most other varieties of shrimp.

The best source I've found for live spot prawns in season is the San Francisco-based Farm-2-Market, which longtime shrimp and oyster merchant Marshall Shnider apparently runs from his home in rural New York State. He points out that, unlike many shellfish and crustacean species these days, spot prawns are plentiful, and since they're caught in traps rather than with nets, there is low bycatch and their harvest has minimal environmental impact.

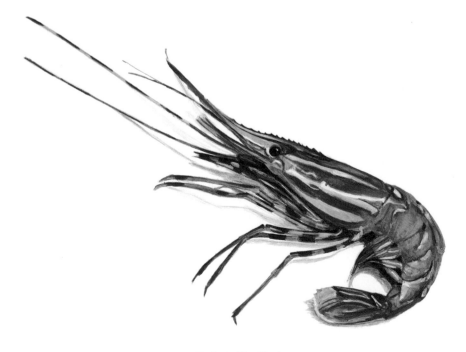

CANNED TUNA

Canned tuna is an American basic, and has been pretty much since its introduction to the marketplace in the early twentieth century. In fact, hard though it is to imagine in this era when "charred rare ahi" (yellowfin or bigeye tuna) and tuna tartare seem to appear on every restaurant menu in the country and tuna-belly sushi is sold in supermarket deli cases, until twenty-five years ago or so, virtually all the tuna consumed in America was canned. Although consumption is down, due partly to changing eating habits and probably partly to concerns about the mercury content of the fish, we still eat around 2½ pounds (about 1 kilogram) of canned tuna a year per capita, packed in oil or (increasingly) in water—about half of that in sandwiches.

Most of that tuna, of course, comes from the large-scale packers, like StarKist or Chicken of the Sea (the latter of which once inspired actress Jessica Simpson to ask "Is this chicken … or is this fish?"). The tuna produced by

Katy's Smokehouse in Trinidad, California, near Eureka on the state's northern coast, is something else again. The smokehouse was established in the early 1940s by Katy State, who had learned smoking techniques from the local Yurok Indians. She sold it to Bob and Judy Lake, who still own it today. As State had done, the Lakes buy fish from Trinidad fishermen and smoke it over alder wood. Their hot-smoked wild king salmon is a marvel—but what really stands out is their unsmoked canned albacore tuna, which they began producing in 1999. This is nothing more than fresh-caught local albacore sealed into cans with a small amount of salt and nothing else—neither oil nor water. (Salt-free and jalapeño spiked versions are also available.) The fish is firm, meaty, and almost fresh tasting. It's too good to mix with mayonnaise, but crumbled and anointed lightly with good olive oil, it's good enough to eat straight.

CAVIAR

I remember very well the first time I tasted California caviar, some time back in the mid-1980s. It was a sample brought to the then-trendy West Hollywood restaurant Ma Maison (chef: Wolfgang Puck) by a nice Swedish couple named Mats and Dafne Engstrom, and as a regular customer of the place who happened to be there at the right time, I was offered a taste. It wasn't bad, though a little salty and a little mushy; the trouble was that at that time there was plenty of top-quality Russian and Iranian caviar for sale in L.A., expensive but not ridiculous in price, so I frankly didn't pay the local version much attention.

Times have changed. Caviar from the Caspian is now pretty much unavailable in America (its production is currently banned in Russia, and Iranian and Azerbaijani caviar is fearsomely expensive), and substitutes from China, Spain, France, Uruguay, and other countries are as pricey now as the best Caspian imports once were. So thank goodness for the Engstroms.

The couple were in the crayfish importing business in Sweden, and on a visit to suppliers in California—the tiny crustaceans are greatly appreciated and enthusiastically consumed in Scandinavia, and much of what gets eaten there comes from our own country—they discovered that there were white sturgeon

in the Sacramento River. Perhaps knowing that much of the caviar consumed in Europe once came from America (though mostly from the Midwest and East Coast), they wondered about the possibilities of producing it here. When they learned that it was illegal to harvest Sacramento River sturgeon commercially, they investigated the idea of farming the fish. What they learned wasn't encouraging: it would take eight or nine years to raise the fish to the proper size. As a result, in 1978 they set up a caviar importing business instead, called California Sunshine Fine Foods.

In the late 1980s, the Engstroms established a partnership with Ken Beer, who had already been farming sturgeon, near Sacramento, for some years. They now raise about 40,000 white sturgeon in massive tanks, in pristine mineral-rich well water, at their own farm, feeding them organically and harvesting the caviar on-site. The roe is processed with a minimum of salt, and sold under the Tsar Nicoulai label. There are several grades available. I'm partial to the Tsar Nicoulai Reserve, a pearlescent gray-black caviar, lightly salty, with a clean, buttery flavor, nicely popping beads, and a long, fresh finish. I'm not sure that it matches the intensity of flavor of the Caspian caviars I used to occasionally enjoy, but it is a luxurious treat nevertheless.

COPPER RIVER SALMON

Though some examples are better than others, farmed salmon in general—and especially that from the factory-level operations in Norway and Chile—is almost always bland and boring. Good-quality wild-caught salmon, however, if very fresh and in peak season, is one of the most delicious fish in the world. Unfortunately, wild is outnumbered by farmed these days by at least three to one.

There is no farmed salmon in Alaska. It isn't permitted. And the state's wild salmon is as good as it gets, in all its varieties. Most notable is the noble king (sometimes called chinook), which is meaty and complex, but also the red-fleshed sockeye with its faint shellfish flavor, and the milder coho. The richest Alaskan salmon, of all types, comes from the Copper River, a 300-mile (482-kilometer) torrent that drains the Wrangell and Chugach mountain regions in the central portion of the state. Because the salmon in this sustainably managed fishery must travel long distances upstream (the ascent is over 1,000 feet, or some 300 meters) against a strong current to reach their spawning grounds, they develop higher than usual stores of omega-3 fatty acids, which make their flesh not only healthier to consume but richer in body and flavor than that of salmon from most other places. Copper River salmon are harvested by gillnetting from small boats and iced as they're caught. Handling is minimized.

The arrival of Copper River king salmon in the marketplace each year—its short season spans just May and June—is a major event at seafood restaurants and fish markets in the Pacific Northwest. It may be as good as salmon gets: firm, almost buttery, with an intense, mouth-filling salmon flavor. Sockeye, which tastes equally salmony but with crustacean overtones and a bit less richness, is the most readily available variety of Copper River salmon because its season runs from May through September. Coho, harvested in August and September, is lighter in color and milder in flavor than king or sockeye, but very high in omega-3s—and from the Copper River, even coho has a lot more character than farmed salmon of other varieties. Much Copper River salmon is sold frozen, incidentally, and though it is a fish that freezes well, the fresh version has a much better texture and more vivid flavor.

The Seattle Fish Company is a good source of Copper River salmon. A fish market with an eat-in dining area known as "The Grill," the Seattle Fish Company also sells their fish through their online store.

CRAB CAKES

The crab cake is a great American regional specialty, invented and made best around the Chesapeake Bay, and especially in and near Baltimore. Nowhere else in the world is crabmeat prepared in the same way. The crab cake is a kind of croquette—or a kind of "burger," if you prefer—made with the meat of its eponymous crustacean, almost always mixed with breadcrumbs and various flavorings, and bound with eggs and sometimes mayonnaise. Old Bay Seasoning (see page 258), an herb-and-spice powder that includes mustard, paprika, pepper, bay leaf, celery seed, and ginger, among other things, is often considered de rigueur in making a crab cake. Indeed, getting the balance of ingredients right is essential to its success. An overly bready crab cake is not very pleasant; on the other hand, if it's all crabmeat, with nothing to hold it together, it's just a mess of crab.

Local blue crab (*Callinectes sapidus*) is the emblematic seafood of the area—an old name for the Chesapeake Bay was Blue Crab Bay—and is considered the ideal (or, in some quarters, only acceptable) basis for real crab cakes. That said, any kind of flavorful fresh crabmeat can be used. I've had very good crab cakes made from the West Coast's superb Dungeness crab (see page 84).

Bethesda, Maryland, is about 35 miles (56 kilometers) southwest of Baltimore, and much closer to Washington, D.C. than it is to the Chesapeake Bay, but Chris Hoge has fished the Chesapeake, and a lot of other places around the world, for many years, and he knows top-quality seafood. The crab cakes he sells at Chris' Marketplace have little or no bread in them, but hold together nicely and are full of crab flavor. Hoge steams the crabs because boiling, he believes, leaves the meat too watery. He makes two kinds of cakes: back-fin, which combine body meat with shreds from the crab's hindquarters, and jumbo lump, which are just body meat in large chunks, and thus offer a particularly intense crab flavor. With their abundance of sweet, salt-kissed meat, these crab cakes are pure Chesapeake Americana.

DUNGENESS CRAB

This superbly tasty creature is named for Dungeness Bay, at the top of the Olympic Peninsula in upstate Washington, and is the official state crustacean of Oregon, but as a native Californian I can't help associating it with my home state and specifically with the place where I first encountered it: Fisherman's Wharf in San Francisco. There, at least when I was younger (I haven't been for a while), the big seafood restaurants that line Jefferson Street and other nearby thoroughfares all had sidewalk stands where you could buy a cardboard container full of Dungeness crabmeat, with cocktail sauce, to eat while you strolled along the piers.

Dungeness, which in fact is harvested all the way from the Aleutian Islands to California's Central Coast, is a delicately flavored crab, with meaty, sweet, faintly salty, faintly coppery flesh and a clean sea-bright finish. (The shells, I've learned, also make first-rate seafood stock.) One of the best restaurant appetizers of my life was served at the tame but well-provisioned bachelor party of a good friend of mine, years back: an entire steamed Dungeness crab for each diner, served with nothing more than lemon wedges and the appropriate implements. Hardly a word was spoken as we all dug into this great treat.

Among the merchants who will ship Dungeness crab, both live and cooked (and in the form of extracted meat, though that takes away half the fun), is i love blue sea, a San Francisco-based company that bills itself as the only online source for 100 percent sustainable seafood. Its founder, Martin Reed, says that it wasn't until he left his native Northern California for college in Tucson that he realized how little good fresh fish and shellfish was available to most of the country. When he looked into sources of seafood supply, he learned for the first time about endangered species and various ecological threats to the quality of Pacific waters. He had been an avid surfer, and when he returned to San Francisco, he and a fellow surfer, Matt Carreira, decided to start a company that would sell fish and shellfish of the highest quality, but only from sustainable fisheries. The company works closely with Seafood Watch as well as the Monterey Bay Aquarium to help promote sustainable species; luckily, the Dungeness crab is on the list.

FINNAN HADDIE

Finnan haddie is cold-smoked haddock (a meaty ocean whitefish, related to pollock and cod), originally from Scotland, and apparently named after the town of Findon in Aberdeenshire. Typically poached in milk, it is still standard breakfast fare in Scotland and parts of England, at least in traditionally minded households. It is also, however, an old favorite in Maine, and especially in that state's northern reaches, where it seems to have been brought either by Scots settlers or, more likely, by immigrants of Scots origin from Nova Scotia and New Brunswick who came to the Pine Tree State looking for work as shipbuilders or fishermen.

The man to know in Maine if you enjoy this specialty—which is lightly smoked, with a flaky, fresh fish texture and good fishy flavor—is Richard Penfold. The Scots-born Penfold learned the art of smoking finnan haddie in the 1980s, working with master smokers in the Shetland Islands while he was a fisheries science undergraduate. He later taught seafood processing in the Shetlands at the North Atlantic Fisheries College, smoking fish with an old-fashioned Torry kiln, of a type designed in Aberdeen in 1939. He moved to Maine in 1997, and helped set up Stonington Sea Products, Inc., in the fishing village of Stonington on Deer Isle off the southern coast of the state. (Stonington Sea Products, Inc. was bought and subsequently re-sold and now Penfold is making his finnan haddie under the Stonington Seafood label.)

Penfold imported a Torry kiln, an exact replica of the original Aberdeen model, in 2001, and also uses an antique brass brinometer to measure the salinity of his brine. The result is a moist, subtly flavored finnan haddie with a perfect balance of salt and smoke.

FLORIDA STONE CRABS

American waters are crawling with crab, from the fearsome looking but rather bland-tasting king crab of Alaska to the flavorful Dungeness of the Pacific Northwest and California (see page 84) to the irresistible blue crab, soft-shell and otherwise, of Chesapeake Bay (see pages 83 and 104), to name only a few—but Florida stone crabs, which in fact are fished as far up the Atlantic coast as Rhode Island and down as far as the Bahamas, are unique. Here's what makes them different: to begin with, they have no back meat, only claw meat; that meat is unusually sweet, firm, and full of flavor, more like lobster than other crabs; the species has thus far resisted efforts to farm-raise it; and, extraordinarily, you don't have to kill a stone crab in order to eat it. The fishermen who harvest the creatures—something that is allowed only between October 15 and May 15 each year—skillfully snap one claw (sometimes two) off each one they catch, then return the crab to the water. If they've done their job

right, the claw regenerates in one to two years. It's against the law, in fact, to bring home a whole stone crab.

Many good seafood stores around the nation now sell stone crab claws, but the name that is indelibly associated with them is Joe's, as in Joe's Stone Crab, a bustling restaurant and mail-order operation in Miami Beach. The establishment was founded in 1918 by Joe Weiss, a Hungarian immigrant who had journeyed from New York to Florida in hopes that the southern climate would be good for his asthma. He and his wife bought a bungalow on Biscayne Street and opened Joe's Restaurant in their front room. The story goes that in 1921, a visiting ichthyologist (ichthyology is the study of fish) arrived with a sack full of stone crabs he'd collected and asked whether Joe knew how to cook them. Joe tossed them in boiling water and served the claws with mustard sauce, and a new culinary treat was born.

GEODUCK

I think it's pretty safe to say that nobody ever forgets his or her first look at a geoduck. This giant clam, native to the Pacific Northwest and British Columbia (there is a related species in New Zealand), is simply bizarre in appearance. Its shell is unmistakably clam-like in shape, though typically measuring 5 or 6 inches (about 12–15 centimeters) in length. The weird part is the geoduck's "foot" or "neck," in reality a kind of siphon for taking in plankton for nourishment while filtering out sand and other impurities. This is a slightly tapered yellowish or yellow-brown, horizontally ridged protuberance extending from one end of the shell, looking unmistakably and graphically phallic. In the case of older geoducks (undisturbed, these bivalves can live for 150 years or more), this "foot" sometimes stretches as much as 4 feet (a little more than 1 meter) in length.

Suffice to say that the geoduck—whose name is unexpectedly, and not very appetizingly, pronounced "gooey-duck"—is not one of nature's more gracefully designed creatures. ("Geoduck" is a mispronunciation of a Nisqually Indian word meaning "dig deep," which is what it does in wet sand.) This phallic-looking siphon, though, happens to be something of a culinary delicacy. The Japanese eat it, peeled and thinly sliced, as sashimi. In China, where it is called elephant-trunk clam and believed to be an aphrodisiac, strips of it are stewed as part of a hot pot or stir-fried.

Around Washington State's Puget Sound, where geoduck is found in abundance, it is served as sashimi (or "crudo"), but also pounded, cut into ribbons, and deep-fried, or even sometimes cooked in chowder—though this is less prevalent than it used to be, simply because geoduck has become very expensive, and is less likely to be wasted in soup than it once was. The meat of geoduck is a little sweet, with a mild flavor and a firm texture that might remind you of conch. More for its daunting appearance than its taste, presumably, geoduck has lately become something of a TV star, appearing frequently as a challenging ingredient on competition cooking shows.

A good mail-order source I've found is Taylor Shellfish Farms. Live geoduck can be ordered online, where the minimum order is 2 pounds (910 grams), or bought through their retail outlets.

HOT-SMOKED TROUT

In the Pisgah National Forest, within the Shining Rock Wilderness Area (North Carolina's largest tract of land thus designated), the Jennings family has farmed trout since 1948. Pure mountain water flows through the ponds and canals at their Sunburst Trout Farms at the rate of 12,000 gallons (more than 45,000 liters) per minute, twice the industry standard. (On request, Sunburst will supply laboratory reports verifying that their fish contain no mercury, PCBs, or pesticides.) The high volume of water flow is important because it keeps the ponds well oxygenated, improving the metabolic rates of the fish and encouraging their growth as they swim against the strong current. The trout are fed a low-phosphorus cereal-based diet—no fish meal or other animal by-products—free from antibiotics and growth hormones. Then they're netted live, bled, and filleted all in the space of about an hour.

In its early years, the farm sold live trout to stock lakes and streams for anglers, but after medical research in the 1960s revealed the cardiovascular advantages of a diet high in omega-3 fatty acids, of which trout are a good source, the farm's proprietors began to investigate ways to produce kitchen- or table-ready trout for the retail market. Family patriarch Dick Jennings traveled to Europe to research trout farming and processing methods there, and in 1980 officially refocused the business, acquiring additional farm ponds and a facility for smoking and otherwise turning the fish into various gourmet treats.

The Sunburst catalogue includes trout in almost any form imaginable: as boneless fillets, in various marinades, crusted (in grits and hemp, sesame seeds and hemp, or crushed peppercorns) and oven-ready, as sausage, as smoked trout dip, as jerky, and as burger patties. There is also trout caviar, plain, smoked, or flavored with blood orange juice. For me, though, the star of the line is Sunburst's premium hot-smoked fillets, smoked over local hickory chips and grapevine cuttings. In addition to the forthright tang of smoke, the fish, flaky and moist, tastes faintly earthy and faintly sweet, with its salt and oil in perfect balance.

LOBSTER STEW

Growing up on the West Coast, I ate much more California lobster (see page 78) than I did the full-clawed Maine variety (see opposite page). I still prefer the former, but on the other hand, I certainly appreciate its Atlantic cousin, especially when it's just-out-of-the-water fresh and correctly (that is, lightly) cooked. Simply steamed, with butter, for instance, Maine lobster is one of those pure, elemental gastronomic basics that needs no fancifying. On the other hand, lobster also lends itself very well to more elaborate preparations, like salad, bisque, spaghetti or risotto, pot pie ... and of course lobster stew.

I encountered a superb example of the last of these back in the 1990s, not at a restaurant, but at a Mainer's Manhattan apartment—and it wasn't homemade. "I can do it, of course," said my friend, "but why bother when LeBlanc's is so good?" She was talking about LeBlanc's Gourmet Lobster Stew, an award-winning packaged version made by Linda LeBlanc in Presque Isle, in far northern

Maine by the New Brunswick border. This rich, lobster-filled concoction is no longer sold under the LeBlanc's label, but fortunately it still exists.

In 2001, LeBlanc put her company up for sale. A small-business consultant named Cal Hancock, originally from York, just over the Maine line from New Hampshire, had recently moved with her husband to Cundy's Harbor, Maine's oldest commercial lobster port, across Casco Bay from Portland. She wasn't looking for a business venture herself, but happened to meet LeBlanc and, since her grandmother had run a well-regarded seafood restaurant and she was a great believer in the quality of Maine's fish and shellfish, she decided to take over the concern. She worked with LeBlanc in Presque Isle for a month, and acquired all her recipes. Hancock now sells a wide range of seafood products, shipped frozen, including crab cakes, cioppino (a San Francisco-style fish stew), lobster mac and cheese, lobster ciabatta, and a famous lobster pot pie topped with a pastry heart.

Today, LeBlanc's Gourmet Lobster Stew has become Cundy's Harbor Lobster Stew, but the flavor is the same. The ingredients include heavy cream, milk, butter, "subtle spices," and more than a lobster's worth of meat in every quart—and no flour or potatoes or other filler. This is not the kind of thing you want to heat up when you're starting your low-fat, low-cholesterol diet. It is positively luxurious in richness, very creamy, very buttery, and full of sweet, flavorful lobster meat that seems to lose nothing in taste or texture from having spent time in the freezer.

MAINE LOBSTER

A lobster lover never forgets his or her first trip to Maine. In most of the country—most of the world—sweet, big-clawed Atlantic lobster is a pricey delicacy, a symbol of luxury and highfalutin tastes. In Maine, it's simply part of daily life. It's not just all the lobsterabilia, the T-shirts and bumper stickers and road signs. In Maine, lobster is hot dogs and hamburgers—almost everyday food, plentiful and inexpensive. Well, OK, maybe not exactly inexpensive, but it was when I first visited Maine in the 1960s, and it's still substantially cheaper and more readily available there than it is anywhere else.

Historically, lobster was so plentiful off the shores of the northeastern United States that whole ones, meat intact, were sometimes plowed into the fields as fertilizer, and workmen's contracts forbade their employers from feeding it to them more than three times a week. According to the lore, it was John D. Rockefeller who changed the lobster's fortunes: Perhaps as a joke he served it at a dinner party attended by New York's social elite—"The 400," as they were called (this having apparently been the number of people the ballroom of Mrs. William Backhouse Astor, Jr., could hold)—and when word of this menu got around, every parvenu in town suddenly wanted to eat lobster, too. Once

it hit the big time, lobster never returned to its humble roots.

Maine lobster is closely related to the lobster of the Brittany coast, across the Atlantic, but many connoisseurs find its flesh even more savory. Any lobster is work to eat, of course; pliers or nutcrackers and long, thin forks for digging meat out of every cavity and limb are necessary tools, and restaurants typically offer patrons bibs to protect their garments, for good reason. Needless to say, most people—myself included—consider it to be worth the trouble. The tender, delicate claw meat is particularly prized, but the slightly sinewy body meat is also full of flavor.

Every good fish market in America seems to have a tankful of live lobsters, though how long they've been sitting in murky water on top of one another—which can't be doing them any good—is always a question. If you want to order live lobster direct from Maine, how could you resist an outfit called Lucky Catch Lobster? Proprietor Tom Martin started lobstering as a summer job in 1984, and liked it well enough to keep at it. Today, his business partner and brother-in-law, Liam McCoy, is in charge of selecting the freshest live hard-shell lobsters for shipment around the United States—at prices, it must be admitted, that won't remind you of hot dogs and hamburgers.

MAINE SHRIMP

More than one observer has pointed out that the term "jumbo shrimp" sounds oxymoronic, since we use the word "shrimp" as a metaphor for something small or underdeveloped. The irresistible wild shrimp that come out of the waters off Maine and northern Massachusetts every year between January and April (the season is extended when stocks are plentiful) will never inspire that oxymoron. They are truly shrimp-size, tiny, about fifty to the pound (half-kilogram), retaining their minute dimensions largely because they live their lives in cold Nothern Atlantic waters, rather than migrating south to warmer climes as do most of their shrimpy cousins. They are also sweet, delicate, and clean-tasting—good enough to eat raw, exquisite when quickly boiled and seasoned with nothing more than a pinch of salt, and so good when deep-fried in a dusting of flour that it's almost worth the effort it takes to shell them first.

The best thing about Maine shrimp, though, is that they are commonly sold—from roadside trucks throughout New England and in select fish markets on the East Coast (and occasionally in the Midwest)—not long out of the water and fresh, at least in the sense of never having been frozen. A lot of these shrimp, mostly sold in Maine, come out of the state's first community-supported fishery, the Midcoast Fishermen's Cooperative out of Port Clyde, just south of Rockland, which started landing shrimp in 2007.

A source that will ship to other parts of the country is New York City-based Wild Edibles. This purveyor of top-notch seafood got its start after Michael Reynolds, a waiter at Jean-Georges Vongerichten's JoJo restaurant in Manhattan, accompanied his boss on a trip to Maine to look for sources of wild seafood. Impressed by the quality of the scallops and sea urchins to be found there, Reynolds contacted his brother-in-law, Richard Martin, a manager at another local restaurant, Trattoria dell'Arte. They decided to go into business bringing fine seafood to the wholesale and retail markets, and opened Wild Edibles in 1992, originally working out of their own refrigerators and cars. Today, having survived bankruptcy after being required to pay a large settlement to former employees, they have an 11,000-square-foot (1,000-square-meter) facility in Queens and a staff of more than forty. The Maine shrimp they get are perfect, a treat worth waiting for each year and worth buying plenty of in the short time that they're available.

OLYMPIA OYSTERS

The first time I saw an Olympia oyster, I had a hard time believing that it really was an oyster and not some obscure variety of miniature shellfish perhaps related to the bay scallop. It was tiny, about the size of an old U.S. fifty-cent piece (about 1 inch, or 25 millimeters, in diameter), with delicate deckled edges. It certainly didn't look like it had anything in common with the first oysters I had fallen in love with—those big, meaty, crevice-shelled ones the French call *creuses*.

The first time I tasted an Olympia oyster, I didn't care what it was, I just wanted a lot more of them. It captivated me immediately with its sweet, salty flavor, finishing with a vague metallic tang, but at the same time it frustrated me because it was so small, not even a real bite's worth. It was so good, but so ephemeral. This, of course, added to its appeal.

The Olympia oyster (*Ostreola conchaphila*) is native to the Pacific Coast, with a range extending from Alaska to Mexico—though it takes its name from the onetime oyster capital of Olympia, Washington, on Puget Sound. It was once plentiful, and was much enjoyed by coastal Native American tribes; towering middens of Olympia oyster shells have been found around San Francisco Bay. During California's Gold Rush in the mid-nineteenth century, overharvesting decimated the Olympia in that state, but local gourmets didn't have to suffer: more than 1,000,000 pounds (a little more than 45,000 kilograms) of Olympias a year were shipped from Washington to San Francisco between 1850 and 1879.

In the twentieth century, the Olympia began disappearing from Washington, too, and it remained a rarity for decades. Today, Olympia oysters are coming back, both naturally and through concentrated restoration projects in both Puget Sound and San Francisco Bay. The Olympia will probably never be as common on American tables as, say, the ubiquitous Blue Point (see page 77)—among other things, it's particularly hard to open—but it is a genuine wonderment, well worth seeking out.

The prime supplier of the Olympia is Taylor Shellfish Farms in Washington State. Taylor traces its origins back to the 1880s, when J. Y. Waldrip started harvesting Olympias near Shelton, west of Tacoma (still a Taylor stronghold). When the oyster beds became depleted, he gave up the shellfish game and went off to become a rancher in Arizona, where family legend has it that he partnered with the fabled Tombstone sheriff Wyatt Earp shortly after the legendary "Gunfight at the O. K. Corral." A few years later, he returned to Washington and began farming oysters. Waldrip's grandsons, Justin and Edwin Taylor, took over the family business in the 1960s, and expanded it to include more kinds of shellfish. Today, Taylor Shellfish is one of the largest aquaculture companies in America, raising more Manila clams and more varieties of seafood than any other producer, including blue mussels, Mediterranean mussels, scallops, shrimp, crab, and many varieties of clam, as well as those treasured Olympias.

QUAHOGS

"Quahog" isn't a word you see a lot on menus or at the fish shop. But if you're a seafood lover—especially in the Northeast—you've certainly eaten the things, probably under one of their size-specific names, the most common being "littlenecks" or "cherrystones." Quahogs, then, are hard-shell clams—*Mercenaria mercenaria* in scientific parlance, which doesn't make them sound very nice. But nice they are, full of briny flavor, versatile, pleasantly chewy. (Their Latin name is not a reference to mercenary behavior on their part, but comes from the Latin word for wages or price, applied because quahog shells were used in trade by Native Americans.)

The smallest available quahogs, not seen very often, are countnecks. Littlenecks are slightly bigger, and are tender and sweet enough to be eaten raw, on the half-shell, though they're also great in pasta and seafood stews. Topnecks (another name not often seen) and cherrystones are progressively larger, and while they can be eaten on the half-shell, too, they are sometimes served steamed (though the term "steamers" usually refers to related soft-shell clams), or else chopped up for chowder or stuffed clams. They're also perfect for clams casino, a Rhode Island specialty of clams stuffed with bacon, breadcrumbs, and other ingredients and broiled. As for the largest of all, called chowder clams, well … you can probably figure that out.

Quahogs range all along the Atlantic Coast of North America, from Canada down to Florida, but the majority of the hard-shells that reach the marketplace come from the stretch between Massachusetts and northern New Jersey. The shellfish beds of Rhode Island are particularly productive, and in fact the quahog is Rhode Island's official state shellfish. "Captain Tim" Handrigan, who fishes out of Narragansett, on the state's south-central coast, styles himself "The Lobster Guy," and he and his family have been lobstering in New England waters for three generations. His lobsters are excellent, but he's also a dependable source for top-quality littleneck clams, dug daily from cold-water bays and salt ponds in Rhode Island and points north. They're available pretty much all year long, but they always taste like summer—summer in New England.

The Taste of America

RAINBOW TROUT

"Trout" is sort of a catchall term covering freshwater fish of three genuses and dozens of species, and anglers and gourmets alike may endlessly dispute which particular variety is best to eat. In my experience, there's a simple answer to that: whichever one you've just caught and can fry up over a campfire or on the stove within an hour or so.

For those of us who don't fish or have access to just-caught trout, I'd argue that wild-caught rainbow trout is the most delicious of all. The rainbow's close relation, the steelhead, is even tastier, because—like its cousin, the salmon—it spends time at sea (another name for it is salmon trout), where it feeds on tiny shrimp and other crustaceans before returning to fresh water to spawn and perhaps be hooked. Steelhead, unfortunately, is currently endangered. Rainbow isn't, and

while its flesh is definitely milder in flavor than that of the steelhead, it is still fresh-tasting and slightly nutty—if it's wild, in any case. Much rainbow trout is farmed, and these fish sometimes—only sometimes—have a muddy flavor that isn't very appealing. Their meat is also often red, which makes it look like that of steelheads, but this is an indication that they've been fed a supplement to lend them this hue. The meat of good-quality wild-caught rainbow trout may have the faintest tinge of pink, but it is mostly grayish-white.

Seattle's legendary Pike Place Market is full of fish purveyors, some better than others. Pure Food Fish Market, one of the larger and older fishmongers there, was founded as a small stand in 1911 by Jack Amon. His son, Sol, is in charge today, and among the fish he can supply, both on site and by mail order, is wild rainbow trout.

ROCK SHRIMP

Another misnamed crustacean, like California spot prawns (see page 79), rock shrimp aren't shrimp but, yes, prawns—and particularly meaty, delicious prawns at that. The only problem with them is that they are virtually never sold fresh. Until the latter part of the twentieth century, in fact, they were seldom sold commercially at all, simply because they were entirely too hard to peel.

The man who changed the game for rock shrimp was a Titusville, Florida boat-builder and part-time shrimper named Rodney Thompson. As he tells the tale, he built himself a 73-foot (22-meter) fiberglass-hulled shrimp trawler, but had a hard time bringing up shrimp. One day, pulling into Port Canaveral, he happened to dock next to a National Oceanic and Atmospheric Administration (NOAA) research vessel, whose captain—noting Thompson's empty hold—said, "Come out with us tomorrow and I'll show you how to make a million dollars." The next day, Thompson's trawler followed the research ship to a point about 20 miles (32 kilometers) off the coast. They lowered their nets, and started pulling up hundreds of pounds of a kind of deep-water shrimp known derisively as "hardheads," "peanuts," or simply "trash." The problem was that they had very hard shells. "If you can figure out a way to sell those," said the NOAA captain, "you'll make that million."

Thompson tried to figure it out, and one day his daughter, Laurilee, had the idea of splitting the shrimp as you might a lobster and butterflying it. This time the shell lifted off easily. Instead of approaching the problem from the top or sides, she went at it through the underbelly. Thompson devised a machine that could split the shrimp open quickly, in quantity. He set up a processing plant, Ponce Seafood, at Port Canaveral, contracted with another shrimper to bring in what he referred to as "rock shrimp," and employed a staff of local women to clean the shrimp by hand.

In 1983, Thompson opened Dixie Crossroads Seafood Restaurant in Titusville, specializing in locally caught shrimp of all kinds, and today his Wild Ocean Seafood Market sells rock shrimp (flash-frozen on board the fishing vessels) and other fresh and frozen seafood, both retail and wholesale. It has become a cliché to say that certain kinds of shellfish and even fish "taste like lobster," but rock shrimp does have a flavor not unlike that of its much larger cousin, and is one of the few crustaceans that really tastes like something even after it's been frozen.

SHAD ROE

The shad is a bony fish, basically a sort of overgrown herring, that runs up the Eastern Seaboard in March each year to spawn in fresh water. (The shadbush, a relative of the rose and also known as the serviceberry, was so named because it blossoms exactly when the fish begin to spawn.) From the Chesapeake Bay up into New York State, the annual spring coming of the shad is greeted happily by fishermen and lovers of the delicacy called shad roe. Its skeletal structure makes the fish itself difficult to eat, and while it has its champions, many find that its flesh is rather muddy-tasting (alternatively, I once heard a diner describe it as tasting like seaweed). Its roe, on the other hand, is greatly appreciated, both for its flavor and for its emblematic role as a harbinger of spring.

Shad roe isn't eaten like caviar or other fish eggs. It is cooked in its sac, which appears in fish markets in the form of two connected lobes, blood-red and veined and frankly not very appetizing to look at. When prepared in the traditional manner, slowly sizzled in bacon fat or butter, then served with crisp bacon or in a lemon butter sauce, it turns a warm, gleaming light brown, with a rosy-pink interior (assuming that it hasn't been overcooked). In flavor, it tastes a little fishy, a little earthy, a little nutty, and maybe even a little livery. The Victorians ate it for breakfast, in place of kippers, and it has a similar heartiness.

There's something old-fashioned about shad roe beyond its association with the Victorians, and it wasn't much seen outside of mainstream East Coast seafood houses in the late twentieth century. More recently, though, younger chefs trying to connect with regional and traditional ingredients have discovered it and revived its popularity, and it is now as inevitable a part of spring menus as morels, ramps (see page 176), and asparagus (see page 150). Many good fishmongers, especially on the East Coast, stock or can order shad roe in season (it is nearly always sold fresh; it doesn't freeze well). One mail-order source is Captain Marden's Seafoods in Wellesley, Massachusetts, a family-run enterprise founded in 1945 by Captain Roy Wilfred Marden.

SHE-CRAB SOUP

She-crab soup is a Lowcountry specialty, a bisque of blue crab, sometimes thickened with puréed rice; it earned its name and its uniqueness from the fact that into it is stirred crab roe. The basic idea of a crab and rice soup may have been inspired by partan bree, a traditional Scots concoction introduced into the Carolinas by Scots settlers in the early 1700s. The addition of roe, however, was apparently the inspiration of William Deas, a cook and butler to an early twentieth-century mayor of Charleston, R. Goodwyn Rhett. The story is that Rhett was entertaining William Howard Taft, then president of the United States, and Rhett asked Deas to do something to enliven the rather pallid-looking crab soup that was on the dinner menu. Deas thought that the bright orange crab roe might be just the thing, and a new tradition was born.

There are many recipes for she-crab soup available, but finding fresh blue crab with its roe can be a challenge. (That may be why some recipes suggest stirring in crumbled hard-cooked egg yolks as a substitute—not a good idea.) A more than credible canned version, sold condensed to be thinned with milk, is available under the Harris label. The company grew out of the Blue Channel Corporation, which was started in the 1930s by Sterling Grover Harris in Port Royal, southwest of Charleston. This became the region's largest processor of blue crabs, and Harris patented a method for canning the crabmeat as well as developing a recipe for she-crab soup. In 1964, an old friend of Harris's, the California-based businessman and philanthropist Girard Brown "Jerry" Henderson (Avon Products, the Alexander Dawson Schools)—who had run a 600-acre (242-hectare) farm near Port Royal during World War II—invested in the company, taking it over in 1968. Today it is owned by Bost Distributing Co., Inc., of Sanford, North Carolina, but the recipe remains Harris's. It is a medium-rich soup with good crab flavor and a scattering of shredded crabmeat and blended-in roe—not egg yolks.

SMOKED CATFISH PÂTÉ

Catfish is big business in the Mississippi Delta. Raised in ponds installed where once corn and cotton grew—Belzoni, Mississippi, in the heart of the Delta, calls itself the Catfish Capital of the World—it's pretty hard to avoid in the region's restaurants. The great blues singer and guitarist B. B. King was raised in Indianola, about 20 miles (32 kilometers) north of Belzoni, and Indianola honors him today with the beautifully designed B. B. King Museum, full of Smithsonian-quality interactive exhibits that trace the arc of this musical giant's life and music. When King comes to visit, as he does at least once a year, he always stops for lunch at his favorite local restaurant, The Crown. And the specialty at The Crown is ... catfish. The Crown has a large repertoire of catfish recipes, and serves it in a number of ways, alternating preparations weekly. There's catfish Florentine, with spinach and Swiss cheese sauce; catfish Allison, luxuriating in Parmesan butter;

catfish pie; catfish bisque; shrimp-stuffed catfish; catfish casserole ... and there's smoked catfish pâté.

Wild catfish (see page 106) feeds in river silt, and its meat often has a strong, muddy flavor. Farmed catfish goes in the other direction. It's too "clean" for my taste, to the point of blandness. It adapts just fine, however, to being skillfully smoked. Tony and Evelyn Roughton, proprietors of The Crown, report that they were inspired by an English friend who makes smoked salmon pâté, and that they visited smokehouses in England, Scotland, and Ireland before developing their own smoking technique. They sure got it right. A lot of smoked fish pâtés are heavy, oily, and woody in flavor. The Roughtons' offering, by contrast, is full-flavored but also subtle, with a mild, sweet smokiness and a touch of elusive spice that may be nothing more than white pepper. Buy a box of good crackers and a tub of this stuff and you won't need dinner.

SMOKED MULLET SPREAD

Fishing for flathead mullet, whether the black (or striped) variety (*Mugil cephalus*) or its white cousin (*Mugil curema*) is something of a religion among Florida "Crackers"—as locals whose roots in the state go back to the original Anglo-Saxon settlers like to call themselves. So is eating it, fried, baked, and especially smoked. Because mullet is an oily fish, it takes to the process particularly well, staying moist as it takes on smoky flavor. And once it's smoked, it flakes easily into pieces and practically begs to be mixed with cream cheese and mayonnaise and properly seasoned to make a nonpareil garnish for crackers or chips. Mullet-lovers sometimes call this Florida caviar, or even Florida foie gras.

An excellent example, said to be made from "Gram's Recipe," comes from Walt's Fish Market and Restaurant in Sarasota. Walt's traces its origins back to 1918, when a young Swedish immigrant named Claus Wallin joined the Ringling Bros. Circus and ended up falling in love with Sarasota, where the circus wintered. He also fell in love with, and married, an Irish-Indian woman, whose brother was a commercial fisherman in the area, and Wallin took up the trade. His son, Walter, and grandsons, Walt and Tom, followed suit, eventually opening a small fish market and then a larger one. In 1979 they added a restaurant. The operation is now run by Tom's son, Brett. The large Walt's menu offers everything from wild 'gator bites and spicy conch chowder to hog snapper sandwiches and fried Florida pink jumbo shrimp, but Walt's Famous Smoked Mullet Spread remains a customer favorite for its rich, smoky flavor.

SMOKED SALMON

Salmon takes to smoking better than any other fish. It is oily enough that it doesn't dry out, and has enough flavor of its own to stand up to the smoke. The best smoked salmon I've ever had was Irish, back in the days when fish smokers on the Emerald Isle had ready access to locally caught wild salmon (there is now very little of it legally taken in the country). Scotland does a very nice job with smoked salmon, too, of course, as does Norway. In America, a number of small artisanal smokers produce good smoked salmon in various styles, but for consistency and balance of elements—salt, smoke, oil, salmon flavor—I'm a big fan of what's produced by the Acme Smoked Fish Corporation of Greenpoint, Brooklyn.

You may well have had Acme's smoked salmon even if the name isn't familiar. They produce private-label salmon for Costco and for premium grocery stores all over the country, including such New York City legends as Zabar's and Balducci's. Acme dates its origins from the early twentieth century, when a Russian immigrant named Harry Brownstein went to work distributing smoked fish to small delis and groceries around Brooklyn. He was soon able to open his own smokehouse, and by mid-century, the business had grown enough that his son and son-in-law were able to open the 80,000-square-foot (just under 7,500-square-meter) plant Acme occupies today under the management of Brownstein's grandchildren and great-grandson.

Acme sources salmon and other fish from Europe, South America, and around the U.S. The best of the several salmons they market is their wild Pacific king salmon, cured in a mild salt and brown sugar brine for about a week, then cold-smoked over wood chips for several days. The result is meltingly smooth, with a delicate smoke and not too much salt—a smoked salmon with the accent on the second word.

SMOKED SALMON JERKY

Smoking and drying are both ancient methods of preserving foodstuffs, and seafood is one of the aliments that has most often been subjected to one or the other over the centuries, with drier varieties better suited to drying and oilier ones to smoking. Salmon is an oily fish, so it's not surprising that smoked salmon has become commonplace. We tend to think of it as a European product, particularly from Scotland and Ireland, or as a staple of Jewish deli food, but Native American tribes in Alaska and the Pacific Northwest have been smoking salmon in their own manner since before the first Europeans arrived in the area—and sometimes drying it, too. A staple of the local indigenous diet, in fact, was a honey-sweetened cold-smoked salmon desiccated into what we would now call jerky.

Salmon jerky, sometimes called "Indian candy," is made today by brining salmon fillets with salt and sugar before the smoking and drying process. One producer that ships this specialty all over the country is SeaBear, founded in 1957 in Anacortes, in northern Washington, by local fisherman Tom Savidge and his wife, Marie. They started with a backyard smokehouse, selling smoked fish locally, but have grown into a full-scale operation, with a product line including other fresh and smoked seafood, fish and shellfish dips, and soups. Sockeye salmon is commonly used for jerky, but the Savidges make theirs with wild-caught Alaskan king salmon, hand-filleted, cured with both white and brown sugar, and smoked over alder wood—the traditional smoking wood in this part of the country. The resulting jerky is medium-salty, only faintly sweet, and noticeably smoky; it is chewy enough to qualify as jerky, but remains slightly moist so it doesn't require an excess of jaw power to consume.

SMOKED WEATHERVANE SCALLOPS

The largest scallops in the world are weathervanes, fished exclusively in Alaska. The state's commercial scallop fishery began only in 1990, with two vessels harvesting weathervanes from the east side of Kodiak Island. Today, the scallops are taken, with deepwater dredge-nets, from a stretch of sea off the coast between Cape Spencer and Yakutat, off the finger of the state that extends down along the Canadian border. Weathervanes are plump, juicy, and clean-tasting, with a mild but pronounced scallop flavor. Because they start with high moisture content, they also turn out to be ideal for smoking—and I doubt that anybody smokes them more successfully than the Seattle-based smoked seafood company called Gerard & Dominique Seafoods.

The two men were acclaimed French chef-restaurateurs in the Seattle area in the latter part of the twentieth century, Gerard Parrat with Gerard's Relais de Lyon and Dominique, whose last name is Place, with the doubly eponymous Dominique's Place. The two got talking one day about how they couldn't find a locally produced smoked salmon they liked, and eventually, in 1990, decided to go into the business of making it themselves. Both closed their restaurants soon thereafter to concentrate on the business. They started in a 2,000-square-foot (185-square-meter) facility in Kenmore, just west of Bothell, where Parrat's restaurant had been, and later moved into a 10,000-square-foot (930-square-meter) plant in Woodinville, not far away. Parrat retired in 1998, and in 2008 the company was sold to SeaBear (see opposite page), with Place as president of the brand.

The smoked salmon is very good, but the weathervane scallops, smoky and sweet and not at all dried out by the smoking process, are really something special.

SOFT-SHELL CRAB

The soft-shell crabs for which the Chesapeake Bay is famous are simply the area's highly regarded blue crabs (see page 83), harvested when they're molting and have shed their exoskeleton. They go through this process from May through September each year (the old folklore held that they began molting with the first full moon of May), becoming not just softer to the tooth but also fattier (they bulk up as insulation in their unprotected state) and thus particularly flavorful.

Soft-shells are increasingly available at good fish markets, especially on the East Coast, but it is also possible to order them by mail, either cleaned and frozen or—much better— live. Some of the best in the latter state come from a company based not on the Chesapeake at all, but in Swatara Township, Pennsylvania, near Mechanicsburg, 80 miles (128 kilometers) or so north of Baltimore. One-time engineer Curt Engle, who liked to fish and go boating on the Chesapeake, missed good crabs, soft- and hard-shell alike, when he got back home.

In 2001, he quit his job and set up shop as a distributor of crabs and other Chesapeake-area seafood under the name Harbour House Crabs. Twice and sometimes three times a day, his trucks bring crab, shrimp, and clams back to his plant, where they are prepared for shipping around the nation.

Engle will ship soft-shells steamed and packed in coolers, but he thinks that live crabs taste better, and are more fun. "You're going to make an afternoon of it," he says. "You want to invite some friends over and have them enjoy the entire experience with you." His crew picks through the crabs every afternoon and packs them late in the day for maximum freshness, always including some extras to account for the inevitable mortality rate (as much as 15 percent) when shipping them still crawling. What do you do when you get a box of the things? If you don't know your way around live soft-shell preparation, Harbour House has a helpline available seven days a week.

WALLEYE

The sweet-fleshed fish known by millions of Midwesterners as walleye pike isn't really pike at all, it's a member of the freshwater perch family, sometimes called pike-perch. It's "walleyed" because its eyes reflect white. Looking into them is rather like looking at a blank wall.

I first encountered walleye in Des Moines, Iowa, at a long-departed local institution called Johnny's Vet's Club (it was swept away when the Des Moines River flooded in 1993), and I was surprised by how mild it tasted. (There's an old joke that goes, "What does fried walleye taste like? Tartar sauce.") It does have a sweetness to it, though, and a faint but pleasant flavor that isn't fishy at all but to me almost suggests white rice, as strange as that may sound.

Iowans love walleye, as do their neighbors in South Dakota, Nebraska, and Wisconsin, but it is appreciated above all in Minnesota. In fact, two towns, Garrison, on Mille Lacs Lake, and Baudette, to the north, near Lake of the Woods, call themselves "Walleye Capital of the World." The oldest and largest walleye processing plant in the country (it dates from World War I) is just southwest of Baudette, and is owned by the Red Lake Band of Chippewa Indians, whose reservation is considered the most isolated in America. Red Lake walleye is harvested by hook and line or occasionally gill net from Upper and Lower Red Lake, which together form the sixth largest body of freshwater in the country, after the five Great Lakes. Red Lake Nation Fishery, owned by the Chippewa, ships walleye both fresh and frozen.

WILD CATFISH

The term catfish applies to a large number of species of the order *Siluriformes*; they are so named because their long barbels (tactile organs extending from the area around the mouth) are thought to resemble cat whiskers. Catfish of various kinds are caught and eaten all over the world, in Asia, Africa, Europe, and our own country. Here, they used to be enjoyed mostly in the South. In other regions, the fish, caught in rivers and sometimes in saltwater estuaries, were thought to taste too "muddy" or "dirty." In the 1970s, though, methods of farming catfish were developed, resulting in fish that were meatier and "cleaner" than their wild-caught cousins. Today, catfish is popular all over the U.S. One catfish-lover, President Ronald Reagan, even established a National Catfish Day, on June 25.

Some wild catfish still reaches the market, most of it fished in Louisiana's Cajun country, often using hoop nets much like those employed centuries ago by local Indians. I'm sure that some catfish has an unpleasant flavor—the fish are opportunistic feeders, meaning that they eat pretty much whatever they want, not all of it what we'd consider savory—but the wild catfish I've enjoyed in Louisiana has been very good, richer in flavor than its farmed counterpart, with buttery, medium-firm flesh.

The wild catfish purveyor who gets written about most is a colorful character named Raymond Joseph "Joey" Fonseca, Jr., who runs what he calls Des Allemands Outlaw Katfish Co. The "outlaws" in question were Cajun fishermen of an earlier era who caught catfish in oil drums instead of with fishing lines. Fonseca uses hoop nets, sunk into the Bayou des Allemands, and sells his take to some of the best restaurants in the region and in New Orleans. The Florida-based Wild Ocean Seafood Market (see page 96) sometimes has wild catfish available by mail order.

YELLOWFIN TUNA

Bluefin tuna, both the Atlantic and Pacific species, are the most expensive fish in the world—a massive Pacific bluefin sold for the equivalent of $1,238 (£1,681) a pound (half-kilogram) at Tokyo's Tsukiji fish market in early 2012—and also one of the most environmentally threatened. Though it has long been a staple at fine sushi bars around the world, it is being taken off more and more non-Japanese menus, and its commercial sale may very well be banned, at least in the U.S., in the near future. A close second to the bluefin in flavor and succulence, however, are the yellowfin and closely related bigeye tuna, both often sold under the Hawaiian name, *ahi*—and according to the Monterey Bay Aquarium's Seafood Watch program these tuna, troll- or pole-and-line-caught (as opposed to that caught by longline or purse seine), qualify as the "Good Alternatives."

That takes care of the ethical considerations. Now, what about flavor? Both varieties are very good, but the best Hawaiian bigeye, dark ruby red in color, is astonishingly rich in flavor, buttery and viscous like wagyu beef (see page 147), with firm flesh (it has a very low moisture content) and a meaty aftertaste. It makes superb sashimi or tartare, and is very good slow-baked. Grilled? "Waste of money,"

says Wayne Samiere of the Honolulu Fish Company. And he should know, because his 1++ grade Hawaiian Ultra Ahi Sashimi is about as good as bigeye gets.

Trained as a marine biologist, Samiere graduated from San Francisco State University and worked for the National Oceanic and Atmospheric Administration (NOAA). A trip to Hawaii in 1987 convinced him that he should move there, and he started a small business selling good Hawaiian fish to mainland wholesalers. He launched the Honolulu Fish Company out of his garage in 1995, and two years later, with his friend, Damon Johnson, a veteran of the seafood business, as partner, he expanded and relocated. Today, he operates out of a 5,000-square-foot (465-square-meter) facility near the Honolulu docks, and sells eco-friendly sashimi-grade fish to top restaurants all over the world—including Jean Georges and Le Bernardin in New York City.

"The deep, cold waters surrounding the Hawaiian Islands," says Samiere, "are the richest location in the world for high oil content, bright red meat sashimi grades of ahi." He adds that only 2 percent of the ahi catch qualifies for the 1++ rating.

POULTRY

FREE-RANGE CHICKEN

When the term "free-range" first started appearing, in the latter decades of the twentieth century, usually attached to chicken, I suspect most of us envisioned ample barnyards or even pastures in which happy flocks strutted around at leisure, nibbling grass and worms in the sunshine. The truth is that there is no government-mandated definition of the term other than that, according to the United States Department of Agriculture (USDA), to describe their birds as free-range, "Producers must demonstrate to the Agency that the poultry has been allowed access to the outside." There are no stipulations as to how much access they must have (does five minutes a day count?) or as to how much ground must be allotted to each bird. Undercover reports from poultry farms suggest that all too often, the "range" of each chicken is only a few inches, and the conditions under which they are raised are scarcely better than those in poultry battery cages with no outside access. This is a distressing fact for anyone who cares about animal welfare to discover.

True free-range, or pastured, chickens are not just (presumably) much happier animals than their restricted kin, but end up yielding firmer, more flavorful flesh. Delicious proof of this fact may be found in Mary's Free-Range California Bronze Air Chilled Chickens, raised by Pitman Farms in California's San Joaquin Valley. These birds truly range freely on pasture land that gives them four times the usual space. They're fed a vegetable diet with no animal by-products or additives and, after slaughter, are cooled individually with cold air instead of being immersed in a communal ice-water bath as are most commercial chickens. This greatly reduces the possibility of bacterial contamination and prevents the flesh from getting water-logged.

Don Pitman started raising chickens and turkeys in 1954. His son, Rick, took over the business, and named the birds Mary's in honor of his wife, an avid student of nutrition and animal welfare practices. Their son, David, and his brothers continue the family tradition. Mary's Free-Range Chicken is a member of the 5-Step Animal Welfare Rating Standards Program run by the Global Animal Partnership, and its California Bronze birds are the first American product to earn a Step-5 rating. They also taste very good, juicy and clean, and full of pure chicken flavor.

GUINEA HEN

The occasional specialty dinner or TV reality show aside, there are very few occasions on which Americans will knowingly consume insects, though they are an important source of protein in some countries and can actually taste rather good. The guinea fowl and his mate, the guinea hen, on the other hand, are great connoisseurs of bugs, happily devouring spiders, worms, ants, and other creepy-crawlies—and even reportedly helping to reduce the population of disease-bearing deer ticks on the Eastern Seaboard. This diet is sometimes said to account for their rich flavor. Modern farm-raised guinea hens, probably eat much more grain and alfalfa than insects, but the guinea hen remains a pretty tasty bird, with faintly sweet, firm-textured, medium-dark meat that, but for its color, suggests that of pheasant (though it is generally not as dry as that bird can get). The female of the species, being plumper than the male, is more appreciated at the table, by the way.

Guinea hens are curious-looking critters, with bodies that look vaguely like footballs with tails, white-spotted (almost polka-dotted) black feathers, red helmets, and blue wattles (the pendulous bits of flesh that hang on each side of their beaks). They're apparently not good game birds, constantly fighting other birds and refusing to fly when flushed, and they're apparently also annoyingly noisy and difficult to raise—though the nineteenth-century poultry expert D. J. Browne noted that the bird is "one of those unfortunate beings, which, from having been occasionally guilty of now and then a trifling fault, has acquired a much worse reputation than it really deserves."

The French are great lovers of guinea hen, which they call *pintade*. In traditional households it was once—and possibly still is—considered a "Sunday bird," the centerpiece for a Sunday night family meal in place of chicken or roast meat. The best American-raised guinea hen I've had comes from Steve and Sylvia Pryzant's Four Story Hill Farm in Honesdale, in northeastern Pennsylvania—but it is sold only to a small number of restaurant clients around the country. (Many restaurant menus identify sources these days, of course; if you see guinea hen—or for that matter chicken—tagged with Four Story's name, don't miss it.) A good guinea hen source for home cooks is D'Artagnan (see page 117), which sells lean, humanely raised hens from French breeding stock to mail-order customers.

QUAIL

The quail is a tasty little bird, with tiny wings and legs that are great fun to gnaw on and dark, juicy breast meat that tastes a little gamy if the bird is wild but more like the most intensely flavored chicken you've ever had if it's properly farm-raised. In recent years, the quail farmed around Bandera, Texas—a little south of the middle of the state, not far from San Antonio—has earned a good reputation, largely thanks to the efforts of Tom and Polly Herrington, who established their Diamond H Ranch there in 1992. The couple originally raised northern bobwhite quail and a small number of Tennessee red quail, both intended primarily to be sold to hunters to stock coveys. On the advice of Texas A&M AgriLife Extension Service, they began to raise Coturnix, or Japanese, quail (an Asian species that grows comparatively large and is known for its tasty meat), and added dressed quail to their product list. The Herringtons registered the Texas Gourmet Quail trademark, and, processing the birds in one of only two state-inspected game bird processing plants in Texas, soon began shipping frozen quail in various forms all over the country.

In 2009, the Herringtons decided to retire, and initially it looked as if the farm might close down. Then Chris Hughes of Broken Arrow Ranch (see page 146) in Ingram, about 25 miles (40 kilometers) north of Bandera, stepped in and took over the operation. Under Broken Arrow's stewardship, the Diamond H raises about 150,000 quail at any time, selling the birds whole or partially boned, as well as in the form of legs and—a real luxury—boneless breasts.

ROCK CORNISH GAME HEN

Some good friends of mine, a husband and wife, used to own a restaurant in West Hollywood, a wonderful, eccentric place where the crowd was always interesting and the food was always ethnically diverse and hearty. The couple's young daughter spent lots of time at the restaurant, drawing with crayons at one of the back tables, falling asleep on one of the banquettes as the evening wore on, and in general absorbing the spirit of the place. The extent to which she was a restaurant child may be seen from the fact that one day at school—her mother later told me—when the teacher was talking about birds and asked students what kind of avian creature they liked best, doubtless expecting hummingbird, eagle, robin, or suchlike, my friends' daughter replied, "Rock Cornish game hen."

Fair enough. As the centerpiece of a meal, that bird is presumably considerably more savory than robin. It isn't "game," of course. It's chicken with a fancy name, specifically a young, small one (typically no more than five weeks old and weighing less than 2 pounds, or less than 1 kilogram), crossbred from White Plymouth Rock and Cornish chickens. It's what the French would call a *poussin*.

Rock Cornish game hens were first bred by Alphonsine Makowsky, also known as "Thérèse" and "Te." A French-born one-time farm girl, she married a Russian refugee who had become an artisanal printer in Paris, then immigrated with him to New York. When her husband retired in 1946, the couple moved to northeastern Connecticut, buying the 200-acre (80-hectare) Idle Wild Farm. There they raised chickens, and there Te had the idea of breeding a small, round-breasted bird called the Cornish game chicken with other birds. The offspring of a Cornish chicken and a White Plymouth Rock was most promising, producing a small but meaty white-fleshed bird suitable for a single serving. By the mid-1950s, they were moving 3,000 hens a day. The Makowskys sold their business and retired to Florida in 1967.

Another early Connecticut-based champion of game hens was the Danish-born comedian and musician Victor Borge, who started raising them on his farm in Southbury—"Because I was hungry," he later said. (He also noted that, while he knew nothing about breeding birds, "I didn't have to know. They knew all about it themselves.")

All the major supermarket poultry producers market game hens now, but some of the best are raised by Eberly Poultry, in Lancaster County, Pennsylvania, and sold under their own name as well as under the D'Artagnan and Bell & Evans labels. Harvey Eberly started the business in the 1940s, selling birds he'd raised at the Lancaster Farmers' Market. Eberly Poultry, which works with more than eighty small farmers, became Certified Organic in 1998, and Eberly birds regularly win taste tests. Their game hens are plump and juicy, and have very good flavor.

SMOKED TURKEY

Turkey can be an insipid bird, plump but lean and often dry, borrowing most of its flavor from its accompaniments. Because it is something of a blank canvas, though, it soaks in strong flavors, which is exactly what Samuel Isaac Greenberg figured out how to infuse into the birds. A Jewish immigrant from Poland, Greenberg arrived in Texas as a teenager in 1903. He ended up in Tyler, in East Texas, near the Sabine River that separates the state from Louisiana, and became a member of the town's sole Jewish congregation. There, he assumed a number of roles, among them circumcising babies and slaughtering animals—turkeys among them—according to kosher imperatives.

Like most of Texas, the Tyler region is serious about its barbecue—which in those parts means not grilling but long, slow smoking over hickory or oak fires. At some point, in the 1930s, Greenberg had the idea of using local techniques to smoke kosher turkeys, and he built a barbecue pit in one corner of his barn. Smoked poultry was hardly unknown in Texas, but Greenberg rubbed his turkeys with a spice mixture his wife had developed and gave them an unusually strong smoke, so that they acquired a deeper flavor than that of their counterparts. He sold them locally at first, but in 1938, someone he'd never heard of in Dallas placed an order for six of his birds. That was the beginning of Greenberg Smoked Turkey, still a thriving enterprise, now run by Greenberg's grandson, another Sam.

Sam Greenberg no longer processes kosher fowl as his grandfather did. He buys commercially raised Broad-Breasted White turkeys, basically supermarket birds, then his employees trim them by hand, perforate their flesh so that the spice mixture soaks in, and truss them before hanging them to smoke over hickory wood. The vast majority of Greenberg's sales come in November and December each year, and he typically ships at least 200,000 birds every season. He calls his turkey "the holiday aristocrat." The birds are very smoky in flavor and nowhere near as dry as you might expect, with a delightful peppery bite. Their meat makes terrific sandwiches and a perfect filling for tamales (see page 197) or enchiladas, but it's good enough to pick right from the bone.

TURDUCKEN

There's an old joke that in an ordinary zoo, the placard outside each animal's cage gives common name, scientific name, and habitat, while at a Cajun zoo, the sign offers common name, scientific name, habitat, and recipe. One beast found on many a Cajun table (among other places), but not, presumably, in a Cajun zoo, is turducken. There's no such animal in nature: the name is a portmanteau of "turkey," "duck," and "chicken," and it describes a heroic preparation that is itself a portmanteau. Turducken is a boned-out chicken fit into a boned-out duck, with the whole then inserted into a boned-out turkey. Various layers of stuffing are generally involved.

The idea of serving one bird or other creature stuffed inside another probably dates back to the Romans, and the elaborate French cooking of the late eighteenth and early nineteenth centuries included recipes for birds inside larger birds. Turducken, though, seems to have been invented by Sammy and Junior Hebert at their original Hebert's Specialty Meats, a butcher shop and Cajun charcuterie in Maurice, Louisiana, just southwest of Lafayette. The story is that a local poultry farmer, who had perhaps been studying up on classical French cuisine, brought the Heberts three birds and asked them to prepare them one inside another. Their experiment was a success, and over the years they refined the process. What is today known as Cajun Ed's Hebert's Specialty Meats, with outposts in Houston, Texas, and Tulsa, Oklahoma, as well as the original location, sells more than 10,000 turduckens annually, many of those by mail order. The birds are filled with a cornbread and pork sausage stuffing and seasoned with mouth-warming Cajun spices, but there are also versions involving chicken sausage with and without jalapeños. What does a turducken, properly roasted so that the chicken hasn't dried out by the time the turkey has cooked, taste like? Meaty. Baroque. Crumbly. A little spicy. Pretty darned good.

TURKEY

There's no mystery about where the Bourbon Red turkey gets its name. Its feathers are a handsome mahogany-red color, and it was first bred in Bourbon County, in the Bluegrass country of Kentucky—also home to and namesake of bourbon whiskey. The Red Bourbon was developed by poultry farmer J. F. Barbee in the late nineteenth century. He originally called them Bourbon Butternuts, but the name had little appeal to the public and the birds didn't sell well. Barbee was savvy enough to rebrand them as Bourbon Reds, and then they, as it were, took off. In the 1930s and 1940s, the Bourbon Red was an important turkey commercially, nearly as popular as the Broad-Breasted Bronze. In the latter half of the twentieth century, though, both were eclipsed by the Broad-Breasted White, now our standard holiday turkey, a bird so plump that it can't breed without human assistance.

With increased interest in so-called heritage breeds in the late twentieth and early twenty-first century, the Bourbon Red has been making a tentative comeback, though it is still on the American Livestock Breeds Conservancy watch list. One avid breeder of the bird is Kathy Wheeler, at her STAR Farm in Hardyville, Kentucky, northeast of Bowling Green.

Wheeler and her husband, Scott, moved to the area from Baltimore in 2004 and bought a 32-acre (13-hectare) property there with the idea that they'd grow their own food and live a rural lifestyle. They started with a couple of horses, ten calves, and a cow, later adding hens, pheasants, and four young turkeys. Kathy soon realized that she liked the turkeys best of all. "Chickens run away when you go out to feed them," she once noted, "but the turkeys run toward you."

When she learned about Bourbon Reds, she thought she should try raising them, since they were a homegrown bird. She ended up producing some specifically for Mark Williams, leader of Kentucky's Slow Food chapter and executive chef for Brown-Forman, which owns many bourbon and other whiskey brands. She is now raising seventy or eighty of the turkeys annually, and selling at least a few of them by mail order. Her biggest obstacle to growth, she says, is that there's only one USDA-approved processing plant for farms her size in the entire state. It's worth reserving one of Wheeler's Bourbon Reds early: They're not overgrown like Broad-Breasted Whites, but they're plenty meaty, with a rich, outdoorsy flavor that will make you forswear your usual turkey for good.

WILD TURKEY

I live in suburban Connecticut, in a bedroom community about 40 miles (65 kilometers) northeast of New York City. It is hardly a wilderness area. The I-95, full of long-haul trucks and speeding commuters, cuts through town. Houses are often built two or three to the lot, and there are plenty of large, if discreet, condominium complexes. And yet there is wildlife among us—and not just the usual birds and squirrels. The parks are infested with Canada geese, rabbits scamper across lawns, deer somehow find forage in our little stands of woods and sometimes dart across a busy town street, and every fall, we see big, skinny, gawky-looking birds, brownish-black in color, pecking for nuts and seeds and bugs along the roadway. They don't look much like anything you'd want to have for dinner, but they're turkeys, wild ones, and they're the bird the Pilgrims would have consumed at the first Thanksgiving (if indeed they ate turkey at all)—the one that Benjamin Franklin once vigorously defended as the best choice for our national bird, in lieu of the inedible bald eagle.

Wild turkeys were pretty much absent from the eastern landscape for more than a century, until around 1950, but they've definitely made a comeback—there are said to be at least seven million of them around America—and remain a common sight around the region, especially in the fall. They shouldn't start feeling too safe and secure, though. After many decades of preferring the pumped-up white meat of commercially raised domestic turkeys, some Americans, in their quest for more authentic "heritage" food, have taken to roasting these wild birds instead of their tame cousins.

It sounds like a nice idea, but there are two problems. First, wild turkey is a lean bird, smaller than supermarket turkeys, with entirely dark or darkish meat, and its diet gives it a pronounced earthy, forest-floor sort of flavor that isn't immediately identifiable as what we've come to know as turkey. It also dries out quickly when roasted, and can be tough and stringy; it all depends on the bird. The second problem, if that description doesn't deter you, is that American wild turkey cannot be sold legally in this country. To eat it, you'd have to know a hunter who shoots it. The good news is that several producers sell farmed "wild" turkey—birds of the same species, raised free-range.

A good source is D'Artagnan, based in Newark, New Jersey, and run by Ariane Daguin. Daughter of the acclaimed French chef André Daguin, who ran the two-star Hôtel de France in Auch, in the heart of foie gras country, Daguin launched D'Artagnan in 1985, becoming the first purveyor of fresh foie gras and game meats in modern-day America. Her wild turkey, like any example of the bird, must be roasted carefully, basted frequently, with the breast tented in foil or shielded with cheesecloth soaked in stock or white wine so that it doesn't dry out while the legs cook through. The result will be very much worth the effort, yielding dense, slightly gamey meat that really tastes like something.

MEATS

ALLIGATOR

The comedian Robert Francis "Bobcat" Goldthwait has a bit about foods that taste like chicken. "If it tastes like chicken," he finally says in exasperation, "then why don't you give me some goddamn chicken?" Well, for one reason, then you wouldn't be able to say that you'd eaten alligator.

Alligators are freshwater reptiles with broad snouts and hidden teeth. (Their surprisingly distant relatives, crocodiles, live in estuaries and salt water and have tapered snouts and exposed teeth. Of the two, crocodiles are the more dangerous to human beings, though you wouldn't want to stick your foot into an alligator's maw.)

Allen and Patty Register and their son, Benjamin—of Palmdale, Florida, in the lower middle portion of the state, just west of Lake Okeechobee—know alligators, and crocodiles, too. The Register family, fifth- and sixth-generation Florida "Crackers" (descendants of the original Anglo-Saxon settlers), run Gatorama, an old-style "roadside attraction" on U.S. Highway 27. One of what once were dozens of such tourist traps, Gatorama was started in 1957 by a colorful character named Cecil Clemons, who had a reputation as something of a scalawag. Clemons realized that alligators were one of the things tourists wanted to see when they came to Florida, so he penned in a colony of local specimens, later bringing Florida crocodiles—not yet an endangered species, as they are today—to join them. David and Marietta Thielen, Patty Register's parents, bought Gatorama from Clemons. The Registers themselves moved there in 1989 and took over management of the property, finally buying it in 2006.

Gatorama has evolved mightily from its days as a seedy amusement. The Registers are active in alligator and crocodile breeding programs and conservation, offer gator-themed entertainment to visitors, and are in the process of turning the enterprise into a "green" showcase. They also sell alligator meat—tail and riblets. I've never had the ribs, but the tail is delicious. The meat is firm, sweet, lean, and clean in flavor (it makes great kabobs). It doesn't exactly taste like chicken, but it does taste more like that than it does beef or game.

ANDOUILLE

Along with boudin (see page 126), ponce (see page 138), and tasso (see page 143), andouille is a staple of Cajun charcuterie. Just as *boudin* means something different in Cajun country than it does in France, Cajun *andouille* is a different animal from its Gallic counterpart—or, rather, different parts of the animal. In France, andouille is made from a pig's stomach and intestines and isn't smoked; the Cajun version is composed of coarse-ground pork with pork fat, garlic, and various seasonings (always including cayenne or red pepper flakes). Some authorities, mostly locals of German descent, claim that, though it bears a French name, andouille is really a German-style sausage.

LaPlace, Louisiana, just up the western shoreline of Lake Pontchartrain from New Orleans, styles itself "The Andouille Capital of the World," largely on the basis of being hometown to a number of noted purveyors of the sausage—among them Bailey's World Famous Andouille, Wayne Jacob's Smokehouse and Restaurant, and Jacob's World Famous Andouille & Sausage. Probably only because it was the first one of the three that I was taken to by a Cajun food-savvy friend of mine years ago, I'm loyal to the last of these.

The Jacob family came to southeastern Louisiana in 1753 as part of a wave of German immigration to the region. They settled around the area that came to be known as Des Allemands ("from the Germans" in French), a little south of LaPlace. The first recorded sausage-maker in the family was Jean Adam Jacob, who was making andouille as early as 1846. The lineage of Jacob's in LaPlace begins with Nelson and Camille Jacob, who in 1928 opened a store a few miles away—the store, it is claimed, that was the first place to sell andouille commercially. Their son, Henry "Diddy" Jacob, opened the LaPlace shop at its current location with his daughter, Mary Ann, in 1979. Today, Mary Ann's son, Aaron, is in charge. (Wayne Jacob's was opened by another branch of the family, but is no longer in the hands of a Jacob.)

Jacob's andouille, stuffed into beef casings, is smoked for about a dozen hours over aged pecan wood, taking on a deep mahogany-brown color and a strong, woody smoke flavor. It is mildly garlicky, mildly spicy, and thoroughly satisfying.

BACON

The word bacon derives ultimately from the Proto-Germanic term *bakkon*, meaning "back meat" (that is, from a pig). The Chinese who first salt-cured pork as many as 3,500 years ago, were smoking it by 200 BC, and the ancient Romans salted and air-dried theirs before smoking, but bacon more or less as we know it in America today was probably developed by our English forebears and brought to this continent in the 1600s. In any case, it has been a popular food here for centuries, as flavoring for beans and stewed dishes and more recently as an essential element of classic sandwiches (the BLT), the bacon cheeseburger, and of course part of an old-fashioned breakfast. In the twenty-first century, in fact, the nation has succumbed to baconmania. We've got bacon chocolates, bacon ice cream, tempura bacon, even toothpaste and soap redolent of it.

This is all a bit crazy, of course. But good bacon made in the traditional style and eaten in the traditional manner remains one of the most immediately appealing foods we know, a masterful blend of salt and sweet and smoke and fat. There are fine examples of this kind of bacon made in many parts of the country, and folks tend to have regional favorites. The South, where cured meats of many kinds are a time-honored art, is particularly rich with examples. But for many of us bacon-lovers,

the ultimate expression of this indulgent food comes from the town of Wittenberg in central Wisconsin, from Nueske's Hillcrest Farm.

When the Nueske family arrived in the area from Germany in 1882, they already knew how to cure and smoke meats, and in 1933, enterprising young Robert Carl Nueske started driving around Wittenberg in his pickup truck, selling turkeys, hams, sausages, and bacon processed on the Nueske farm. Pretty soon, customers starting coming to him, and in 1940, the Nueskes bought a butcher shop and constructed a series of smokehouses, fueled by locally abundant applewood.

Today, the Nueskes sell a wide array of smoked meats and fowl, but their reputation rests above all on bacon. Sold thin- or thick-sliced and also in "super-thick" form (this is sometimes called knife-and-fork bacon, because it can be eaten as a dinner meat), the bacon is cured with hand-mixed spices and smoked for twenty-four hours (far longer than most bacon) with applewood logs, not sawdust as is the norm. (They also produce a more strongly smoky cherrywood version.) Nueske's bacon is unusually lean, so it doesn't shrink and shrivel like most bacon. It does get nicely crispy, though, when cooked with patience, and its flavor is meaty, with a perfect balance of smoke and sweetness.

BEEF BACON

Everybody knows that martinis are made with gin and bacon is made with pork, right? Oh. Never mind. We live in a world of vodka martinis (with chocolate or apple, no less, or who knows what else added) and of "bacon" made from lamb, duck, turkey, even vegetable protein. And beef.

Of all the alternatives to the real thing, beef bacon, long a staple at kosher and halal butcher shops, is about the best there is. It lacks the gorgeous fat of pork bacon, the part that fries up so nice and crispy, but well-made examples have plenty of meaty flavor, and you can get them fairly crisp as well. The problem is that, compared with its porcine cousin, beef bacon is undeniably rather dry, more like Canadian or back bacon than the usual kind.

The leanest but also the most flavorful beef bacon that I've encountered is made from grass-fed beef, whose natural sweetness and herbal character translate nicely into this form. A particularly good version comes from Menefee Ranches in Carthage, in the grassy plains of southwestern Missouri. Three generations of Menefees work on the ranch (a fourth generation is currently a toddler, but will no doubt be moving into position before too long), raising 100 percent grass-fed and organically raised Black Angus cattle. It is processed by a small, family-owned, United States Department of Agriculture (USDA)-approved plant a few miles away, and the Menefees promise that they personally inspect every carcass. Menefee Ranches meats are sold under the Pops Natural Grass Fed Beef label.

BEEF JERKY

The idea of preserving meat by drying and smoking it is an old one—"jerky" derives ultimately from the Quechua Indian word *ch'arki*, meaning burned or dried meat—and variations on the theme are found around the world, from Italy to India to South Africa. In our own country, it is possible to find jerky made from turkey, goat, bison, deer, salmon (see page 102), tuna, and just about any other variety of meaty animal or fish flesh. By far the most popular kind, though, is beef jerky.

There are countless varieties of beef jerky available around the country, from mass-produced, nationally distributed brands like Jack Link's (the world's largest), Oberto, and Matador, to smaller regional labels and handmade smokehouse versions. Then there's Velma Willett's jerky, from Kirbyville, Texas. There is nothing else remotely like it. It comes not in flat sheets or irregular shards like most jerky, but in long, thick, squared-off pieces. It is so heavily smoked that when you unwrap a bundle, it smells as though somebody has just doused a campfire with a bucket of water. The flavor varies slightly from sample to sample,

because it's made in small lots, a few pounds at a time, and neither the marinade recipe nor the particulars of the smoking process are written down or regulated. Willett improvises. (For one recent batch she stirred pineapple preserves into the marinade.) Her jerky is always strongly flavored, though, with a touch of sweetness, some heat, and enough acidity to offset the richness of the beef with which she starts.

Unfortunately, though Willett still makes her jerky, she doesn't sell it regularly anymore, by mail order or otherwise. The next best thing might be the jerky from Woody's Smokehouse, also in Texas—this time from Centerville, northwest of Houston. Dudley "Woody" Wood, a butcher since the age of eighteen, turned what was once a roadside gas station and convenience store into a jerky haven. He makes jerky from buffalo, elk, and venison as well as turkey and pork—and he produces six variations on beef jerky. His thick-cut version, hickory-smoked and seasoned with lots of black pepper, is the standard—not as complex in flavor as Willett's, but deliciously beefy and rich, with just enough peppery fire.

BISON

Bison is America's meat. For centuries, beginning as early as 8500 BC, it was being hunted for food throughout the so-called Great Bison Belt (stretching from Alaska to the Gulf of Mexico and covering more than two-thirds of what is now the United States), and sustained Native American populations across the Plains States. Later it became an important food source for interloping European pioneers, and eventually for gourmands even on the Eastern Seaboard.

A lumbering, out-of-proportion beast (its front half is considerably heftier than its aft, and it is magnificently maned and bearded), the bison is, of course, what we more commonly call the buffalo—though true buffalo are found only in Africa and Asia. The bison feeds on grass and shrubbery, and its meat is tasty and nutritious. Before the Spanish introduced horses to the continent in the sixteenth century, Indians hunted buffalo by herding them over cliffs, where they'd fall to their deaths. (The practice is memorialized in the rather graphic name of a UNESCO World Heritage Site in Alberta, Canada: Head-Smashed-In Buffalo Jump.) Horses, and then firearms, made the process much easier. Europeans took up buffalo-hunting enthusiastically, more for commerce than for sustenance (buffalo tongue was once a great delicacy on the restaurant tables of New York City and Washington, D.C.), and by the latter 1800s, the bison had almost disappeared.

A Scottish-born South Dakota rancher named James Philip is credited with having saved the animal from extinction, buying a small herd around the turn of the last century and propagating them on his property near Fort Pierre. It is fitting, then, that some of the best-tasting contemporary bison meat is raised not far to the southwest of Philip's land, at the 28,000-acre (11,300-hectare) Cheyenne River Ranch, just west of Badlands National Park, near the Wyoming and Nebraska borders. Here, Dan and Jill O'Brien have established their Wild Idea Buffalo Company. Dan is a veteran wildlife biologist, rancher, and author (and also a celebrated falconer, instrumental in restoring the peregrine falcon population to the Rocky Mountains). Jill grew up on a dairy farm and worked in the restaurant business for many years.

The couple originally raised cattle, but little by little the idea of specializing in the bison native to the area began to seem like a good idea, and in 2005 they started putting together their new business. In 2007, they equipped a mobile harvesting truck and brought it to the property, and in 2011 they built their own packing plant. Today, Wild Idea sells a complete range of bison products, including steaks and roasts, sausages, cured meats, and organ meats (including that once-prized tongue, as well as heart and liver). Bison meat is similar to beef, but with a slightly "wilder" flavor, herbaceous and earthy. It is leaner than beef, but has enough fat to keep it moist and savory. My favorite cut is what is known as uncut short rib plate: buffalo in the form of meaty Flintstonian bones, great oven-roasted or smoked for a few hours over indirect heat.

BOUDIN

In France, boudin comes in two flavors, *blanc* and *noir*. The former is a mild sausage of finely ground pork and pork parts, often moistened with milk; the latter is blood sausage. The two correspond to what in Ireland and the United Kingdom are known as white pudding and black pudding, respectively—and in fact the word "boudin" shares an etymology with "pudding," both deriving ultimately from a Latin term for sausage, *botellus*.

Now forget all that. In Louisiana's Cajun country, and anywhere else where gourmands of Acadian descent have gathered, boudin means an assertively spiced sausage, nothing like its European counterparts, made with ground pork, sometimes with innards and sometimes not, rice, and often scallions, onions, and/or green peppers. (There are also Cajun boudins made of shrimp or crayfish, but that's another story.) Boudin finds its apotheosis in southern and southwestern Louisiana, and many of the establishments listed and graded by the Web site called www.boudinlink.com—yes, boudin has its own Web site—are in that region.

On a trip through that part of the world some years ago, I became particularly fond of the boudin produced by Rabideaux's Sausage Kitchen in Iowa (that's "RAB-a-dooze" in "Io-way"), run by a former residential contractor named Glenn Daigle. Daigle produces a number of traditional Cajun pork products as well as a savory crayfish boudin, but his classic version of the sausage is the one to try. All his pork is smoked over oak; he gets the wood from the state prison, he once told me, where it is harvested by convicts. To extend the law-and-order theme, the local sheriff grows scallions for him. His boudin has a thin, crisp casing and the interior, which seems to be almost half rice, is sweet and perfectly spiced. You should taste the heat after you've eaten the boudin, says Daigle, not while it's in your mouth. If your cardiologist isn't anywhere in sight, incidentally, you might want to try one of Daigle's other specialties: boudin balls. These are simply the filling of the sausage formed into squash-ball-size spheres and deep-fried. Deadly, I'm sure, but oh, so good.

BRATWURST

The most popular variety of sausage in many corners of the Midwest is bratwurst, a mildly but authoritatively spiced link typically made from veal, pork, or a combination of the two. The name comes from the German *Wurst*, meaning sausage, and the Old High German *Brät*, meaning lean, finely ground calf or swine flesh. In America, bratwurst, known informally and collectively as "brats," is particularly associated with Wisconsin (the city of Madison holds what it claims is the world's largest bratwurst festival every year, and Usinger's in Milwaukee makes a definitive veal-and-pork version). Nevertheless, I think the most delicious bratwurst I've ever found in this country is an all-pork version produced by Dewig Meats in Haubstadt, Indiana.

Dewig (pronounced "DAY-wig") was started as Dewig Bros. Packing Co. in 1916 by John Dewig and his brothers. Their father had been an itinerant butcher, traveling from farm to farm to slaughter animals, so the boys grew up in the meat-cutting trade. It is family lore that when the first small storefront packinghouse opened for business, the only tools used were knives. As the business expanded, more equipment was purchased and the Dewigs built their own slaughterhouse.

The Dewigs's part of western Indiana has a substantial German-American population, and German pork products became their specialty. In the 1960s, they were asked to supply bratwurst, which hadn't yet become popular in America, for the *Bierstube* (beer hall) at their town's annual *Sommerfest* (summer festival). A family friend named Jewell Steick, an accomplished sausage-maker, gave them his recipe, and after it was a hit at the Bierstube, the Dewigs began producing it year-round. It's a juicy, finely textured sausage with an unusually complex flavor, with hints of nutmeg, sage, and oregano.

BREAKFAST SAUSAGE

One of my strongest taste memories from childhood is of Sunday breakfast, which for some years consisted, almost ritualistically, of waffles, made from a mix on our big old electric waffle iron, and served with Arden Farms butter, Log Cabin maple syrup (which came in cabin-shaped tin cans), and Little Pig Sausages. The waffles were crisp, the butter was creamy and slightly cheesy, the syrup was full of flavor, the sausages were peppery and sweet, and the whole taken together in one bite was paradise.

Little Pig Sausages had their origins in Vermont. In the 1830s, a surveyor named Milo Jones moved with his family to Wisconsin's Rock River Valley, where the town of Fort Atkinson now stands, buying a farm there with gold coins he'd carted in wooden buckets from his New England home. He brought in dairy cows and turned the farm into a self-sufficient property, complete with brickyard, blacksmith shop, tannery, and tavern. His wife, known as Aunt Sally Crane, was a good cook, and one of her specialties was sausage made from an old family recipe from Vermont, based on young pig meat and home-ground spices. Milo Junior

came along, growing up to be a surveyor like his father—but he was stricken with rheumatoid arthritis, and could no longer travel easily or work the farm, so in 1889, he decided to try making sausage according to his mother's recipe and sell it to other local farmers.

His enterprise was a success. Initially grinding meat by hand, and later with the help of a patient workhorse operating a large grinder, he eventually built a sausage factory in Fort Atkinson, and added ham and bacon to his product line. He was very proud of the fact that only the finest quality pork went into his sausage, even sometimes including bacon and ham; the lesser parts of the animal, such as hearts and tongues, which other sausage makers used, he'd sell off to large-scale producers.

Today, the Jones Dairy Farm remains family-owned, and it still produces a range of ham, bacon, and sausage (and also an excellent liverwurst). Little Pig Sausages aren't sold by that name anymore, but Jones All Natural Little Pork Sausages, whose ingredients include only pork, water, salt, and spices, in a lamb casing, are close enough to stimulate delicious childhood memories.

CHORIZO

Like boudin (see page 126), chorizo is a different thing in the Americas than it is in Europe. Spanish chorizo is a firm-textured, comparatively lean, cured and fermented pork sausage flavored with *pimentón* (paprika); Mexican chorizo, an essential ingredient in Tex-Mex and other border state cooking as well as that of its home country, is a crumbly, fatty pork sausage, usually made with fresh chiles, along with garlic and assorted herbs and spices (oregano, cumin, and even cinnamon are common). When used for cooking, it is removed from its casings and prepared in the same way as is ground meat. (There is something vaguely similar in Spain called *chorizo fresco*, which may have been the original inspiration for the Mexican interpretation.)

In neighborhoods with Mexican meat markets, there is often freshly made chorizo available, and this is the best kind to seek out. A good commercial brand, though, is El Popular—headquartered, I was surprised to learn, in the Chicago area. Actually, I shouldn't have been surprised: Chicago has a large Mexican and Mexican-American community (Illinois boasts a Hispanic population approximately equal to that of Arizona), and it's a great city in which to eat Mexican food—not all of it prepared by Rick Bayless.

El Popular's founder, Vicente F. Garza, immigrated to the Windy City in 1925 from Nuevo Léon. Two years later, he set up a small food business, specializing in chorizo, mole sauce, and chocolate, in East Chicago, Indiana, a few miles down the Lake Michigan shoreline from Chicago itself. His son, Richard, took over the company in 1982, in turn handing it on to his sons. El Popular produces chorizo in mild, regular, and "super picante" versions, as well as a beef chorizo. All are made without preservatives or artificial colors or flavors, and all are superb—rich but not gristly, with a complex herb-and-spice flavor and, in the super picante entry, at least, spicy enough to make you sit up and take notice.

CINCINNATI CHILI

A Transportation Security Administration (TSA) agent seized a can of Cincinnati chili that I was transporting from Fort Myers, Florida (the nearby community of Naples has a substantial Cincinnatian constituency), back to New York. "But it's canned chili," I protested. She shook it vigorously. "Sounds like liquid to me," she announced, "and you're not taking it on the plane." I'll bet that wouldn't have happened with Texas chili (see page 144).

Cincinnati chili, in fact, isn't chili in any sense that a Texan or New Mexican (or even a Californian like me) would intuitively understand it. It's more or less Greek-style meat sauce, made with finely ground beef in a, er, liquid spiced with cinnamon and other "sweet" spices, and possibly some bitter chocolate. (Everybody who makes Cincinnati chili claims to have a "secret recipe.") Scholars of the subject trace the original preparation to Tom and John Kiradjieff, immigrants from Greek Macedonia, who started serving a variation on a traditional meat stew with hot dogs and spaghetti in 1922 at their hot dog stand—which became known as the Empress, after the burlesque theater next door.

Another Greek newcomer, Nicholas Lambrinides, later went to work at what had grown into the Empress Chili restaurant. In 1949, in partnership with three of his sons, he struck out on his own and opened Skyline Chili. His recipe for chili, which differed from the Empress formula, appealed to locals and the business grew. By the year 2000, there were more than a hundred Skyline outlets, in Ohio, Kentucky, Indiana, and Florida. Lambrinides's sons continued to run the business after his death in 1962, until they sold it to a New England investment firm in 1998.

Besides Skyline and Empress, which is still going strong, other Cincinnati chili chains include Dixie and Gold Star, and there are also one-offs like Camp Washington and Price Hill. Cincinnati chili is eaten in various ritualized manners, rarely just by itself in a bowl but more frequently in one of these manners: two-way (over spaghetti), three-way (with spaghetti and shredded Cheddar), four-way (with onions added to a three-way), and five-way (with the addition of beans). Like Texas chili, the Cincinnati version is perfectly good canned. And the best one you'll find in that form is Skyline's. As long as you're not expecting anything spicy or too meaty, it's good stuff, undeniably Balkan-tasting, with a not-unpleasant sweetness and a lingering finish. And did I mention that you probably shouldn't try to take it with you on a plane?

COUNTRY HAM

Cured in salt and sugar and hung to age in smokehouses for as long as two years, country ham is one of the great gastronomic treasures of the American South. Allan Benton, of Benton's Smoky Mountain Country Hams in Madisonville, Tennessee, about 60 miles (97 kilometers) northeast of Chattanooga, makes a version so good—so pure and vivid and right in flavor—that even Thomas Keller buys it.

Curing, drying, and smoking was the best way to preserve meat in the days before refrigeration, and Southern farmers, especially in Tennessee, Kentucky, and Virginia, elevated the process to an art. Benton remembers his grandparents butchering hogs on Thanksgiving Day each year and transforming them into hams, sausages, and bacon. He had aspirations to escape farm life himself, though, and went to college to earn degrees in education and counseling. Returning home to Madisonville in the early 1970s, he realized that he couldn't live on a guidance counselor's salary, so he bought a small smokehouse that had been in operation since 1947, and set about producing good pork products. He experimented with various rubs for his ham, settling on a mix of salt, brown sugar, and red pepper—exactly what his grandparents had used. Benton uses only heritage breed pork, mostly from Berkshire, Duroc, and Tamworth pigs, and smokes his hams over hickory and applewood before aging them for at least eighteen months.

In 1991, Benton took his ham and bacon to Blackberry Farm (see page 65), a celebrated inn and restaurant property in Walland, Tennessee, not far from Madisonville. John Fleer, then chef at the inn, liked the products so well that he created a special menu around them. After that, word got out, and today, Benton's ham is found—and proudly name-checked—on menus all over America. About a hundred New York City restaurants use it, and the smokehouse sells regularly to chefs in Chicago, New Orleans, and the San Francisco Bay area. At least 70 percent of his production is shipped out of state, Benton estimates.

The ham's appeal is easy to see: It's sweet, pale, and very tender, with a good balance of salt and smoke. It's also, unfortunately, pretty near impossible to stop eating.

GOETTA

Goetta (pronounced "get-uh") is a sort-of sausage, apparently of northwestern German origin, that has become the emblematic regional specialty of the Cincinnati area. Made of finely ground pork parts (shoulder commonly predominates) or a blend of pork and beef, along with pinhead oats and various herbs and spices (among them thyme, rosemary, and black pepper), goetta is a cousin to the Pennsylvania Dutch specialty called scrapple—in which cornmeal and flour take the place of oats. It's also not at all dissimilar to the white pudding of Ireland and the United Kingdom (as I discovered when I brought some goetta over to serve to friends in County Tipperary one St. Patrick's Day).

Many independent butchers in and around Cincinnati—including some a few miles from the city, across the Ohio River, in northern Kentucky—make their own goetta, and there is considerable variation in flavor and texture. The standard interpretation, though, is Glier's, made in the Kentucky city of Covington. This is the one found in supermarkets all over the area, and the one homesick Cincinnatians order over the Internet wherever they might be.

Glier's started as a small family-run butcher shop in Newport, Kentucky, and first sold goetta apportioned into 1-pound (450-gram) log-shaped packages—a novelty—in the early 1960s. Their product was so popular that within a few years they had to build a plant to produce it exclusively. Today, they effectively own the commercial goetta trade, turning out more than 1,000,000 pounds (about 450,000 kilograms) a year.

Goetta was traditionally eaten for breakfast, cut into slabs and fried, then anointed with various condiments either sweet (maple syrup, honey, apple butter) or savory (mustard, ketchup, butter, and salt). Every summer, there are not one but two "Goettafests" held on the Kentucky side of the river, one of which is sponsored by Glier's. These feature recipe contests, which have yielded formulas for everything from goetta-stuffed wontons to goetta fudge. Perhaps inspired by these creations, local eateries have begun expanding the idiom with dishes like goetta chili and goetta burgers. Personally, I like it fried crisp in bacon drippings, with spicy salsa on the side.

The Taste of America

GRASS-FED BEEF

We do love our beef in America. The United States Department of Agriculture (USDA) estimates that something close to 35,000,000 head of beef cattle are processed annually for eating purposes, and our per capita beef and veal consumption each year is around 80 pounds (36 kilograms). That doesn't mean we're the beef-eating champions. Brazil and Paraguay have a slightly larger consumption rate; Argentina manages about 120 pounds (54 kilograms) per person per year, and Uruguay makes everybody look bad with around 135 pounds (61 kilograms). The big difference is that virtually all South American beef is grass-fed, while about 90 percent of ours is fattened on corn and other grains.

What difference does it make? There's nothing wrong with grain-fed beef per se. Such meat tends to have the big, round, beefy flavor Americans like in their steaks and roasts; the strip loins and rib eyes from California's grain-fed Brandt Beef, for instance, are some of the best I've ever tasted. But the vast majority of grain-fed cattle are also fed with antibiotics, which help them plump up faster (an estimated 70 percent of all the antibiotics used in America are fed to livestock), and with growth hormones, including estrogen and testosterone. It is naive to think that these substances, lodged in the meat, don't deleteriously affect those of us who eat beef, at least a little. Grass-fed animals rarely receive these enhancements, both because it's too difficult to administer them to pastured beasts and because the farmers and ranchers who raise grass-fed cattle tend to be a bit messianic about organic, sustainable practices.

The USDA defines grass-fed cattle as those that have continuous access to pasturage, and are never fed with grain or grain products. Lack of additives aside, the meat cut from animals like these is leaner than that of grain-fed beef and higher in beneficial linoleic and omega-3 acids. What about flavor? Some folks simply don't like grass-fed meat; it's not what they're used to, and to some palates it seems to lack that rich, primal flavor they've come to associate with beef. Some people even think it tastes "fishy"—not suspicious, but piscine. I've never picked up that quality in it myself, and while I hardly eat it exclusively, I always enjoy grass-fed beef very much.

One of my favorite producers is, like Brandt, from California, and it bears a name famous around the world for something other than ranching: Hearst. The story began in 1865, when George Hearst, a businessman and U.S. senator, bought the 48,000-acre (just under 20,000-hectare) Piedra Blanca Rancho just northwest of San Luis Obispo on California's Central Coast. Over the next twenty years, he acquired neighboring properties until the ranch had grown to 270,000 acres (just under 110,000 hectares) and become a massive integrated farming and ranching operation. George's son, the illustrious, notorious William Randolph Hearst, began building his legendary Hearst Castle on one part of the property in 1919. Portions of the original acreage were sold off or repurposed over the years, but 82,000 acres (about 33,000 hectares) of ranchland still surround the castle, and in 1965, the corporation also bought the 73,000-acre (just under 30,000-hectare) Jack Ranch in Cholame, inland from San Luis. Both properties, now run by William Randolph's great-grandson, Stephen Thompson Hearst, today raise grass-fed beef and pork, as well as various crops, including wine grapes. The cattle feed on rye, soft chess, filaree, clovers, brassicas, purple needlegrass, and birdsfoot trefoil, as well as pasture grass. I haven't tasted Hearst Ranch pork, but the beef is a marvel, with a mouth-filling flavor that says Beef with a capital B, and a clean, faintly herby aftertaste. The Hearst crew likes to say that, like wine, their meat expresses *terroir*—the French term for the unique characteristics bestowed by climate, geography, and soil.

HOT DOGS

I was sitting at the Brasserie Lipp on the Boulevard Saint-Germain in Paris one day some years ago when an American couple sitting next to me, who had just been served their food, started laughing. I looked over and immediately guessed what had happened: Thinking that it was some exotic local variety of charcuterie, they must have ordered *saucisse de Francfort*—because on each of their plates, unadorned, were two long hot dogs.

Well, they may have been seasoned slightly differently from an American dog, but they were more or less identical. This isn't surprising when you remember that the old-fashioned name for hot dogs in this country was frankfurters. Indeed, most authorities agree that the hot dog's ancestor was a pork sausage served in a roll that had been known for centuries in Frankfurt, Germany. As to who brought it to the U.S. and adapted it into its present form, there is much disagreement. A German immigrant named Charles Feltman sold sausages in rolls on Coney Island in the early 1870s. In St. Louis, it is maintained that they were first introduced to America at a street stand in 1880. They were also seen at the World's Columbian Exposition, as the Chicago World's Fair of 1893 was officially known. A few years later, a vendor at the New York

Polo Grounds sold sausages-in-buns that he dubbed "dachshund sandwiches" for their shape. This might be the origin of the term "hot dog." In 1916, Nathan Handwerker, who had worked for Charles Feltman on Coney Island, went off on his own and started what was to become Nathan's Famous, possibly the best-known hot-dog purveyor of all.

A good hot dog pops a little when you bite into it, lacks gristle or bits of bone, has recognizable pork flavor, is properly seasoned with salt and pepper (with a hint of garlic), contains no fillers, and is juicy enough that a little of its flavor soaks into the bun. This is a pretty good description of the dogs made by Liehs & Steigerwald in Syracuse, New York. An old-style meat shop, specializing in sausages of many kinds, it was opened in 1936 by German immigrants Curt Liehs and Ludwig Steigerwald. Steigerwald's nephew, Bob, and Liehs's son, Curt Jr., assumed control of the shop in the 1980s. Today it is owned by Jeffrey Steigerwald, Bob's son, in partnership with Chuck Madonna, who started working at the shop when he was fifteen. They promise to preserve the shop's food traditions while modernizing the business, and so far, at least judging from their hot dogs, they're doing a good job.

LIVERWURST

For no particularly good reason, given my white-bread ethnic background and my parents' extremely conventional tastes in food, I grew up loving liverwurst. Liverwurst is an anglicization of *Leberwurst*, a German word that literally means "liver sausage," and under either name it's a semi-soft, spreadable sausage traditionally made with at least a small percentage of strong-tasting pork liver along with pork and/or other meats and a blend of spices.

I'm perfectly happy eating supermarket liverwurst, but by far the best and most unusual interpretation of this traditional pork product comes from, of all places, a microbrewery in North Carolina. Actually, Weeping Radish Farm Brewery—the oldest microbrewery in the state, located in Jarvisburg, between Norfolk, Virginia, and the Carolinan barrier islands known as the Outer Banks—is rather more than just a place that makes beer. It's also a pub-style

restaurant, a vegetable farm selling retail to the public, a shop featuring North Carolina food products, and a first-rate butcher shop.

The operation was launched by German-born Uli Bennewitz, who came to the United States as an agribusiness executive but who, he says, "got suckered into opening a craft brewery" by his brother in the mid-1980s. Little by little, he expanded, moving from a dry town nearby to his present 24-acre (10-hectare) property. Weeping Radish meats and charcuterie—nitrate-free and based on animals sourced from area farms—are the preserve of another German, butcher Frank Meusel, and his masterpiece, at least to me, is his "liver pâté with a Southern flair". This is liverwurst made not just with pork and pork liver but sweetened with a touch of sweet potato. The effect is brilliant: a mouth-filling concentration of flavors neither sugary nor livery, but just right.

PASTRAMI

My New York friends would never admit this in a million years, even if they had a chance to make the comparison for themselves, but I'm convinced, on the evidence of not a few taste tests, that the delis of Los Angeles (full disclosure: my hometown) serve better pastrami than their East Coast counterparts.

Its association with delis, and thus with American Jewish cooking, notwithstanding, pastrami has its origins in the Eastern Mediterranean and Eastern Europe, and particularly in Romania, by way of Turkey. Its etymology goes back to *bastirma*, a form of the Turkish verb meaning "to press." Some variation on the word is used today to describe spiced air-dried meat all over the Balkans and the Middle East. We inherited the term from Romanian Jewish immigrants to New York in the last quarter of the nineteenth century, and the modern-day technique for producing what we now call pastrami was probably developed by its importers around that time. The model may have been cured goose breast, which was popular in Romania, where geese were commonplace.

Pastrami is a labor-intensive meat to prepare. Beef (often brisket or boneless plate) is first brined with salt and sugar, then allowed to dry a little and seasoned with garlic and assorted herbs and spices, such as black pepper, paprika, and mustard seed—every maker has his or her own recipe. Next, it is smoked. Then it is steamed. If the basic idea of pastrami was originally to preserve meat, as it almost certainly was, then somebody wanted to make sure that this stuff *stayed* preserved.

Pastrami sandwiches, with the meat thinly sliced and piled high on rye bread or a roll well slathered with mustard, were sold from pushcarts in lower Manhattan and Brooklyn, and later from delis. There is no question that New Yorkers were eating pastrami before Californians were (the famous Katz's Delicatessen opened in 1888, almost certainly with pastrami on the menu). I'm not sure when the first deli opened in the Los Angeles area, but the oldest one still operating there, as far as I can tell, is Greenblatt's, at the eastern end of the Sunset Strip, and descended from a deli established by Herman Greenblatt in 1926. Although celebrity-magnet Canter's was founded in 1924, in New Jersey, it did not open in Los Angeles (at its now-iconic Fairfax Avenue location) until 1931.

Canter's Deli has pretty good pastrami, as do such other local favorites as Nate 'n Al's, Langer's Delicatessen-Restaurant, and Art's Delicatessen & Restaurant. But Greenblatt's Deli, owned by the Kavin family since the early 1940s, has the best pastrami in town (and thus the best in the country), in my opinion. Like Canter's, Greenblatt's has long catered to local royalty, serving the likes of Marilyn Monroe, Errol Flynn, Janis Joplin, Marlon Brando, Billie Holiday, Rita Hayworth, and even onetime Hollywood screenwriter F. Scott Fitzgerald. I'd like to think that at least a few of them enjoyed the pastrami as much as I do. It's just meltingly tender, with sweet fat and meaty meat and just enough salt. It's great in classic sandwich form (on rye, with coleslaw and Russian dressing), but it's good enough to nibble right off the butcher's paper. Is it really better than anything in New York? I think so.

Deli expert David Sax, in his exhaustively researched book *Save the Deli: In Search of Perfect Pastrami, Crusty Rye, and the Heart of Jewish Delicatessen*, wrote that "Los Angeles has become America's premier deli city." He's from Brooklyn, so he ought to know.

PEPPERONI

How many Americans, asking for pepperoni on their pizza while traveling in Italy, have been disappointed to find no trace of meat at all, but just some strips of yellow, red, and/or green pepper? That, of course, is because pepperoni doesn't exist in Italy; *peperoni*, bell peppers, do. Pepperoni is an Italian-American invention, dating from around 1920. It is fine-grained and usually moderately spicy, with a dark orangish color. Unlike the southern Italian *salame* on which it is apparently modeled, it is rarely eaten by itself, but usually goes into sandwiches or, of course, on pizza.

The vast majority of the pepperoni made and consumed in America is an industrial product, mass-produced and full of preservatives (not that it isn't also pretty tasty). I recently discovered an excellent, unusual artisanal version, though, made by Vermont Smoke and Cure in South Barre,

near the Vermont state capital of Montpelier. The operation began in 1962, under a French-Canadian smoker named Roland LeFebvre, who brined his meats with maple syrup and smoked them with corn cobs and maplewood. In 1999, Lefebvre sold the smokehouse to Chris Bailey and his partners, operators of a well-regarded restaurant called The Farmers' Diner. The current Vermont Smoke and Cure label was created in 2006, and the company still uses LeFebvre's recipes and methods. Their pepperoni, though, is a recent creation. What's uncommon about it, besides the fact that it's dry and almost lean (though still plenty flavorful), is that it's smoked—over the same corn cobs and maplewood LeFebvre used—giving it a depth of character that ordinary pepperoni just doesn't have. This is one that deserves to be eaten by itself, though it sure won't do a pizza any harm.

PONCE

I've never understood why haggis, the classic Scots dish of ground, seasoned lamb parts packed into a sheep's stomach, inspires all those jokes, all those expressions of horror. We've all been eating ground, seasoned pig parts packed into a pig's (or some other animal's) intestines—that is, sausage—forever, and I'm not sure why that should seem any less unappetizing. I bring this up because ponce (also called pounce and chaudin) is the Cajun haggis, a kind of hybrid of that dish and sausage, if you will, in which the meat and stomach come from pigs.

Ponce is a specialty of rural southern Louisiana, and not one you're likely to find in New Orleans. It's sold at the same kinds of butcher shops that offer boudin (see page 126) and andouille (see page 121), and it's more likely to be served at communal suppers or at home than at any restaurant. Besides pork, which should be coarsely ground, the filling for ponce typically includes white bread or breadcrumbs and sometimes an egg or two as a binder, as well as finely chopped garlic, scallions, and green pepper, and a dose of hot sauce or cayenne. Some recipes add diced yam. The filling is loosely packed inside the stomach, then boiled or steamed and, in some regions, smoked. The cooking tightens the stomach so that the ponce can be cut into crumbly slices. Ponce tastes like a kind of super-rich, slightly spicy meatloaf. If you don't like pork fat, it's probably a good idea to avoid ponce, but it's a real taste of Cajun country.

The only mail-order source I've found for ponce is Poché's Market and Restaurant in Breaux Bridge, opened by Lug and Eleanor Poché in 1962 and now run by their son, Floyd, and his wife, Karen. Their ponce, which they call chaudin, contains both crushed red pepper flakes and jalapeños, so it is a little warmer on the palate than some versions.

RABBIT

My first father-in-law, a former grocery executive, was a sophisticated eater, at home in the best restaurants of South America and France, but he wouldn't go near rabbit. He'd grown up during the Depression, and rabbit was the cheapest meat available, so it ended up on the family table three or four times a week. "I've had enough rabbit to last a lifetime," he'd say. Our own economic downturn notwithstanding, that's not a complaint today's fathers-in-law are likely to make: 3-pound (about 1-kilogram) rabbit fryers now typically cost $25 to $40 (about £15 to £25).

That's not the only reason that rabbit remains a minority meat in American diets. There's also what I call the Thumper Factor, after the gregarious cartoon rabbit in the Walt Disney movie *Bambi*. Rabbits are cute, furry, cotton-tailed little creatures—how could you even *think* about eating one? Easily, once you grow out of your animated movie phase. Rabbit is delicious meat, mild and very lean and extremely versatile. You can deep-fry rabbit, roast it, grill it, stew it, turn it into pasta sauce or pasta filling, and more.

The Rare Hare Barn's Eric Rapp is a third-generation farmer who has been helping raise rabbits since he was a kid. His wife, Callene, is on the board of the American Livestock Breeds Conservancy, and is senior zookeeper at the Children's Farms at the Sedgwick County Zoo in Wichita, Kansas. In the late 2000s, the Rapps started raising rabbits for their own consumption on their farm in Leon, Kansas, in the Flint Hills due east of Wichita. They also have horses, chickens, a small herd of Pineywoods cattle, and some Jacob and Navajo-Churro sheep— but it is rabbits they have come to specialize in, now producing enough to sell. They raise five breeds: Blanc de Hotot, American Chinchilla, American, Silver Fox, and Crème d'Argent, all of which make good eating.

The rabbits are raised humanely, in large, well-ventilated pens, and fed on fresh greens, hay, and grain-oat pellets. They are never dosed with antibiotics or growth hormones. Their meat is very clean-tasting, moist despite its low fat content, and very faintly earthy. Does it taste like chicken? No. Better.

SMOKED BEEF TONGUE

Don't tackle beef tongue if you're on a low-fat diet: almost 75 percent of its calories (a little over 1,000 of them a pound, or a little over 2,000 per kilogram) are from fat. That's precisely what makes it so meltingly delicious, of course, especially when it's braised or slow-roasted and thinly sliced. Beef tongue also lends itself well to pickling in brine, but until I encountered it at Café Rouge in Berkeley, I had never before had beef tongue smoked. It is remarkable, delicate in texture but beefy and smoky in flavor, with a faint woody sweetness and a pleasant bite of salt.

Café Rouge is a lively restaurant with a beguiling menu—typical dishes include kale Caesar salad, asparagus vichyssoise, and a mixed grill of goat chop and merguez sausage with black chanterelles and pecorino bread pudding—but there is an ambitious meat market attached. The establishment was opened in 1996 by Marsha McBride,

a University of California, Berkeley, graduate who had gone on to the California Culinary Academy with the intention of becoming a pastry chef, only to discover that she preferred meats to sweets. She ended up in charge of charcuterie at Judy Rodgers's classic Zuni Café in San Francisco, a post she held for nine years. When she opened her own restaurant and market, she was determined to make cured and smoked meats an important part of her repertoire, and to ensure a supply of organically raised animals to work with, she established relationships with farms and ranches around Northern California. Organically raised beef from Angus-Shorthorn cattle comes from Magruder Ranch in Ukiah, and it was their tongues that Scott Brennan, then the Café Rouge butcher (he has since opened his own business), used to make the product that won a 2011 Good Food Award; the judges thought it "epitomized the art of hand-crafted charcuterie."

SUMMER SAUSAGE

I always used to wonder why Christmas gift baskets—the kind that get sent by suppliers to their customers in various businesses every holiday season, and to families by relatives who haven't a clue what else to send—inevitably seem to contain something called "summer sausage," usually from an Ohio-based outfit called Hickory Farms. Wasn't there a seasonal disconnect there? Where was the *winter* sausage?

Summer sausage, at least the gift-basket variety, came wrapped in a kind of papery plastic (or plastic-y paper); once you stripped that off, it had an edible rind and its filling was finely ground, firm, and generously seasoned with salt and pepper, among other things. It was very aromatic, and the smell of smoke and animal fat would linger on your fingers after you'd eaten some. It wasn't too bad if you sliced it thinly enough.

What I eventually learned was that "summer sausage" simply means one that can be kept without refrigeration—presumably even in hot summer weather. This has to do with how it's cured (it is usually smoked) and its acidity. That summer sausage from Hickory Farms is a taste of my childhood, and I still find it pretty good. But several years ago, in my adopted state of Connecticut, I discovered a summer sausage that changed the game. This is a venison version prepared by Nodine's Smokehouse in Goshen, in the northwest corner of the state, not far from Litchfield. Nodine's is a family-owned business started in 1969 by Ronald and Johanne Nodine as a custom smokehouse serving the needs of local hunters and fishermen. Today, they have a 20,000-square-foot (about 1,850-square-meter) processing plant and they smoke fish, poultry, cheese, pork, and game over apple, juniper, and hickory wood. They also produce a good range of sausage and several varieties of bacon that give Nueske's (see page 122) stiff competition. I love their summer sausage most of all, though, because it's so unusual. Made with red deer venison imported from New Zealand, blended with beef fat, and flavored with orange zest and lemon, it is both foresty and fresh.

SURRYANO HAM

The Spanish word *serrano*, meaning more or less "of the mountains," is shorthand for *jamón serrano*, dry-cured Spanish ham. Surry is a community in eastern Virginia, across Cobham Bay from Jamestown. Put them together, and you've got Surryano, a sort of cross between traditional Southern country ham and good Spanish *jamón*, produced from heritage-breed Six-Spotted Berkshire pigs at S. Wallace Edwards and Sons' Surry Farms.

Tradition holds that Native Americans in the area cured fish and venison with salt evaporated from sea water and smoked it over oak and hickory fires to preserve it. It is certainly true that European settlers in the seventeenth century—Jamestown was founded in 1607—brought not only hogs but some knowledge of meat-curing with them, and by the eighteenth century, Virginia hams were being shipped back to England. In 1926,

S. Wallace Edwards, captain of the Jamestown-Surry ferry, started selling his passengers sandwiches made with ham that he'd cured himself on the family farm. Demand became so great that he began curing hams full-time.

Edwards's grandchildren now run the farm, producing conventional Virginia ham, bacon, and other products. Several years ago, though, they added Surryano to their line. Their pigs are raised on a network of sustainable independent family farms in Missouri. The hams are cured with salt, then washed and coated with pepper before being smoked over hickory wood for seven days. Then they're hung and aged for more than a year. The results don't taste quite like Virginia ham *or jamón serrano*, but when thinly sliced, Spanish style, the meat—with a good balance between its seasonings and its sweet pork flavor—is hard to stop eating.

TASSO

Tasso, an essential ingredient of Cajun cookery, is often called tasso ham, but it isn't really ham at all. It's a hunk of pork—often the so-called "Boston butt," or "pork hand," as it is known in the United Kingdom, though other cuts are sometimes used. The pork is sliced into pieces about the size of a dinner steak, cured, spice-marinated (the mixture always includes plenty of garlic and cayenne, along with salt, sugar, and black pepper), and then hot-smoked, to yield a piquant, assertively flavored meat. This is not eaten by itself but used to flavor everything from crab cakes to gumbo, shrimp and grits to jambalaya.

In the old days, tasso was made with strips of pork left over from a Cajun *boucherie*, or hog-killing, and was smoked for much longer than is common today. The result had a texture approaching that of beef jerky (see page 124). Today, tasso tends to be a little closer to, well, ham in its consistency. Many Louisiana cooks make their own tasso; the process isn't particularly difficult if you have access to a smoker. There are also a number of good commercial brands available, however. One comes from Manda Fine Meats, founded by three brothers in Baton Rouge, Louisiana, in 1947. The company, now under the leadership of one of the founders' three grandsons, makes a wide range of meat products, including Cajun andouille and boudin (see pages 121 and 126, respectively) and an array of smoked sausages, all of good quality. Their tasso is forthright in flavor and medium-firm in texture, with a true pork taste and a peppery burn.

TEXAS CHILI

The late Fort Worth-born disc jockey, musician, record producer, raconteur, and passionate epicure Joe Gracey once told me, "The reason chili doesn't have beans is because down in south Texas, where it comes from, they had too much beef, not too many beans." Chili was invented—and canned—as a commercial product, he believed, as a way to ship beef north (and east and west) that was a lot less trouble and expense than driving cattle on the hoof. I'm not sure whether chili historians, of whom there are many, would agree, but I do know that canned chili has been around for well over a century and that—while I like to make my own chili, and have had some great ones made from scratch by other folks—the kind that comes in a can is sometimes pretty darned good.

It seems reasonable to assume that the native peoples of Central and South America, to which chiles are native, started using them to flavor meat and other foods as soon as they started cooking. The first written reference to *chiles con carne*—literally "chile with meat" in Spanish—comes from a Spanish explorer's diary in 1519. A mixture of meat, chiles, and spices that was dried into a thick paste and shaped into blocks or bricks later became a staple trail food for Texas cowboys; it could easily be reconstituted with water added in a kettle over a campfire. In 1895, Lyman T. Davis, of Corsicana, southwest of Dallas, started dishing up chili from a local range cook's recipe, spicy and rich with beef suet, from the back of a wagon. He later opened a butcher shop, where he sold the chili in traditional brick form.

In 1908, down in the Texas Hill Country, one William "Willie" Gebhardt, a saloon-keeper who had already invented commercial chili powder, became the first entrepreneur to can chili. In 1921, Lyman Davis began canning his chili, too, calling it Wolf Brand Chili in honor of his pet wolf, Kaiser Bill. In 1923, after oil was discovered on his ranch, Davis retired from the chili business, selling Wolf Brand to a couple of Corsicana businessmen. In 1957, it was purchased by Quaker Oats, and today it is part of the massive Nebraska-based ConAgra Foods (as is, incidentally, the Gebhardt brand). Wolf Brand is obviously a mass-produced chili, and I doubt that it has very much to do with the original version (Davis probably didn't use tomato paste, rolled oats, or soy flour in his recipe, and I doubt that he had access to soy lecithin or sodium tripolyphosphate), but as canned foods go, this one (need I specify the "no beans" kind?) is a good thing to have in the cupboard.

TEXAS HOT LINKS

The Texas Hill Country was largely settled by German, Austrian, and Czech immigrants in the nineteenth and early twentieth century. Their influence can be seen in the local architecture, heard in the polka-accented music of the region, and tasted in Hill Country baked goods and, most vividly, sausage-making. Charles Kreuz opened a grocery store and meat market in the Hill Country town of Lockhart in 1900, and began curing and smoking his own meats and making his own smoked links, in the German style. Over time, he adapted to Texas tastes by spicing up his sausages, and he eventually added tables so that his customers could sit down and eat the meats he sold.

Edgar "Smitty" Schmidt bought the operation from the Kreuz family in 1948, and turned Kreuz's into an internationally known barbecue institution. Like his predecessor, Schmidt was a purist: meats were served on waxed butcher's paper, not plates; there were no utensils; and don't even think about asking for barbecue sauce. When Schmidt died in 1999, a family dispute arose over the ownership of Kreuz's. Basically, Schmidt had sold the business to his sons, but left the market building to his daughter, and the two sides were unable to compromise. Schmidt's son, Rick, won rights to the name, and decamped to a new, larger location not far away. Schmidt's daughter, Nina, and her husband, Jim Sells, stayed put and changed the sign outside to Smitty's Market. (The market's motto is "Where it all began.") Barbecue aficionados argue ceaselessly over which enterprise has the better 'cue—when the Travel Channel program *Food Wars* staged a comparison of the brisket and sausage from both places, Kreuz's won— but in truth both are excellent, and many of their food items are frankly pretty hard to tell apart.

That said, I think Kreuz's sausage is about the best the Hill Country has to offer. Produced in hand-tied horseshoe-shaped rings weighing about a third of a pound (150 grams) each, it's about 85 percent beef and 15 percent pork, seasoned with salt, pepper, and cayenne, and packed in pork casings. The meat ratio makes it slightly leaner than more pork-heavy sausages in the area, but it is still plenty moist, with a meaty flavor and a memorable cayenne kick.

VENISON

In America these days, the term "wild game" is widely misapplied, usually meaning battery-raised rabbit or farmed quail or pheasant. There's nothing wild about these creatures, and they're certainly not "game." The sad fact—sad for food-lovers, anyway—is that for a variety of health and environmental reasons, indigenous hunter-shot wild birds and animals may not be sold commercially for food in this country. Some purveyors do bring in genuine game birds (look out for buckshot!), occasionally fresh in season but mostly frozen, from Scotland, New Zealand, and other countries, but real hooved game is a rarity. Except for what comes from Broken Arrow Ranch.

Broken Arrow, in Ingram in the Texas Hill Country, is Mike Hughes's second-generation family-owned operation, an enterprise that has cleverly figured out a way to supply fresh, wild (well, sort of wild; more on that below) venison and other hooved game meats to American diners pretty much all year round. Eighty years ago or so, a group of wealthy Texans imported non-native species of deer, antelope, and boar from Europe and Asia to the Lone Star State to hunt on their sprawling ranches. Broken Arrow, established in 1983, bought some of the descendants of the original beasts—wild boar, blackbuck and nilgai antelope, and axis, sika, and fallow deer—to raise for food. Today, the stock lives and roams on over 100 ranches, covering a total of about 1,000,000 acres (400,000 hectares). They may be technically fenced in, but the properties are so large that they are truly free-range, feeding on grasses and wild plants.

Almost as important to the quality of the meat is that they are field-harvested. When wild animals are captured and transported to slaughterhouses, so-called stress chemicals like adrenaline and lactic acid flood their flesh and toughen it. Broken Arrow pioneered a better means of processing them: animals are dispatched in the field by marksmen using long-range sound-suppressed rifles, then dressed, inspected, and refrigerated within the hour in mobile units set up in central locations. From there, they are taken to Broken Arrow's main plant in Ingram for aging and packing.

The star of the Broken Arrow line is its axis deer venison. The species, native to India, was first brought to Texas in the mid-twentieth century; today there are more than 150,000 of the animals on the company's contract game ranches. This venison has a dense texture but is unusually tender, and has a vivid flavor, not overly gamy, that farm-raised venison simply can't match.

WAGYU BEEF

Twenty years ago in America, Kobe beef was a legend. Gourmands who had never traveled to Japan, Kobe's homeland, would speak in reverential tones about cows fed on beer and massaged daily, yielding unimaginably flavorful and tender meat. Gourmands who *had* made the trip sometimes came back disappointed; they'd imagined huge, juicy steaks they could cut with a fork, and instead learned that Kobe beef was apt to be cut into small strips and seared on a *hibachi*, or even tossed into a stir-fry.

Today, Kobe beef is everywhere in America; it seems to have all but crowded good old Yankee beef off restaurant menus these days. Even food trucks sell wagyu burgers—wagyu being a catchall term that simply means "Japanese cow," but that is frequently considered to be virtually a synonym of Kobe. Real Kobe disappeared from America in early 2010 after the United States Department of Agriculture (USDA) banned all imports of Japanese beef of any kind. The ban was relaxed in the fall of 2012—but only tiny quantities are now brought in, most going to high-end steakhouses, which charge high-end prices for it. Another issue, though, is whether so-called Kobe from Japan is really Kobe.

Real Kobe is beef from pure-bred Tajima-gyu cattle raised in Hyōgo Prefecture, of which Kobe is the capital. Tajima-gyu, along with other breeds like Matsusaka and Sanda,

are part of a herd that has been closed to crossbreeding by imperial decree since 1635 (except for a brief period in the nineteenth century). Their meat, and above all that of Kobe, is densely marbled with sweet unsaturated fat, and is rich in omega-3 and omega-6 fatty acids. It is remarkably tender, very juicy, and full of beefy flavor. Beef labeled as Kobe but raised in this country, or Canada, or Australia, may be very good, but it isn't what it claims to be. And wagyu? Most American wagyu is actually a crossbreed of Japanese breeds and Angus. There's nothing wrong with that, but the crossbreeding reduces the marbling and, while the flavor is still good, the meat simply isn't anywhere near as moist or tender as what you'd find in Japan.

That said, Japanese cattle can produce excellent beef in American pastures—like that produced by the Morgan family of Burwell, Nebraska. Refugees from drought-stricken New Mexico, the Morgans went into the cattle business in 1934. They came to specialize in Herefords (which they still raise), but in 1992, at the urging of a number of their Japanese customers, they introduced one of America's first wagyu herds into the state. Exactly what breed these cattle are, they don't reveal—they call wagyu a breed, which, as noted, it isn't—but the beef they produce from their Japanese cattle, which are purebreds and not crosses, is juicy and full-flavored, and about as good as American wagyu gets.

FRUITS & VEGETABLES

ASPARAGUS

Asparagus, a flowering perennial native to parts of Europe, North Africa, and western Asia, was eaten as long ago as about 18,000 BC in ancient Egypt, as both a food and (for its diuretic powers) a medicine. The Greeks and the Romans were fond of it, and it was much appreciated in the Arab world. The French considered it a gastronomic treasure (Louis XIV had it grown in greenhouses for the royal banqueting table), and it seems to have reached the United States around the time of the Civil War. Its name derives from the Persian *asparag*, meaning sprout, but in parts of New England, as in England beforehand, it was known as "sparrow grass."

Today, California leads the country in the production of asparagus (as it does with so many fruits and vegetables), and it thrives above all in the state's agricultural heartland,

the Central Valley. Mister Spear, the Stockton-based produce company started in 1978 by Chip Arnett, is far from being one of the largest producers of the vegetable, but it ships some of the very best. Mister Spear's specialty is thick, or "jumbo," asparagus—not the pencil-thin, often fibrous ones that are most prevalent in our supermarkets today, but fat, tender spears three-quarters of an inch or so (about two centimeters) in diameter at the base. According to Arnett, the first thick shoots sent out by a mature asparagus plant each spring are the tastiest; as the season progresses, the plants tire, the diameter of the shoots shrinks, and their meat starts toughening.

Mister Spear asparagus is sold nationally through several large supermarket chains, including Whole Foods, but is also shipped direct to the consumer from Stockton. Arnett suggests that his customers bathe their asparagus in ice water for thirty minutes, then drain and dry it, and refrigerate it wrapped in damp paper towels in a cloth vegetable bag. The stalky ends of the asparagus should be trimmed or at least peeled before cooking, and the cooking shouldn't go on too long (the Roman emperor Augustus used the expression "faster than cooking asparagus" for something done quickly). Asparagus can be added to various dishes or elaborately sauced, but to me some nice plump sparrow grass from Mister Spear, cooked just long enough, drizzled with melted butter, and sprinkled with coarse salt, is pure heaven.

AVOCADO

The avocado is an ancient fruit whose origins have been traced to the Mexican state of Puebla, where fossil remains suggest that it was eaten as early as 10,000 BC. Though it grew wild in abundance, it has been cultivated for more than a thousand years. A chance occurrence in the late 1920s, though, changed its nature all over the world. That's when a mailman named Rudolph Hass, who lived southeast of Los Angeles in La Habra Heights, California, near Whittier (where both Richard Nixon and legendary food writer M. F. K. Fisher grew up), bought an avocado seedling of uncertain species from a local nurseryman. Hass planted the seedling in his small orchard, planning to graft another variety onto it. His attempts at grafting failed to take, and he decided to cut the tree down. His children talked him out of it, and sampled the mystery tree's fruit, of which it produced a lot. It was of daunting appearance, with pebbly green-turning-to-black skin, not at all like the smooth green exterior of the popular Fuerte variety, but it was delicious—more flavorful than the Fuerte, with a buttery richness and nutty aftertaste.

In 1935, Hass took out a patent on this avocado and named it after himself, striking a deal with a Whittier grower to cultivate the trees commercially. By the time the patent expired in 1952, the Hass had become popular all over America and beyond. Hass's original tree died of root rot in 2002, but her children today produce about 80 percent of all the avocados eaten worldwide. (California is the avocado capital of the United States, but the Hass is also now grown in substantial quantities in Chile, Peru, Mexico, the Dominican Republic, and New Zealand.)

The first avocados were first planted in Goleta, California, in 1928, the same year that a runway was built for what is still the Santa Barbara Airport, and cultivated in nearby Aguajitos Canyon in 1973, on property once owned by James Arness, star of the long-running TV western *Gunsmoke*. Locally raised Landon Stableford bought 500 acres (about 200 hectares) in the canyon in the 1970s and planted his own trees, and today his Aguajitos Ranch ships excellent Hass avocados around the country. His trees are raised naturally, without pesticides or herbicides. And they are irrigated, as he proudly points out, by water from a reservoir stocked with koi, the ornamental carp so prized for their appearance by the Japanese, which add nutrients to the water and thus to the trees on which the avocados are grown.

BEEFSTEAK TOMATOES

Tomatoes come in many sizes; they can be as small as green peas, or as large as grapefruit. "Beefsteak" (or simply "beef," in Britain) is a catchall term for the really big ones, tomatoes that can weigh a pound (about half a kilogram) and sometimes more. In general, beefsteaks are the ideal tomato for BLTs and burgers, and they're part of the classic steakhouse salad of sliced tomatoes, thin-sliced red onions, and sometimes crumbled blue cheese, all draped in vinaigrette. They are a hefty, manly tomato, all too often forgotten in our current mania for strangely colored and shaped boutique varieties.

The original beefsteak was apparently developed by a Swiss-born farmer named Johann Heinrich Muster at his farm in Marathon, New York, just north of Binghamton, sometime in the early years of the twentieth century. Among the most popular beefsteak varieties today are the Big Beef, the Beefmaster, the Brandywine (a pinkish tomato bred by Amish farmers in Pennsylvania), the purple-red Cherokee Purple, the deeply furrowed Coeur-du-Boeuf ("beef heart" or "ox heart"), and—my nominee for Best Tomato Name Ever—the hefty Mortgage Lifter. This is a bright red, juicy, full-flavored tomato with a touch of sweetness and a nice acidic bite.

Some sources maintain that the Mortgage Lifter was developed by William Estler in 1922 on his farm in Barboursville, West Virginia, near the Kentucky border; Estler registered the name in 1932. The other contender for the honor of having come up with the tomato is M. C. "Radiator Charlie" Byles, from Logan, West Virginia, about 50 miles (80 kilometers) southwest of Barboursville. In the early 1930s, he reportedly set out to breed the largest tomato he could, starting with a variety called the German Johnson and going from there. It took him seven years to come up with his own giant fruit, but when he did, he sold the seedlings for a dollar apiece, big money at the time. "I didn't pay but $6,000 for my home," he later said in an oral history, "and paid most of it off with tomato plants."

Beefsteaks, including Mortgage Lifters, are rarely found in supermarkets; they're too difficult to handle on a large-scale commercial basis. Look for them at farmers' markets— or grow your own, using seeds from Burpee Seeds or another supplier.

CANNED TOMATOES

In Italy, and especially in the south, cooks make tomato sauces and add tomatoes to soups and stews all year long. They don't use the wan, cottony "fresh" tomatoes so many Americans buy most of the year, however; they use canned tomatoes, either put up in jars at home or commercially packed in metal. This is simply considered good sense. Tomatoes can well—the process was invented in Italy in the mid-1850s, and the proliferation of canned tomatoes helped popularize the fruit in areas where it had not been well known. And it is obvious to any sensible Italian that good-quality tomatoes preserved at the height of the season are preferable to pale out-of-season ones.

The best Italian canned tomatoes are San Marzano, a term that refers to both the plum-shaped variety of that name and the region of Campania, east of Naples, where they're best grown. These are readily available in specialty stores in America, but we also produce first-class canned tomatoes of our own in this country—the best of them coming from Muir Glen, in California's San Joaquin Valley. Now part of Minneapolis-based Small Planet Foods (which also produces the Cascadian Farms line of frozen organic vegetables), Muir Glen—named for the celebrated naturalist and Sierra Club founder John Muir—was founded in 1991 by a partnership of entrepreneurs with extensive tomato-growing experience. The company sources organically grown tomatoes from numerous area farmers, beginning the packing process within eight hours of picking, and canning without artificial preservatives.

Muir Glen sells what they label Crushed Tomatoes with Basil (seasoned only with sea salt), among other products, but their real prize product is their Fire Roasted Crushed Tomatoes. These are roasted at high temperature, then hardwood-smoked. They remain remarkably firm and bright in color, with a rich tomato flavor, a lightly caramelized sweetness, and a hint of smoke. They make excellent tomato sauce, and vivify cooked dishes of many kinds.

CHERRIES

More than any other fruit—more than peaches or raspberries or watermelon—cherries seem somehow emblematic of summer. Maybe it's their unusually short growing season, which is more or less mid-June through late July in most of the northern hemisphere; maybe it's their unambiguous deep red color; maybe it's the sheer lusciousness of a ripe one bursting in the mouth.

The United States is the second largest producer of cherries in the world—after Turkey, which is perhaps appropriate, since the word "cherry" comes from the old Roman name for the northern Turkish city of Giresun, from which the fruit is believed to have been first exported to Western Europe. In the U.S., the West Coast leads the country in sweet cherry production, with Washington State in first place, followed by California and Oregon. It was an Oregon farmer named Henderson Lewelling, in fact, who first bred what has become the most famous sweet cherry in America, the garnet-red Bing—which he named for one of his Chinese workmen. The Bing, in turn, became the parent, with a hardy Bing-like pollinator called the Van, of a particularly delicious variety called the Rainier. Developed in 1952 by Dr. Harold W. Fogle at the Washington State University Research Station in Prosser, it was named for the imposing summit of Mount Rainier, and like that peak has become a symbol of the Pacific Northwest.

The Bailey family has been growing premium cherries on their Orchard View Farms in The Dalles, Oregon, east of Portland near the Washington border, since Walter and Mabel Bailey founded it in 1923. Their great-granddaughters, Bridget Bailey and Brenda Thomas, and great-grandnephew, David Ortega, now oversee what has become a 2,000-acre property packing as much as 10,000 pounds (4,530 kilograms) of cherries annually. Some of these are Rainiers, which have two-tone golden-red skin and are bursting with acidic-sweet cherry flavor. These are special cherries, so delicate and subject to bruising and temperature damage that they are picked only by the most trusted workers on the farm, who make premium wages—and as a result, sell for three or four times what Bings bring.

The height of Rainier picking season usually comes around the Fourth of July, and with their sunburst color and luscious juicy flesh, these cherries seem to define summer.

CHIMAYO CHILES

Chiles are grown all over New Mexico, and many communities are justly proud of the unique characteristics of their own varieties (see page 163)—but the farmland around the town of Chimayo, roughly 25 miles (40 kilometers) north of Santa Fe in the north-central part of the state, produces perhaps the most highly regarded (and thus priciest) of all.

Named for the nearby hill of Tsi Mayoh, a sacred place to both the indigenous Tewa Indians and later Hispanic Christians, Chimayo is a tranquil town, surrounded by apple orchards and private vegetable gardens as well as fields of chiles. The local variety has been grown here for centuries, perhaps imported from Mexico by a colonial entrepreneur named Don Juan de Oñate in 1598. Chile seeds are considered a valuable resource, and many local families have stores of them, their origins going back several generations; they are literally heirloom seeds. Probably for precisely that reason, the chiles they produce vary substantially in size, shape, and heat. Some are 6 or 8 inches (15–20 centimeters) long, others not much more than 3 inches (just under 8 centimeters); some are straight and tapered, others curve or twist; and while Chimayos are never seriously spicy, some will leave a definite mild burn on your palate, while others offer but a wisp of fire.

Unless you travel through this part of New Mexico, you'll have a hard time finding fresh Chimayo chiles, but El Potrero Trading Post, in Chimayo itself, sells Chimayo heirloom chile powder, made from chiles grown from the original Chimayo seed. El Potrero descends from the Vigil Store, opened by Alfonsa and José Manuel Vigil in 1921. Their grandchildren, Vikki Bal Tejada and Raymond Bal, run the enterprise today; Raymond is a well-known dealer in and collector of nineteenth-century religious art, but is also famous for his acuity in sourcing the best chiles from all over New Mexico.

CHIPOTLES

There's no such thing as a fresh chipotle. The chipotle borrows its name from *chilpoctli*, a term in the native Mexican Nahuatl language that means smoked chile—and that's exactly what a chipotle is. Specifically, it's a smoked, dried red jalapeño. There are numerous subvarieties of jalapeño, but all ripen toward the end of the growing season into a dark red hue; as they redden, they lose moisture, and so become more suitable for smoking than plump green chiles would be.

Chipotles turn deep reddish brown as they smoke, and acquire a wizened appearance. (It takes about 10 pounds (4.5 kilograms) of fresh chiles, to produce a pound, or half a kilogram, of chipotles.) They are sold both dried and partially reconstituted in a vinegary *adobo* (marinade). Depending on the variety of jalapeño used, chipotles can be quite spicy, reaching a heat level of as much as 10,000 Scoville units (the Scoville scale measures the heat of a chile pepper, based on the amount of capsaicin present). They are usually used sparingly in salsas and stewed dishes, their heat moderated by other ingredients. In addition to their heat, in any case, they have a wonderful rounded smoky flavor, so identifiable that it has lately become a recognized flavoring for everything from potato chips to salad dressing.

Brother and sister Wayne and Lee James and Wayne's wife, Evie Truxaw, produce what might well be America's most famous chipotles, from chiles grown on their 20-acre (8-hectare) Tierra Vegetables farm near Windsor in California's Sonoma County. They turned to chipotles about ten years ago when a customer came up to their stand at the Marin County Farmers' Market and asked if they had any. They'd never even tasted them, but they made it a point to find some and give them a try. They were unimpressed, finding the chipotles to have an unpleasant flavor (some big commercial producers air-dry the chiles and flavor them with liquid smoke, and it may have been these they first came across)—but thought they could figure out how to make good ones.

They settled on a process of smoking their chiles for five days over a smoldering fruitwood fire in a brick smoker (they reportedly sometimes throw dried basil stems on the fire for added flavor), then further drying them for up to two weeks. Tierra Vegetables, it should be noted, uses the term "chipotle" loosely, applying it to several varieties of smoked chile, not just jalapeños. It's their fiery jalapeño chipotles, though, that win the prize, with their rich smoky flavor, forthright bite, and fruity aftertaste.

COLLARD GREENS

Canned vegetables don't get any respect in our locavoracious age, but certain kinds of produce take to this honorable preservation process quite nicely—collard greens, for instance. Collard greens are a *Brassica*, related to broccoli and cabbage, and are close cousins of kale. The word "collard," in fact, seems to be a corruption of "colewort," or cabbage plant. Collards are a rich source of vitamin C and contain vitamin E and calcium, and are believed to have antibacterial and anti-carcinogenic qualities. That makes them one of the healthier staples of the cooking of the American South, where they are typically seasoned with ham hocks or fatback and traditionally served with black-eyed peas or other field peas and corn bread—the latter of which is used to sop up the so-called pot liquor, or collard broth.

In 1989, a Columbus, Ohio-based chef-restaurateur and sometime hotel food and beverage manager named William F. Williams was talking with friends about African-American family meals, and how much time it took and trouble it was to properly prepare collards—an essential part of any celebratory repast in the African-American community. He realized that nobody was canning good-quality greens, and thought there might be a market for such a product. With several partners, he launched Glory Foods, and the first products—including seasoned collards—appeared in 1992. Today the company has about eighty-five products in its line, including numerous varieties of greens, field peas, beans, cooking bases, and hot sauces.

Williams was community-minded, and devoted much time and effort to bringing young African-Americans into the culinary and hospitality trades; after his death, Glory Foods established a scholarship program in his name to pursue these same goals. The company is also a generous contributor to inner-city food banks. All of that, while admirable, would be of passing interest in the present context were it not for the fact that Glory products are really good, especially the collards. They're well-seasoned but not excessively salty, and the greens maintain good texture and color and plenty of earthy, slightly (but nicely) bitter flavor.

COWPEAS

Call them cowpeas, field peas, crowder peas, cream peas, pigeon peas, stock peas, clay peas, black-eyed peas; get more specific and call them Dixie Lees, Early Scarlets, Red Rippers, Mississippi Purples, Whippoorwills, Calicos, Rattlesnakes … whatever their size, color and flavor, all are legumes of the genus and species *Vigna unguiculata*, and all are essential to the traditional cooking of the American South.

Cowpeas—let's use that term for the sake of convenience—are probably African in origin, though as a drought-tolerant, warm-weather crop, they are grown today not just in Africa and in the southern United States but in many parts of Asia, Mediterranean Europe, and Central and South America. They were almost certainly introduced to our shores by slaves imported from Africa, and there are records of their cultivation in Jamaica as early as 1675 and in Florida by 1700. Because they were easy to grow, and because the gentry usually preferred the brighter, fresher-tasting English peas, cowpeas became known as a food of the poor. Like so many other "poor foods," however, they're actually nutritionally rich, being high in protein and amino acids.

What do cowpeas taste like? They vary considerably from one variety to another, but they tend to be starchy, with an earthy and sometimes nutty flavor and often a faint metallic tinge.

It's easy to find cowpea seeds, if you have the room and the inclination (and the climate) to grow your own. Otherwise, Carolina Plantation, purveyors of Carolina Gold rice (see page 198), has excellent dried ones available by mail order.

CRANBERRIES

The old radio comedy duo Bob and Ray used to do a routine in which the reporter Wally Ballou, one of their stock characters, interviewed a cranberry farmer. Ballou asks the man whether he has his own factory for squeezing cranberry juice and making cranberry jelly. The farmer is incredulous. "Squeezing juice out of cranberries?" he says. "I never heard of that. ... Jelly out of cranberries? What is there, pectin in them or something?" Finally Ballou asks him what he *has* been doing with them. "Selling them out of a basket like strawberries, for cranberry shortcake," he says, adding, "You know, they never did sell that way, either."

Behind the joke, of course, is the plain truth that cranberries are one of those rare fruits that aren't very pleasant to eat unless you do something to them, preferably something that involves adding sugar to counter their mouth-puckering sour and bitter character. That's why 95 percent of the North American cranberry crop each year is sold in processed form—and it's a pretty fair bet that the remaining 5 percent is bought by people who want to process the berries themselves in one way or another.

Cranberries are one of only three important fruits native to this continent (the others are blueberries and Concord grapes). Native Americans ate the berries in various forms (it was an ingredient in the dried jerky-like meat called pemmican), but also used it medicinally and as a dye for baskets and blankets. The fruit was first referred to as "craneberry" by early English settlers, who thought that its stems and blossoms suggested the neck and head of a crane. (They were also sometimes called bearberries, not because any part of the plant resembled a bear but because the animals often fed on them.) The earliest recipe for cranberry sauce appeared in 1667, and cranberry juice was first mentioned in 1683—but both would have depended on foraged wild fruit since cranberries weren't farmed until around 1815.

Wild cranberries grow in bogs and marshes, and the earliest cultivated plantings were made in wetlands as well. Today, the fruit is grown commercially in sand-bottom pens surrounded by dykes, and flooded. Massachusetts is perhaps the best-known source of cranberries, but they are also grown in New Jersey, Wisconsin, the Pacific Northwest, and many parts of Canada. Cranberry farmers have marketed their fruit through cooperatives since at least 1904. Ocean Spray, the cooperative whose name is most vividly associated with cranberries, went into business in 1930, through a merger of three other cooperatives. Today it accounts for at least 65 percent of all the cranberries and cranberry products sold in the United States and Canada.

Willows Cranberries, founded by the DeGrenier family in the early 1900s in Onset, Massachusetts, is a much smaller operation, today based in Plymouth and Wareham with contract farms on Cape Cod and elsewhere on the Bay State's coast. Willows sells fresh cranberries in season, as well as cranberry-based dressings, syrups, candies, and other products, along with dried, sweetened cranberries that I find deftly encapsulate the flavor of the fruit. They're so good, you probably *could* use them for shortcake.

DATES

I have a blurry childhood recollection of standing near a grove of tall date palms that faintly rustled in the hot breeze, while ladies clad like Scheherazade strolled on the sand and boys in burnooses slouched by on camels. This wasn't a fantasy: this was the Indio Date Festival (now the Riverside County Fair & National Date Festival), an annual celebration first held in 1921 in the Coachella Valley city of Indio, California, 20 miles (32 kilometers) southeast of Palm Springs. The event has grown into an immense celebration, with live music and even monster-truck rallies and bull-riding, but it still focuses on the date, with date-related displays and competitions and of course plenty of the honored fruit to eat (and drink: Date milkshakes are an absolute marvel).

Dates are, to my mind, the most exotic non-tropical fruit imaginable. First cultivated as early as 6,000 BC on the Arabian peninsula, they have long been a staple of the Middle Eastern desert diet (the Bedouins are said to have a hundred ways of eating them). The Spanish brought the fruit to California in the mid-eighteenth century, but dates didn't flourish there until they reached the Central Valley in the 1850s. About sixty years later, the first date palms, Algerian seedlings, were planted in the Coachella Valley. This was outside the appropriately named town of Mecca, a dozen miles southeast of Indio,

and there the dates behaved as if they'd just come home. Today there are about 5,000 acres (2,000 hectares) of date groves in the Coachella Valley, producing about 95 percent of the American date crop.

The first date varieties grown in the region, and still among the most important, were the Deglet Noor and the Medjool. The former is in the majority by far, because it's easier to grow, but the Medjool—the so-called King of Dates—is sweeter and softer, with a faintly spicy, almost caramelized flavor. In the Middle East, it is considered something of a special-occasion date and is eaten sparingly, almost as though it were too good to consume promiscuously.

In 1930, a couple of Glendale, California schoolteachers, Tom and Florence Brown, bought a plot of valley land on which to grow Medjools and other dates as a weekend hobby. In 1941, after gas prices had skyrocketed (by the standards of the day) and the couple could no longer afford the weekly round-trip drive to their date trees, they moved to the farm full-time. After the Browns died, Tom's nephew, Ted Fish, took over the property with his wife, Donna. Then their son, "Little Ted," and *his* wife, "Little Donna," joined the business, and Brown Date Garden remains a family enterprise to this day—selling, among other things, jumbo Medjool dates that are as rich and irresistible as a chocolate truffle.

FIDDLEHEAD FERNS

For the past fifteen years or so, on the better restaurant menus of the East Coast of America, fiddlehead ferns and the wild leeks called ramps (see page 176) have joined other predictable culinary harbingers of spring such as shad and its roe (see page 97), morels, and asparagus (see page 150). Fiddleheads are simply the tender young curlicued tops of certain varieties of fern (their shape is often compared to that of the top of a bishop's crozier, or staff, or the scroll at the top of a violin). They can be steamed or boiled or sautéed as a vegetable, and are typically eaten with hollandaise (like asparagus) or mixed with morels or other spring vegetables. They tend to have a grassy, slightly bitter flavor, a bit like that of okra, and retain an appealing crunch if not overcooked.

At least half a dozen varieties of fern are eaten in this manner in the U.S., France, and various Asian countries. Most are high in antioxidants, omega-3 and omega-6 fatty acids, iron, and potassium, and thus are often touted for their health benefits. Ironically, the Centers for Disease Control and Prevention in Atlanta reported incidences of foodborne illnesses linked to the consumption of undercooked fiddleheads in 1994, and certain varieties have since been identified as potential carcinogens. The latter is probably not a matter of great concern, since the fiddlehead season lasts only a few weeks each spring, and very few people eat them more than two or three times a year.

There is no significant commercial cultivation of fiddleheads in the U.S., but wild-harvested ones are sometimes sold in supermarkets as well as at farmers' markets. They were part of the local diet in Maine and parts of eastern Canada for many generations before they became trendy in New York and Boston. Earthy Delights in DeWitt, Michigan, sells fiddleheads both frozen (they freeze well) and, during their brief annual appearance, fresh.

GOLDEN RUSSET APPLES

When a friend brought a few golden russet apples to my office in Manhattan, from the Union Square Greenmarket, I have to admit that I wasn't impressed at first glance. This is not a picture-book apple. It's medium in size, a little squat, with patchy skin ranging from tepid green to sandpaper brown (or russet) in color. The golden russet is an excellent cider apple, and, looking at a handful of them for the first time, I admit that my first thought was, yes, pack them off to the mill, they don't look like anything you'd want to eat. But I had to try one, of course, and when I bit into it, I had an epiphany. This was what apples were supposed to taste like, I thought—supernally crisp, tart, sweet, luscious.

The golden russet is apparently English in origin, and there are a dozen or more other russet varieties. (They were sometimes known as "leathercoats" for their rough skin.) It may also be related to another English variety, Ashmead's Kernel. Golden russets seem to have reached New York State, where the majority of the American crop is still grown, in the mid-nineteenth century, and for a time they were grown on a commercial scale. More cosmetically attractive cultivars eventually pushed them out of the marketplace, but they may still be found at farmers' markets and farmstands around the Northeast in the fall, and they are well worth looking for.

North Star Orchard, in Chester County, Pennsylvania, was founded in 1992 by Ike and Lisa Kerschner on a leased 4-acre (1.6 hectare) plot, and now farm 30 acres (12 hectares) in and around the town of Cochranville. They specialize in apples and pears, but also grow peaches and plums and a variety of vegetables. Golden Russets are among the 300 or so apple varieties they grow. According to the Kerschners, the variety may be as much as 400 years old.

HATCH CHILES

New Mexico boasts two particularly celebrated kinds of chile, both named for their places of origin—Chimayo (see page 155) and Hatch. Of the two, the latter has a much more extensive production and so is more widely available. In fact, there are several varieties sold as Hatch chiles, but the quintessential one is the NuMex Big Jim, developed by Dr. Roy Nakayama at New Mexico State University, in collaboration with Hatch farmer Jim Lytle, for whom it was named. A mildly spicy but extremely flavorful yellow-green chile, maturing to a brilliant red, the Big Jim is slender, tapered, and commonly as much as 8–10 inches (20–25 centimeters) long; an example exceeding 1 foot (30 centimeters) in length won the variety the title of world's biggest chile in the *Guinness Book of World Records*.

Hatch, a small town about 40 miles (just under 65 kilometers) north of Las Cruces, calls itself "The Chile Capital of the World" (which it certainly isn't in terms of size of production), and hosts an annual chile festival each Labor Day, attracting as many as 30,000 visitors. Hatch chiles make superlative *chiles rellenos* (stuffed chiles) because of their size and flavor. Roasted over an open fire and peeled, they're also excellent in salsas or puréed into New Mexican-style chili.

Widely sold around New Mexico in season (late summer through the fall), Hatch chiles are hard to find elsewhere. For anyone willing to make a serious commitment, however, large boxes are sold by mail order—fresh in season, otherwise frozen (which affects their texture slightly but not their flavor)—through Hatch Chile Express, a company that happens to be run by Jimmy Lytle, Jim's son. "I praise God," says Jimmy's wife, Jo, "that Jimmy grows a product that is addictive *and* legal!"

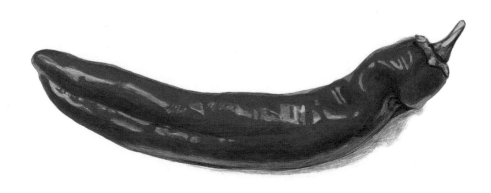

HEIRLOOM POTATOES

Long before Idaho became known for its "famous potatoes," the rocky farmland of Aroostook County, Maine, in the far northeastern corner of the state, bordering New Brunswick and Quebec, was producing large quantities of excellent spuds. The English and Irish farmers who settled here in the eighteenth and nineteenth centuries recognized that the soil was sandy enough to produce good potatoes and that the climate, cool and damp, was suitable for their cultivation. In the 1920s, 1930s, and 1940s, the county was a major source of potatoes for commercial processing, but beginning in the 1950s, the potato farming business began to move west, to regions whose climate and soil yielded the more regularly shaped potatoes increasingly required by the fast-food industry.

Jim Gerritsen moved to the Aroostook County town of Bridgewater from California, where he was studying forestry, in 1976, because land was cheap—precisely because so many potato farms were going under—and he wanted to be an organic farmer. Ironically, he ended up growing potatoes himself, though very differently from the way his neighbors had done. Gerritsen and his wife, Megan, at first tried growing a variety of organic vegetables and cider apples on their Wood Prairie Farm, but when these proved less than profitable, they decided to try potatoes, and specifically as many local heirloom varieties as they could find.

After several years of research and sample plantings, the Gerritsens settled on sixteen varieties that they could sell both as seed potatoes to other farmers and home gardeners and as ready-to-eat spuds for cooking. Among these are Elbas, Cranberry Reds, Island Sunshines (from Prince Edward Island), Rose Golds, Yukon Golds, and several small, elongated fingerling types, including the superb Russian Banana fingerling, first grown by Russian settlers in New England. Maybe the most flavorful of all, though, is the Yellow Finn, brought to the region by Finnish immigrants in the nineteenth century. This is a dry, floury potato with golden-yellow flesh and an intense potato flavor. When you steam and mash it, it almost doesn't need butter. Almost.

LIMA BEANS

West Cape May, New Jersey, which juts out towards Delaware at the far southwestern tip of the state, is almost certainly not the largest lima bean-growing region in the country, but it holds an annual festival to celebrate this oft-maligned legume. Walking around this low-key, folksy fête one October afternoon some years ago, it occurred to me that attendance here, which affords visitors the opportunity to sample lima beans in myriad forms—soups, stews, casseroles, succotash, dips, and on and on—would doubtless be considered punishment, if not outright torture, by a good many Americans. The lima beans of our youth, as a nation, were inevitably canned or frozen. Foisted upon us by our mothers and/or our school cafeteria cooks, they represented everything we hated about vegetables: They were pale, squishy, gassy-tasting, and thoroughly unpleasant.

Happily, I was able to evolve beyond my early dislike of lima beans largely by taking over the preparation of the vegetables and not overcooking them—with frozen lima beans being greatly preferable to the canned variety. At some point, I also started buying them fresh at farmers' markets in the summertime, and, after the admittedly laborious chore of shelling them, I found that they had a vivid, meaty flavor that reminded me a little of fresh green peas, but with an earthy overtone. I realized, in other words, that lima beans were really pretty good.

Lima beans come from Central or South America (yes, they really are named for Lima, Peru, not because they were grown there but because that was the point from which they were exported); they apparently reached what is now the United States as early as AD 1300. A couple of hundred years later, limas were being grown tentatively in Europe, but they never really caught on there; I once served some to a French friend who refused to eat them, because he'd been told since childhood that they were toxic (they are, but only when raw). The most common variety today is the Fordhook, which comes in normal and miniature sizes; large white (actually more beige) limas, particularly popular in the South, are often called butter beans.

I don't think anybody sells fresh limas by mail order. Look for them at farmers' markets—or else buy them frozen, and cook them until they're just tender (four or five minutes in boiling water is usually long enough for unthawed beans, but tasting them is the only sure guide). A good brand is Pictsweet, from the family-owned, Tennessee-based frozen food company of that name, and especially their All Natural Fordhooks.

MANGOES

The mango is the national fruit of India—appropriately enough, since the Indian subcontinent was almost certainly its birthplace. Mangoes, which exist in more than a thousand varieties, are eaten both ripe (in which form they are one of the most luscious of fruits, as drippingly sweet as summer peaches) and unripe or green, in salad form. They're an immensely popular fruit in Asia and Latin America, and account for about half of all the tropical fruit produced worldwide each year; some sources even claim that they are the single most widely consumed fruit on earth.

Though the fruit is grown primarily in India, China, Thailand, Indonesia, and Mexico, the state of Florida occupies an important place in the mango world: many of the world's most successful commercial varieties, including the Tommy Atkin, the Keitt, the Van Dyke, and the Haden, were developed there. Mangoes are believed to have first reached the state in 1833, arriving from Mexico, but they failed, and it wasn't until the 1880s that choice grafted trees from India began to thrive. There was once extensive cultivation of the fruit around the state, but hurricane damage and then the new availability of Mexican and Central American mangoes at lower prices pretty much wiped out the industry. The celebrated Fairchild Tropical Botanical Garden in Coral Gables has a splendid mango tree collection, however, and hosts an annual International Mango Festival, while a few small mango orchards still grow excellent fruit.

One of these is Erickson Farm (formerly Erickson Groves) in Canal Point, on Lake Okeechobee, inland from West Palm Beach. An immigrant Swedish couple, Alfred and Elfrida Erickson, settled here in 1911. They and their four children grew an assortment of vegetables for the northern market. In the course of agricultural studies at the University of Florida, one son, Floyd, became interested in avocados and mangoes, and in 1961 started his own business, Erickson Groves. In turn, his son, Dale, and Dale's wife, Lynn, took over mango production and launched Lyn-Dale's Fruit & Gifts. Now, with the participation of their daughters, Krista and Kimberly, they ship top-quality Florida mangoes by mail order under the banner of Erickson Farm.

The large, greenish Keitts, which mature from late July all the way into November, are particularly recommended. They announce themselves with an intense tropical-fruit aroma, are very sweet and juicy, with little fiber, and they have a vivid, pleasantly metallic flavor that seems to define mango-ness.

MARIONBERRIES

Pay attention, because this gets a little complicated: The olallieberry is the offspring of the loganberry (descended from the raspberry and the blackberry) and the youngberry (progeny of the blackberry and the dewberry). The Chehalem blackberry, meanwhile, counts the Himalayan blackberry and the santiam berry as its parents and the Pacific blackberry and the loganberry as its grandparents. Then the olallieberry and the Chehalem blackberry got together and the marionberry was born. It was named for Marion County, Oregon, site of Oregon State University, where the berry was developed in partnership with the United States Department of Agriculture (USDA).

Big, purple-black, juicy, and complex in flavor, balancing a pronounced sweetness with a mere hint of astringency, the marionberry is basically a super-blackberry. It is so highly thought of in Oregon, in fact, that it was very nearly named the official state berry. (The Oregon Raspberry & Blackberry Commission apparently thought such recognition might hurt the sales of other varieties, and saw to it that the motion was withdrawn.)

Marionberries are grown in neighboring Washington State, but Oregon remains the main producer, accounting for about 90 percent of the annual crop. The fruit sometimes finds its way into supermarkets around the country in the summertime, but it rarely seems at its best—at least compared to the marionberries bought from roadside farmstands in their home state. The berries do make excellent fruit butters, jams, and jellies, though. I particularly like the ones produced by Oregon Hill Farms, headquartered in St. Helens, Oregon. The original property was a 400-acre (about 160-hectare) strawberry farm run by two brothers, who produced strawberry and other fruit syrups, selling commercially for the first time in 1987. Tom and Carmen McMahon bought the property in 2005, and now buy fruit from other small farms in Oregon and Washington to supplement their own. They sell a wide range of products, including fruit in various forms, baking mixes, sauces and condiments, and even their own custom-blend coffee.

MEYER LEMONS

Imagine the acidity of a lemon, but softened slightly, combined with suggestions of an orange's aroma and tart sweetness. That's a Meyer lemon. In fact a hybrid cross of lemons and oranges (or mandarins), the Meyer lemon is native to China, where it was cultivated mostly as a fragrant houseplant. In 1908, Frank N. Meyer, a United States Department of Agriculture (USDA) agricultural explorer— is that a great job description, or what?— discovered the tree growing near Beijing and thought enough of it to import it to the United States, where it was named in his honor. (He is said to have introduced as many as 2,500 new plant species to our shores.)

In time it was discovered that Meyer lemons grew particularly well in California's Central Valley, and that's the center of their production today. It's where Alice Waters and other pioneers of California cuisine discovered them and helped make them popular around the nation. (Meyer himself never saw the fruit come into prominence: He died on a plant-gathering expedition near Shanghai in 1918.) The Meyer lemon's path to success wasn't a smooth one, though. In the 1940s, it was discovered that the trees carried a citrus virus that was devastating to other varieties, and most of what had been planted had to be destroyed. A virus-free clone was later discovered and put into production in 1975.

Meyer lemons are slightly smaller than most conventional lemons, and have a much thinner skin, more orange in hue than that of their cousins and soft and smooth enough to bite into if you're so inclined. They're more aromatic than other lemons, and lower in acid. They're also great for marinades, and make delicious lemonade and sorbet.

Larry and Ralene Snow grow excellent Meyer lemons—along with Owari Satsuma mandarins, Sanguinelli (blood) oranges, kumquats, pomegranates, and other fruits— at their Snow's Citrus Court, founded in 1974 in Newcastle, in California's Sierra Nevada foothills. They farm sustainably, without pesticides or chemicals, and both hand-pick and hand-pack their fruit, shipping it around America immediately after harvest.

OKRA PICKLES

Okra, a vegetable of African origin that has become almost an object of religious veneration in the American South, is a weird entity. With its ridged sides, tapering into a rounded-off snout, it looks more like some strange widget fashioned in a machine shop than something grown on a plant. In cross-section, it seems scarcely less mechanical, with its wheel of tiny chambers, usually between six and nine, some of them almost heart-shaped. On the other hand, it has two qualities that make it appear frighteningly organic: Fresh-picked okra is faintly hairy, and when it's cut open, it oozes slime. Only its flavor—a little grassy, a little meaty—has saved it from obscurity, I suspect.

There are many ways to tame the okra, of course. When it's cooked in soups and stews, its gooey effluent melds nicely into, and thickens, the surrounding liquid; dredged in cornmeal or a batter of some kind and deep-fried, it turns crisp and is no longer sticky. Another way to deal with the slime is with acidity: it dissolves

in tomato juice, lemon juice, or vinegar. Hence the popularity, especially throughout the South, of pickled okra.

I've eaten a lot of pickled okra over the years, both homemade and commercially produced, from Georgia to Texas to Southern California. Ideally, it maintains the crunch and unmistakable flavor of the vegetable itself while banishing its stickiness and adding a counterpart of spice. About the best store-bought version I've ever had comes under the Talk o' Texas label from San Angelo in the Lone Star State. For them, okra isn't just one in a large line of pickled vegetables—they make pickled okra, period, in mild and hot versions, and their only other product is Hickory Liquid Smoke (go figure!). They are, in other words, pickled okra specialists. It shows in the perfection of the crunch and the tang of the pickling solution. My only quarrel with Talk o' Texas is that their "hot" version is about as spicy as a stalk of celery.

PAWPAWS

Pawpaws aren't papayas, though the term is a synonym for papaya in Australia, and though pawpaws probably take their name from a perceived resemblance between the flesh of the two fruits (from the outside, pawpaws look more like mangoes than papayas). Bright, juicy, and luscious in flavor, pawpaws are like a tropical fruit that has somehow lost its way. The pawpaw tree is native to the temperate forests of the East Coast of America, and was probably spread across much of the country, from the Great Lakes to Texas, by Indians. Today, pawpaws grow wild in at least twenty-five states and the Canadian province of Ontario.

If pawpaws aren't better known or more popular, it's probably because they don't keep well and turn blotchy and eventually black, like an overripe banana, as they age. (A slang name for them is "Hoosier banana.") There's certainly nothing wrong with the way they taste. They're not a timid fruit: They have a sexy floral perfume and a flavor that seems to blend hints of pineapple, mango, and maybe cantaloupe. They'd fit right in at a luau.

The Spanish conquistador Hernando de Soto describes seeing Indians eating pawpaws in the Missouri River Valley in 1540. George Washington was reportedly a fan, and Thomas Jefferson cultivated pawpaw trees at Monticello. In the early nineteenth century, Meriweather Lewis, of Lewis and Clark, noted that his men were very fond of pawpaws, which he said were also called custard apples. In fact, the fruit more usually called custard apple is a relative of the pawpaw, as is the cherimoya, or "ice cream fruit."

The bad news about pawpaws is that, probably because of their perishability, they are rarely found in supermarkets, and I've been unable to find a dependable mail-order source. Farmers' markets, especially in Ohio, often sell them in season, from late summer through autumn. Alternatively, if you have a place to grow your own, Edible Landscaping, of Afton, Virginia, sells trees for six different varieties.

The Taste of America

PEACHES

Perfect peaches—juicy, ripe, and fragrant, sweet as a summer morning—are one of the most sensuous and luscious of fruits. Maybe that's why getting a bad one, hard and green, flavorless and dry, can be such a wrenching disappointment.

I've never gone wrong with a Frog Hollow Farm peach. Frog Hollow is a 133-acre (about 54-hectare) certified organic farm in Brentwood, California, in the Sacramento River Delta. The man in charge is a long-time Bay Area resident and graduate of University of California, Berkeley named Al Courchesne. "Farmer Al," as he styles himself, ended up teaching at a school in Hawaii, where a friend convinced him to try small-scale farming on the side. After two years, he moved back to Northern California and bought a small plot of land in Brentwood. He planted peach trees, simply because he loved peaches. The farm grew little by little to its current size, with other fruit added—including nectarines, cherries, apricots, plums, pluots (a plum-apricot cross), Asian and European pears, and table grapes—and in 1989, Courchesne made the decision to go organic. His fruit came to the attention of Alice Waters at Chez Panisse, and she started featuring it in the restaurant.

Frog Hollow Fram grows fifteen varieties of peach that have differing characteristics and ripen at different times through the season. The small, mild-flavored Rich Zee is harvested in the second half of May; about a month later, the low-acid, soft-fleshed Gold Dust comes off the trees; the classic Flavorcrest, intensely sweet, is picked in early July; the deliciously peachy-flavored Cal Red ripens in mid- to late August ... and so on through the Autumn Flame, still on the trees in the last weeks of September. Some varieties are better for canning or baking or drying than for plain eating, but all are excellent and none disappoint.

PERSIMMONS

The American persimmon is a tricky thing. Eat it ripe and it's luscious and sweet, with a flavor reminiscent of Christmas spices; bite into it unripe and you'll get a mouthful of bitter cotton. Persimmons are native to Asia, Europe, and America, but each is of a different species. Our own version of the tree (*Diospyros virginiana*—which translates roughly as "Virginian food of the gods"), grows wild from Florida to Maine and west as far as Kansas and Texas, producing fruit that is both smaller than other varieties (it's often not much bigger than a ping-pong ball) and capable of fearsome astringency, the result of a high tannin content. Indians cultivated the trees and used persimmons—the word comes from the Algonquian *pasimenan*, meaning artificially dried fruit—frequently, in the form of puddings and cornmeal or acorn breads (the pulp is high in pectin, so it thickens nicely). Persimmon wood was also highly prized for building. Colonial settlers adapted the fruit to European recipes, and even used the seeds to make a coffee substitute and to flavor beer.

I've never seen American persimmons in the supermarket—those are Asian ones—so unless you can find a tree growing wild somewhere, your best bet to get some is at autumn farmers' markets in Indiana, where persimmons are widely cultivated, and in some parts of Illinois and North Carolina. It's also possible to buy persimmon pulp by mail order, from operations like Persimmon Pleasures, which is part of Seeds and Such, Inc., of Bedford, Indiana.

Seeds and Such got its start in 1992 when Charlotte and Kent Waltz harvested and shelled bushels of black walnuts (see page 13) to make enough money to take their family to Disneyland. They sold so much that they not only made the trip, but decided to go into the business of selling nuts, tree and shrub seeds, and nut-gathering tools. A distant cousin of Charlotte's, Sam Burton, had discovered a particularly tasty variety of persimmon in the 1950s, which he named after his youngest son, Morris Burton. The Waltzes now sell pots of persimmon pulp, made from Morris Burtons and related varieties, as well as homemade persimmon pudding and persimmon chocolate chip cookies. Flavorful and viscous, the pulp is great for making cakes, pies, ice creams, and jam.

PINQUITO BEANS

In and around the city of Santa Maria, in Santa Barbara County, on California's Central Coast, the aroma of beef sizzling over live oak fires sometimes fills the air, especially on weekends. The aroma comes from restaurants, church and supermarket parking lots, and roadside stands, where the local tradition known as Santa Maria barbecue is being celebrated. Locals like to claim that this style of cooking—this ritual meal, really—derives from indigenous Chumash Indian and Spanish rancho cookouts, but it probably developed after World War II as a kind of charity event. (It should be noted that Santa Maria barbecue is a form of grilling—not "barbecue" in the Southern sense, which is smoking with indirect heat.) In any case, barbecue is taken very seriously in Santa Maria. So much so, in fact, that in 1978, the city's chamber of commerce copyrighted what they call "the traditional Santa Maria Style Barbecue menu": barbecued sirloin (though the most popular cut today is tri-tip, a triangular piece of muscle from the bottom sirloin cut of beef), salsa, grilled French bread dipped in melted butter, tossed green salad, and pinquito beans. That last ingredient is the one that would almost certainly give any non-local pause.

Pinquitos are small pink beans with a tender skin but a rich, slightly firm texture even when completely cooked; they have a faintly herbaceous flavor with an earthy overlay, like a more refined version of pinto beans. Pinquitos are something of a mystery in that nobody knows where they came from or when they were first planted in the area, though they don't seem to grow anywhere other than around the Santa Maria Valley.

Pinquitos are delicious and unusual beans, and a good side dish even if you're not grilling steaks. They're available by mail from several sources, but the one with the best pedigree is Susie Q's Brand, based of course in Santa Maria. The Susie in question is Susan Righetti, daughter of Clarence and Rosalie Minetti, who own the Far Western Tavern— a restaurant devoted to Santa Maria barbecue, famous for decades in the community of Guadalupe but relocated to Orcutt, a few miles to the southeast, in late 2012. The Minettis and Righettis are both old local families of Italian-Swiss origin, and steeped in local lore and culture. Susan launched Susie Q's in 1981 with the idea of selling local products to a national audience. It is not accidental that bags of pinquito beans were her very first offering.

PIXIE TANGERINES

Ojai, California, a town of about 5,000 people nestled in a verdant valley near Santa Barbara about 60 miles (96 kilometers) northwest of Los Angeles, has long been hospitable to what we would now call New Agers. The Indian philosopher Jiddu Krishnamurti lived there, it is home to a Theosophist "colony," and the valley famously stood in for Shangri-La in the 1937 film *Lost Horizon*. But it is also an agricultural community, full of citrus and other fruit-tree orchards. On chilly winter evenings the murky smell of smudge pots, lit to protect the trees from frost, used to fill the air (before pollution laws shut them down); on warm summer afternoons, the much more pleasant aroma permeating the atmosphere is that of orange blossoms bursting into life from one end of the valley to the other.

Tangerines are a kind of mandarin orange, first cultivated more than 3,000 years ago in China. There are five or six main varieties, most of them grown around California. The Pixie is one of the more unusual of these. Its origins date back to the mid-1920s, but it wasn't made widely available until 1965, after citrus specialists at the University of

California, Riverside had spent four decades working with it under various conditions. Even then, it wasn't considered to have much commercial potential, because its fruit came late in the season and crops varied vastly in size from one year to the next. It had one thing going for it, however: It was simply delicious. Intensely sweet without being cloying, it had just enough acidity to make it interesting and a deep, concentrated orange flavor.

Seduced by its quality and either ignorant of its shortcomings or remarkably prescient, two Ojai citrus farmers, Tony Thacher and Jim Churchill, began planting serious numbers of Pixie trees in the early 1980s. Citrus is apparently particularly sensitive to differences in microclimate, and it turned out that the valley was absolutely perfect for Pixies. The fruit was wonderful, and the harvests were more or less regular. Witnessing the success that the two pioneers had with the fruit, other growers also began planting Pixies. There are now more than 25,000 Pixie trees around Ojai, tended by more than twenty farmers, and the Ojai Pixie has gained renown all over California.

PRUNES

The French savor *pruneaux d'Agen* macerated in Armagnac, or filled with prune purée; in Mexico, prunes are salted and sometimes seasoned with chile and lime; in China, variously flavored, they're both eaten as snacks and made into beverages; Moroccans put them in tagines, and in Ashkenazi Jewish cooking, prunes are frequently included in the vegetable stew called tzimmes.

In America, prunes ... well, they're eaten and enjoyed, of course, but also often joked about for their laxative effect. The association of prunes with constipation is so ingrained, in fact, that California prune growers now label their product "dried plums"—which is fair enough, actually, because that's exactly what prunes are. Specifically, they're smallish, dense-fleshed plums, usually of the genus and species *Prunus domestica*, grown specifically for drying. A blue-skin, yellow-flesh variety is sold seasonally in the U.S. as "Italian prune plums," and in fact they taste pretty good fresh. Their chocolate-like richness when dried, though, is very appealing; they're not as chewy as, say, dried figs, but they do a good job of satisfying sugar cravings. The fact that prunes do aid digestion through the various compounds they contain is a bonus. They have also recently gotten some good publicity as a potent source of antioxidants.

Brooks plums are a variety that was developed especially for drying in 1947 by a California nursery worker named Glenn Brooks, who brought the fruit to Oregon's Willamette Valley in the mid-1960s. There, he introduced it to a local cherry farmer named Fred Bowyer, who liked it well enough to plant plum trees and invest in a dehydrating machine. The Bowyer family has since become a major prune producer, and their meaty, intensely flavored fruit defines what good prunes can be.

RAMPS

It has long been said that the name of the great city of Chicago comes from a Native American term (variously rendered as *shikaakwa* or *sheka:ko:heki*), meaning a place where wild garlic or onions grow. Research done in the 1990s, however, suggests that the fragrant plant that once flourished where the city was founded was neither, but rather *allium tricoccum*, known to us as the ramson or, more commonly, the ramp.

Ramps are a kind of wild leek, found growing all over Appalachia and up into Canada. Unlike their cultivated cousin, they have veined, tapered green leaves, which are good to eat when they're young, descending to purple stems with a small scallion-like bulb at the end. They're extremely pungent, with an intense garlicky flavor; everybody quotes the Ohio food writer Jane Snow, who thought they tasted like "fried green onions with a dash of funky feet." Suffice to say that with ramps, a little goes a long way. Most people chop them up and stir them into eggs or vegetables or else pickle them for use as a condiment, and only

the brave (or anti-social) eat them plain or in abundance. Because they have a short season, usually beginning around early April, ramps are known as a harbinger of spring, and many communities, especially in West Virginia and Tennessee, hold annual ramp festivals.

Once known mostly in rural areas, ramps have become, in recent years, a trendy addition to contemporary American menus around the country. *Time* magazine's food writer, Josh Ozersky, calls them "the new arugula," and suggests that their recent popularity is based on cultural rather than culinary values. I'm not sure there's anything wrong with that, and in any case ramps do have a unique intensity of flavor that isn't quite the same as that of garlic, much less of leeks.

Glen and Noreen Facemire operate what they are pretty sure is the only ramp farm in the world (G–N Ramp Farm), on the South Fork of the Cherry River in Richwood, West Virginia. They sell freshly harvested ramps in season, as well as ramp seeds and bulbs, and even a book on the subject.

RUBY RED GRAPEFRUIT

There's something about red-fleshed citrus fruit: blood oranges seem both sweeter and sharper, and certainly more elegant, than their conventionally hued kin. Red-fleshed Texas grapefruit seem to me to have a lusciousness and flavor unparalleled by any other variety. Maybe (in both cases) I'm being seduced by appearances; red is racy, romantic. But I'm convinced that both are something special. Blood oranges thrive in Spain and Italy, and while they are grown in the U.S., they never seem to reach the intensity of flavor attained in southern Europe. Red grapefruit, on the other hand, are a Texas treasure.

In the late 1920s, a citrus farmer in the Lone Star State found a grapefruit with dark red meat growing on a pink grapefruit tree. He recognized its value (and possibly its superior flavor), cultivated it, and patented the variety in 1929. Some sources suggest that it wasn't until this new kind of fruit, called Ruby Red, hit the market that grapefruit of all kinds became truly popular in America.

The subtropical climate in south Texas, where most of the state's citrus crops are grown, is ideal for red grapefruit. Freezes in 1949, 1951, and 1962 destroyed the white and pink grapefruit crop in the region, but the reds continued to thrive.

Grapefruit that are darker in color and (perhaps) more deeply flavored than Ruby Reds have been developed since the appearance of that first red variety. One popular variation, the Star Ruby, appeared in 1970. In 1984, Dr. Richard Hensz, a researcher at the Texas A&I Citrus Center in Kingsville (now a part of the Texas A&M system) used ionizing radiation to produce the reddest possible version, called the Rio Red. I doubt that I could tell the difference between one variety and another by taste, though I think I might be able to distinguish red from white grapefruit blindfolded. Anyway, a good red Texas grapefruit tastes wonderfully citrusy, with a nice balance of tart and sweet. I love scooping it right out of the skin with a grapefruit spoon. Red Cooper, from Alamo, Texas, is one of many growers who ship Ruby Reds. Also recommended: Texas red grapefruit juice and tequila in a tall ice-filled glass with salt on the rim.

SMOKE-DRIED TOMATOES

Larry Butler and Carol Ann Sayle run two agricultural properties in Texas: the celebrated Boggy Creek Farm, on the east side of Austin, and Milam County Farm in Gause, not quite two hours drive to the northeast. One summer back in the early 1990s, in Gause, Butler found himself with a bumper crop of organic Roma tomatoes that had been—as he politely puts it—"compromised" by a wind- and rain-storm. He considered sun-drying them in the Italian manner, but quickly realized that it was too humid in his part of Texas for that to work. Instead, he hit upon the idea of smoking them. This involved building a small smokehouse and then constructing wooden trays to hold the fruit.

He harvested post oak that grew on the farm, and set up a cool indirect fire in the smokehouse. Carefully monitoring the heat, he smoke-dried the tomatoes for three or four days. The results were superb: brick-red, intensely flavored, dried but still slightly moist fruit with a rich, smoky tomato flavor. Butler now smoke-dries a substantial portion of his Roma crop every summer, regardless of storms, and plastic bags of the tomatoes are now seen in the kitchens of discerning eaters all over the Austin area. Butler recommends macerating the tomatoes in good olive oil, which not only softens and flavors them, but yields smoke-tinged oil that's great to use when cooking or dressing salads or vegetables. He and Sayle are vegetarians, so Butler gladly adds that, with their texture and their smoky flavor, his smoke-dried tomatoes make a great substitute for bacon in dishes of many kinds.

SOFTNECK GARLIC

There are two kinds of garlic, softneck and hardneck. The names refer to the fact that hardneck varieties have a central stalk that grows up through the center of each head (before it hardens, this is the green garlic "scape" sold at farmers' markets in late spring and early summer). Softneck garlic lacks this core, which makes it easier to plant and harvest mechanically; almost all supermarket garlic, for that reason, is softneck. Lorz is one you won't find in ordinary commercial channels, though—an heirloom garlic variety brought from Italy (or possibly Ticino, Italian-speaking Switzerland) by a family of that name around 1850, and planted in Washington State's Columbia River Basin, where it thrived. Lorz is a so-called artichoke variety, with a thick outer skin, sometimes splotched with purple, and large cloves. (It is an excellent garlic for roasting whole.) Most artichoke garlics are comparatively mild, but Lorz is fairly hot on the palate, with a peppery aftertaste.

Though the Pacific Northwest was Lorz's original home, it is now grown in other regions as well, including California and even Texas. In fact, Gourmet Garlic Gardens in Denton, Texas, just northwest of Dallas, produces an excellent example, along with many other varieties. The farm's co-proprietor, Bob Anderson, worked in the health insurance, two-way radio, and microcomputer industries, but when his last employer went out of business and no other obvious opportunities appeared, he says, instead of either calling himself a consultant or calling himself unemployed, he became a ranchhand for his father-in-law. With his wife, Merridee McClatchy, he subsequently decided to make a life out of tending the ranch and growing garlic and herbs. Today, Gourmet Garlic Gardens is one of *the* places to know if you're a lover of (as they call it up in garlic-mad Berkeley) "the stinking rose."

SUN GOLD TOMATOES

They positively glow on the vine, deep sunny gold in color, maturing into orange, and they shine from their little cartons at farmers' markets and the occasional grocery store like jewels in a treasure box. They're cherry tomatoes the color of no cherry you've ever seen—they're Sun Golds. Not at all an heirloom variety, though farmstands often label them as such, the Sun Gold is in fact a twentieth-century hybrid, known botanically as *Lycopersicon esculentum* var. *cerasiforme* "Sungold."

Sun Golds have become extremely popular with home gardeners—I grow a couple of bushes of them on my balcony in Connecticut every summer. This is partly because they produce ripe fruit fairly quickly, and plenty of it; partly because they're sturdy creatures, all but immune to wilt and bud rot and other enemies of the tomato; partly because even at peak ripeness, they remain firm, yielding an attractive texture when eaten; but most of all because they are almost supernally sweet. Yellow tomatoes, in general, have a reputation for being sweeter and less acidic than their red counterparts. This may or may not be true—acidity, in particular, seems to be more a function of soil and climate than of variety—but a Sun Gold is undeniably a little ball of sugar, and though it has a faint citrus flavor, it lacks any obvious acid bite. Sun Golds illuminate salads and make unusual but very flavorful sauces; however, my favorite way to eat them is right out of the box, lightly sprinkled with sea salt and popped straight into my mouth.

Look for Sun Golds at farmers' markets in summer and early fall (they're rarely found in supermarkets), or order seeds or plants from the granddaddy of major seed companies, Burpee Seeds—founded in 1878 by a former poultry breeder named W. Atlee Burpee.

SWEET ONIONS

Sweet onions are simply those bred for a low sulphur content. They taste like regular onions, and are more mild than actually sweet. It is said of some varieties that if you bite into a peeled one blindfolded, you'll think it's an apple, but I've tried the experiment a few times over the years, and I have yet to experience that phenomenon.

The varieties most often seen in U.S. markets are Vidalias, first cultivated near Vidalia, Georgia, in the 1930s but now grown in other parts of the state as well; Maui onions, grown in volcanic soil on the Hawaiian island of the same name; Texas Super Sweets, also called 1015s (a reference to their supposed ideal planting date of October 15), developed in the early 1980s in the horticulture department of Texas A&M University; and my favorites, Walla Walla sweets. (There are several other kinds of sweet onion, grown in California, the Southwest, and other parts of Texas and Georgia, but they are rarely seen outside their own neighborhoods.)

Walla Wallas trace their origins to about 1900, when a retired French soldier named Pete Pieri arrived in the Walla Walla Valley in southern Washington State from Corsica, bringing the seeds of a mild onion growing on that Mediterranean island. He planted the variety and went to work to breed it into a large, round, particularly sweet one. One of his farm workers was an Italian immigrant named Joe Locati, who joined him in 1905 and helped propagate the new variety. In 1909, Locati bought his own farm and started raising sweet onions himself. His sons, Ambrose and Pete, and their cousin, Virgil Criscola, set up the first onion-packing shed in the region in 1949. Today, Ambrose's son, Michael F. Locati, carries on the family business at Locati Farms. His onions are plump and almost perfectly round, with a pronounced onion flavor but no sulphuric bite. They caramelize superbly on the grill or in a pan with some olive oil, and they don't taste anything like apples at all.

TANGELOS

Citrus fruits aren't particular about whom they hook up with, and easily interbreed with each other. The grapefruit, for instance, is the offspring of the sweet orange and a Southeast-Asian fruit called the pomelo, which is shaped like a very large pear and tastes like a milder, sweeter grapefruit. The Meyer lemon (see page 168) is a cross between the ordinary lemon and the mandarin orange. The tangelo, as its name suggests, is theoretically part tangerine, part pomelo, though one popular variety counts grapefruit, not pomelo, as a progenitor.

The tangelo is also one of the most unabashedly sweet citrus fruits imaginable, as well as a very juicy one. It is almost certainly the easiest to peel, thanks to its medium-thick, loose-fitting skin and the convenient bump or nipple at its top, which is easy to hold on to when beginning the process. For its shape as well as its sweetness, one variety—officially the Minneola—is also called the HoneyBell. This is the tangelo descended from grapefruit, not pomelo.

The first HoneyBells I ever tasted came from Svrlinga Groves in Zellwood, Florida, near Orlando, and I think of them as the definitive examples of the fruit, tangerine-sweet with the faintest bite of acidity. The Mack family has farmed this land and packed this fruit for three generations. Their original 1911-vintage tin-roof farmhouse stands in the middle of one of their groves. Though they grow other kinds of citrus, the HoneyBells are a specialty. Bulk orders are shipped with a "HoneyBell Bib," a reference to how generously juicy tangelos can be.

TARO

Taro is a tropical plant (*Colocasia esculenta*) with an edible root or corm and large, elephant-ear leaves that are toxic when raw but safe and nourishing when cooked. Although it is commonly thought of as a Polynesian plant, it is in fact native to Southeast Asia, and is eaten in various forms not only in Polynesia but in parts of Asia, Africa, and the Caribbean. It was also known to the ancient Romans, and I once encountered its bulbs, roasted, in inland Catalonia (where it reminded me of Jerusalem artichokes).

The most famous preparation of taro, though, is the Hawaiian staple known as poi. This is made by steaming and mashing the tubers, with added water to adjust the poi's consistency. Poi is an essential part of the traditional diet in Hawaii, and is so important to island culture that the taro plant, called *kalo* in Hawaiian, is believed to have been the ancestor of the Hawaiian people; as such, it has long been said that when a bowl of poi is on the table, no fights or arguments are allowed.

To say that poi is an acquired taste is probably an understatement. While it can be as fluid as gruel, it is commonly served in thicker, paste-like form that sticks to the roof of your mouth like peanut butter. It has a natural sweetness but is frankly quite bland, and it begins to ferment and sour within a day or two of its manufacture (Captain Cook famously described it as being "a disagreeable mess"). That said, it offers a unique taste of Hawaii, and becomes quite palatable when flavored (which no self-respecting Hawaiian native would ever do) with honey and cream, or lightly salted and eaten alongside raw marinated fish. It is also a healthy foodstuff: high in fiber, vitamins, and minerals, and with roughly the same caloric count as that of non-fat yogurt.

Poi was first exported to the American mainland as early as 1900 or so, and by the 1950s it was available in supermarkets in Hawaii and in mainland communities with an appreciable Hawaiian population. Today it's even available in squeeze tubes. It is also baked into cookies, cheesecake, and bagels, among other things, but that seems like cheating. Fresh poi is shipped to the mainland in 2-pound (1-kilogram) bags every Monday by the all-things-Hawaiian enterprise, Maui Direct.

WATERMELON

I've always thought that watermelon was the perfect kids' food: sweet, messy, cheap (it used to sell for a penny a pound in midsummer when I was a boy), and—maybe best of all—full of slippery black seeds that were easy and all too tempting to spit, often competitively. It was a gift of summer, and would have had no more place on the table around Thanksgiving or Christmas than those two-stick blue Popsicles we used to slurp around the pool. Today, of course, watermelon is readily available all year round, and the most popular varieties seem to be seedless (which they are never quite; it's just that the seeds are flat and off-white and worthless as projectiles). It's still a pretty wonderful treat, however.

Watermelon—whose name is appropriate, since the fruit is more than 90 percent water—is native to Africa, where in some regions it still grows wild. It became popular with the ancient Egyptians, and was known in China by the tenth century, and in Europe by the thirteenth. As to how it reached America, the obvious theory is that African slaves brought seeds with them, and there are reports of it being farmed by Indians in the Mississippi Valley as early as the late sixteenth century. There are said to be well over 1,200 varieties of watermelon worldwide, including pricey cube-shaped ones cultivated in Japan, and they come with flesh that is not only the familiar vivid red but also pink, white, yellow, or orange. The major watermelon-growing states are Florida, Texas, and Georgia, in that order; however, all but five or six states produce at least some, and the best examples are usually those sold at farmers' markets, in season.

I can't imagine that anybody sells watermelon by mail order (even the small ones weigh 4 or 5 pounds, or about 2 kilograms, so shipping costs would be prohibitive), but if you've got the ground space, it's a pretty easy fruit to raise. A number of companies sell heirloom variety seeds, among them Victory Seeds of Molalla, Oregon, which offers about twenty kinds, including the Klondike Blue Ribbon, which looks like a delicata squash, and the Moon and Stars, which resembles a cannonball.

WHITE ASPARAGUS

These meaty, ivory-hued spears are basically the same plant as green asparagus. They are blanched while growing by the simple expedient of packing soil around the shoots as they rise up from the ground (the heads of Belgian endive are whitened in the same way). While green asparagus is far more common than white in America (the latter is too labor-intensive for most U.S. producers to bother with), it's the other way around in Europe. In France, Belgium, the Netherlands, and Switzerland, each season, the coming of white asparagus—milder in flavor than its verdant cousin—is a milestone of the gastronomic year. In Germany, the vegetable is hawked at roadside stands around the countryside, and is treated so reverentially in serious kitchens that apprentice chefs aren't allowed to touch it. In Spain, where it is also wildly popular, it is—curiously to most of the rest of the world—sold and enjoyed almost exclusively in preserved form, packed in jars or cans, in water and diluted vinegar with assorted seasonings. Why this should be the case, I have never heard a cogent explanation; Spaniards usually say something like, "The pickling adds flavor"— as though white asparagus needed help.

If fresh white asparagus is a comparative rarity in American markets, the pickled variety is even more so. Tillen Farms, however, in Washington State's Yakima Valley, has recently started packing top-quality Peruvian-grown white asparagus spears in its own mild brine, faintly flavored with garlic and chiles, with a touch of sugar. Tillen had its origins in a family farm started in the late 1960s by the Hogue family, who also launched the Hogue Cellars winery in the region. Tim Metzger, who had supervised the farm's vegetable sales since 1987, bought the property with his wife, Helen, in 2002. They have been slowly expanding the product line, which now includes—in addition to white asparagus—green asparagus, green beans, snap peas, and carrots, among other vegetables. These are all naturally grown and hand-packed. Tillen's white asparagus is a revelation, tender but with a touch of crispness, and full of intense asparagus flavor.

WHITE NECTARINES

The nectarine is basically a peach that doesn't need to shave. It's a peach with a smooth, often reddish skin without a trace of the peach's typical fuzz. Like the peach, the nectarine comes from Asia, but exactly when and where it was first developed is not known. The first mention of the word in English comes in the second decade of the seventeenth century; it literally means "like nectar," and was perhaps inspired by the German term *Nektarpfirsich*, nectar-peach. The fruit was being grown in America at least as early as 1768, when a newspaper mentions it among the produce being cultivated on a farm on Long Island.

Are nectarines sweeter than peaches? It depends on the nectarine, and on the peach, of course, but I believe the sweetest fruit that I've ever tasted was a white nectarine, drippingly juicy, eaten many summers ago in Southern California. Both peaches and plums are bred with white flesh as well as yellow, and in general the white-fleshed varieties are lower in acidity, which may accentuate their natural sugar. From that nectarine paragon of mine, I recall not just an intense, almost honeyed sweetness, but a mouth-filling floral character and what I can only describe as a concentrated essence of fruit.

I'm not sure where that nectarine came from, but something very similar is grown by Ted and Fran Loewen at their Blossom Bluff Orchards in Parlier, overlooking the Kings River in the San Joaquin Valley in central California. Blossom Bluff is an old property, and had already been planted with mature trees when it was taken over by Daniel and Babette Lichti in 1931. Their son, Herb, succeeded them in the 1940s; Fran Loewen is his daughter, and she and her husband are continuing the family tradition. The Loewens grow several varieties of peach and nectarine, as well as cherries, apricots, apriums (an apricot-plum cross), and other fruits.

The original farm was organic, because there was no alternative in those days. Later, like most commercial farmers in America, the Lichtis availed themselves of newly developed pesticides, herbicides, and fertilizers to increase their yield. Ted Loewen began easing the farm back from chemicals, using integrated pest management (a system that in effect uses such agents only as a last resort), and then evolving to organic production. In 2007, after fifteen years of sustainable management, the farm was certified organic by California Certified Organic Farmers (CCOF).

WHITE TRUFFLES

When I was new to this gastronomy business, many years ago, the truffle story that almost everybody believed was simple: white truffles (*Tuber magnatum*) are found by dogs in the Italian region of Piedmont in the fall; black truffles (*Tuber melanosporum*) are found by pigs in Provence and the Périgord in France. Period.

Little did we know. As we have since learned, there are numerous species of truffle, black, white, and in-between, found in many parts of Italy and France, Croatia, Slovenia, portions of Spain, the Australian states of Tasmania and Western Australia, China, and ... the West Coast of America, and particularly Oregon. There are in fact two common species of Oregon truffles, both white, found from Northern California on up into British Columbia: the so-called spring truffle, *Tuber gibbosum*, and the winter version, *Tuber oregonense*. As early as 1983, the estimable James Beard, born and raised in Oregon, opined that the former variety was "at least as good" as anything from Italy or France. He may be permitted some hyperbole as a loyal native son, but the fact is that Oregon truffles can be pretty good—good enough to have inspired an annual festival in Eugene.

The Oregon-based chef-restaurateur and mycologist Jack Czarnecki once told an interviewer that he suspected Oregon truffles weren't better known because wild mushrooms growing in the same forests were much easier to find and harvest.

Oregon truffles are generally found adjacent to Douglas fir trees, with which they have a symbiotic relationship. They are also an important food source for flying squirrels and other forest denizens. Though considered white truffles, they tend to be more yellowish, sometimes tending towards yellow-brown. They are usually smaller than their Italian counterparts, with a pungent aroma that seems more monochromatic than that of *Tuber magnatum*; I always think that they smell a little like garlic, and maybe (though this could be a suggestion) a little like pine needles. On the palate, they're a little gassy and a little sweet, but not bad at all, especially considering that they cost a fraction of what their Italian counterparts do—so far.

Earthy Delights in DeWitt, Michigan, sells white truffles from Oregon. Since they pack the fresh truffles in rice when shipping them, the rice becomes "infused with truffle flavor" and they recommend using it for risotto.

CEREALS, GRAINS, & POWDERS

BREAKFAST CEREAL

Manufactured breakfast cereal is such a peculiarly American concept—"granula" started it all in the late nineteenth century (see page 194), and the Kellogg brothers and then the farm-machinery inventor, real estate mogul, and anti-unionist C. W. Post ran with the notion—that at least one brand-name example belongs in this book. Kellogg's Corn Flakes, which appeared in 1896, were the first big cereal success, but I've always been partial to Grape-Nuts, which came along a year later. These were Post's invention. He had been a patient at John Harvey Kellogg's sanitarium in Battle Creek, Michigan, and while there he was inspired by the idea that a diet rich in grains could save the world.

Grape-Nuts are tiny, crunchy pellets of wheat and barley, with a flavor of whole wheat and nuts and, by breakfast cereal standards, merely a modest sweetness. (They have nothing to do with either grapes or nuts, and are said to take their name from their resemblance to grape pips.) Post made all kinds of health claims for the cereal when it came out, among them that it was "brain food," and that it prevented malaria; the Panama Canal couldn't have been dug without Grape-Nuts, claimed one early advertisement, a reference to the fact that the cereal keeps well in humid climates. In fact, the cereal *was* included in some U.S. Army rations during World War II, precisely because of its stability. Post—whose other brands include the estimable Shredded Wheat—actually sells Grape-Nuts and its other products by mail order, but it would be hard to find a supermarket that didn't stock them.

DRIED CORN

Dried corn is pretty much a lost American foodstuff. In colonial times, to preserve sweet corn after the harvest, farmers sun-dried it in trays on their rooftops or in the falling heat of their wood-burning stoves once the fire had gone out. After drying, it was sometimes further toasted, which caramelized its sugars and made it seem sweeter still. In this form, it would keep indefinitely. Cracked into little shards, it cooked quickly, rehydrating but retaining its caramelized savor.

Unlike other preserved products—pickles, dried fruit, and sauerkraut among them—dried corn didn't survive the advent of canning and freezing. Suddenly there was no reason to dry the kernels anymore, as they could be enjoyed in something approximating fresh form through these new techniques. Only the technology-adverse Pennsylvania Dutch (i.e., German-Americans), in places like Lancaster County, kept processing corn in the old manner. Today, one Lancaster producer, John Cope's of Hanover, continues to produce and sell this heritage product.

John Cope's was established in 1900 by Martin Cope, and is run today by his grandson, John F. Cope. The product gained some notoriety in the 1950s: President Dwight D. Eisenhower, though born in Texas and raised in Kansas, was of Pennsylvania Dutch descent, and he regularly ordered Cope's toasted dried corn for White House meals. It remains a traditional side dish, stewed, creamed, or baked into savory pudding, at Thanksgiving feasts in Lancaster County, and makes splendid corn chowder, too.

FILÉ POWDER

The classic Creole and Cajun dish called gumbo—the name of which seems to derive from a Bantu dialect term for okra (see page 169)—is a dense, intensely flavored stew of vegetables and meat and/or shellfish that has pride of place as Louisiana's official state dish. Gumbo may be thickened in one of three ways: with the aforementioned okra, the characteristic mucilage of which dissolves into the sauce with long cooking; with roux, the fat-and-flour mixture that is the base of much Cajun cooking; and with filé powder, arguably the most traditional means of all.

Filé powder, also called simply filé, is a pungent seasoning made from the dried, ground leaves of the sassafras tree (the roots of which have often been used to flavor root beer). Louisiana's Choctaw Indians first turned the leaves into powder, which they used in cooking but also medicinally. The Choctaw passed it along to their Cajun neighbors, and it became a staple of the region's cooking, used not just in gumbo (which may itself be partly of Choctaw origin) but as a seasoning for seafood, vegetables, and meats. Filé does indeed have a faintly medicinal taste, with a fragrant pungency that reminds me of something between green tea and summer savory. Once you've sampled it, you'll recognize it anywhere, and won't likely mistake a filé gumbo for one thickened in other ways.

Uncle Bill's Creole Filé is one of the last hand-harvested, hand-ground examples of old-style filé powder. The man in charge of producing it today, Lionel Key, is the grand-nephew of Joseph Willie "Uncle Bill" Ricard, who in turn learned how to make it from his own uncle. Uncle Bill passed the secrets of the technique, along with his handmade tools for processing the sassafras, to Key—who says, "A lot of people make filé, but they don't make it like me."

FLOUR

Flour is the definitive staple, found in every cooking household, readily available in every supermarket, essential to so much of what we eat—even beyond baked goods. Because it's white and sold in bulk, we may sometimes tend to think that all flour is pretty much the same. Not so. The type of wheat, the season in which it is grown (there are broadly two types of wheat, summer and winter), the milling process—all these variables affect the texture of the flour and ultimately the texture and the flavor of the foods into which it goes. And any serious baker will tell you that getting to know your flour is as important as getting to know your oven; consistency matters.

In the test kitchen at *Saveur*, we used several brands of flour regularly with good results, among them King Arthur and Heckers. But the flour everybody loved most was Hudson Cream from Stafford County Flour Mills in Hudson, Kansas (population: 125)—one of the last remaining independently owned flour mills in the country. The company was founded more than a century ago by Gustav Krug, an immigrant from the state of Saxony, in eastern Germany, who arrived in Kansas in 1882. Krug's father was a miller, and though the young man bought a farm north of Hudson when he arrived, he found that he preferred milling to farming, and in 1904, opened the Hudson Milling Company in partnership with his brother-in-law. Five years later, the firm reorganized and reopened under its present name. The mill remained in the Krug family until 1968, when a holding company formed by local residents took over a majority interest. In 1992, the mill was remodeled and expanded, and now produces about 240,000 pounds (just under 110,000 kilograms) of flour a day.

Hudson Cream flour is made through an old-style "short patent" milling process, in which the wheat is ground more often and sifted more finely than in standard milling. This results in a lighter flour, and one with fewer impurities. The Jersey cow on the flour bags is, like its name, a reference to the flour's soft, almost creamy texture.

The mill produces a high-gluten bread flour and several other products, but their signature is their regular Hudson Cream bleached flour; an unbleached version is also available. Since flour isn't something people taste in its raw state, it's hard to describe the character of Hudson Cream, but the breads and cakes made from it that I've tasted have been particularly light, fine-grained, and flavorful.

GRANOLA

No food, not even tofu, is as emblematic—rightly or wrongly—of New Age beliefs and good old-fashioned hippiedom as granola. There's no good reason for that, as far as I can see: granola is basically fancy breakfast cereal. But if I call somebody "crunchy-granola," I'll bet you'll know what I mean.

In simple terms, granola is a mixture of baked and crumbled oats (and/or other grains) and nuts with one or more varieties of dried fruit mixed in, and some form of sweetening, typically honey, added. Some people say that it is an adaptation of a Swiss product called muesli, but in fact an early version of granola, called "granula," seems to slightly antedate the Swiss concoction. Muesli was developed in the early 1900s by a Zürich physician and dietician named Maximilian Bircher-Benner for patients in his sanitarium. (Some is still sold as Bircher muesli today.) The first granula had apparently been invented slightly earlier at James Caleb Jackson's sanitarium in Dansville, New York. Shortly thereafter, breakfast cereal and peanut butter pioneer Dr. John Harvey Kellogg of Battle Creek, Michigan, came up with a similar mixture, changing the name to granola.

Both muesli and granola remained specialty items for decades, found mostly in health food shops, but granola made a comeback in the 1960s as an early example of supposedly "whole food" popular in the pantries of the counterculture—hence its association with hippies. In the 1970s, Quaker, General Mills, and, yes, Kellogg's (founded by John Harvey's brother Will) got into the game in a big way, and granola became a supermarket staple.

Granola frankly isn't that difficult to make at home, but for the sake of convenience, there are a number of good packaged versions available. One of the best was sold under the Café Fanny brand, out of Alice Waters's popular Café Fanny in Berkeley. That establishment abruptly closed in early 2012, but Café Fanny Granola is still available and is now manufactured by Cassandra Chen's artisanal caramel company CC Made. A good

substitute is Bear Naked Fruit and Nut Granola, a honey-glazed blend of whole-grain oats, almonds, walnuts, pecans, raisins, and dried cranberries, among other ingredients—very crunchy, attractively varied in flavors and textures, and just sweet enough.

The Bear Naked line was launched by Brendan Synnott and Kelly Flatley of Darien, Connecticut. The two had been friends in middle school, and reconnected after college. Synnott was then working as a talent manager for *Saturday Night Live*, and Flatley had started making granola and selling it at sidewalk sales and a few small markets in Connecticut. Synnott saw the possibilities, and the two joined forces. By the end of 2002, their first year in business, their original product, Fruit and Nut Granola, was in about twenty-five stores in and around Connecticut. Today, it is available nationwide in over 10,000 outlets and has become the best-selling granola brand in America. Just to bring things full circle, in 2007 the company was bought by ... Kellogg's.

GRITS

"If I don't love you, baby," the great Little Milton once sang, "Grits ain't grocery." Grits are definitely grocery, and pretty much indispensable at that in much of the South, especially Georgia and South Carolina. Grits are simply coarse-ground cornmeal, ground corn without the pericarp, or hull. "People used to strain the ground corn through a wire mesh," says Glenn Roberts of Anson Mills in Columbia, South Carolina, "and what passed through was cornmeal and what didn't was grits."

Grits are of American Indian origin, but have become virtually an icon of Southern culture. They're a ubiquitous breakfast food, served with butter and salt, cheese, hot sauce, or with sugar or corn syrup. They're also part of two classic regional dishes, shrimp and grits (so popular that there's a whole cookbook dedicated to variations on the theme) and grits and grillades, a New Orleans specialty in which they are topped with beef or pork stewed with green peppers, celery, and scallions. And they're baked into breads and desserts, and treated like polenta by some "new Southern" chefs. They're such a symbol of down-home Southern virtues, in fact, that Mitt Romney, in his bid for the Republican presidential nomination in 2012, made a point of publicly eating cheesy grits in Mississippi.

The aforementioned Anson Mills produces the grits almost everybody seems to like best these days. Glenn Roberts was a historic restoration consultant and restaurant and hotel designer who decided, in 1998, to embark on an ambitious project to revive some traditional Southern staples. His idea was to grow and mill forgotten heirloom varieties of corn, rice, and wheat, organically, in the hopes that his products would help inspire a revival of some traditional Southern foodways. They have.

Though he now produces Carolina Gold rice (see page 198), a colonial heirloom wheat called Red May, and other grains, Roberts started with grits. He discovered old corn cultivars like Carolina Gourdseed White and John Haulk, and learned how to cold-mill them (both the corn and the millstones are chilled) as the millers of the eighteenth and nineteenth centuries did to minimize heat damage that could rob the meal of flavor. Today, Roberts works with about thirty contract growers in six states, and has helped them bring back about a dozen antebellum corn varieties. Roberts's product line now includes both white and yellow coarse grits made from a blend of varieties, blue corn grits made from a single cultivar grown by the Cherokee Nation, and, best of all, Pencil Cob grits, a hand-milled product from a kind of corn named for its unusually thin cob, one that fairly bursts with sweet corn flavor.

HOMINY

Maybe it was because they'd lived through the Depression and were afraid of running out of food, or maybe it was simply because it saved trips to the store, but when I was young my parents bought canned goods by the case and stored them in an immense walk-in closet, lined with shelves. There were cans of mandarin orange segments, fruit cocktail, orange and tomato juice, yams, baked beans, petit pois, corn "niblets," kidney beans, beets, succotash, green beans, three or four kinds of Campbell's soup, even canned new potatoes. And there was something called hominy, which was one vegetable I'd never learned about in my schoolbooks.

"What is hominy?" I asked my dad one day. "It's good," he answered, and I think it must have occurred to me that he basically had no idea what it was either. I'm not sure where my parents acquired a taste for it, but in any event it became part of the family menu, served hot alongside ham steaks or pork chops. I thought it had sort of a funny consistency, a little powdery, a little squeaky, but I enjoyed its rather earthy flavor. I would never have guessed, however, that it was corn.

I figured that part out years later, when I was in college, and drove across the country one Christmastime, passing through New Mexico on the way. There, in a modest-looking roadside diner, I ordered an interesting-sounding dish called posole—which turned out to be a chile-accented pork and hominy stew. I liked it enough to do a little research, and learned that hominy was indeed corn—dried corn, that had been nixtamalized (treated with alkali). This process helps both to preserve the corn and make it more nutritionally valuable by converting some of its niacin into an assimilable form. Nixtamalization also makes the skin fall off the corn kernels and causes the corn to swell. The resulting hominy, besides being essential to posole, bulks up all kinds of stews, adding a distinctive flavor that I think of as being more like beans than corn.

Canned hominy is available in Hispanic markets, and top-quality dried hominy, which needs to be boiled before using, is sold by Rancho Gordo—a Napa Valley-based business selling heirloom beans, chiles, grains, and herbs and spices. Started by Steve Sando in his Napa living room in 2001, the company has become one of the most important sources for basic New World foods.

MISSISSIPPI TAMALES

Tamales are cornmeal masa formed around meat, cheese, or other fillings, wrapped in corn husks or banana leaves, and steamed or boiled. They were probably invented by the Mayans, possibly as far back as 3,000 years ago, and are today a common feature of Mexican, Central American, and both Tex-Mex and Cal-Mex cooking. But they are also a century-old tradition far from the border, in the Mississippi Delta, birthplace of the blues. Tamales and the blues are intertwined in the region, in fact. Tamale carts used to stand outside practically every juke joint and blues bar in the state; tamales were fuel for blues musicians and their fans, the perfect portable edible accompaniment to too much beer or whiskey. (Their portability also made tamales popular food for field workers.)

Early blues singers paid tribute to the tamale. Red Hot Ole Mose (né Moses Mason) left us the first recorded musical ode to the Mississippi tamale, "Molly Man," released in 1928 ("Two for a nickel, four for a dime / Thirty cents a dozen, and you'll sure eat fine"). Eight years later, the legendary Robert Johnson turned them into a double entendre with "They're Red Hot" ("Hot tamales and they red hot / Yes, she got 'em for sale"). To this day, up and down the Delta, tamales are sold in restaurants, clubs, diners, markets, and even still from carts or stands, outside the occasional remaining juke joint, sometimes, but also outside gas stations and hardware stores.

How did tamales get to Mississippi in the first place? Nobody is quite sure. One popular explanation is that they came with Mexican agricultural workers in the early twentieth century—presumably the same men who are supposed to have introduced the guitar to the region, thus bringing Mississippians both their definitive music and one of their signature foods. Gustavo Arellano, in his excellent history of Mexican food in America, *Taco USA*, suggests that they arrived via San Francisco, where tamales were a craze around the turn of the century. Some historians think they came earlier, suspecting that soldiers from Mississippi who fought in the Mexican-American war in the mid-nineteenth century brought them home. Still others maintain that Mexico had nothing to do with it, and that tamales developed out of a seasoned cornmeal dish of African origin, called "cush," eaten by slaves in the Magnolia State.

The Mississippi tamale is, in any case, distinct from the versions known to the west and south. It is typically small and neatly tube-shaped, unlike the more free-form interpretations common elsewhere. It is usually made from cornmeal rather than the treated corn dough called masa, and always filled with meat, often very finely ground (and sometimes spicy) beef or pork. It is wrapped not in corn husks or banana leaves, but in thick paper—and eaten not with salsa but either plain or, at least sometimes, dipped into ranch dressing! It can even be deep-fried. (The Mississippi tamale also found it's way up the river to Chicago, where it became a sandwich filling, stuffed into a roll with onions and peppers. This is known as a "mother-in-law sandwich.")

Some of the classic Mississippi tamale purveyors, such as Ervin's Hot Tamales in Sledge, Solly's Hot Tamales in Vicksburg, Hicks' World Famous Hot Tamales in Clarksdale, and Teal's Onward Store in Onward, will sometimes agree to ship tamales if you call them up. For a more regular mail-order source, the best bet is Fat Mama's Tamales in Natchez, started by Jimmy and Britton Gammill in the late 1980s. Their tamales are classic, juicy and nicely spiced, though hardly fiery. Put on your best Robert Johnson, or maybe B.B. King, Muddy Waters, John Lee Hooker, Howlin' Wolf, or Elmore James, and eat 'em red hot.

RICE

The people of Charleston, South Carolina once ate large amounts of an aromatic long-grain rice called Carolina Gold (referring to its color in the fields). Rice came to the region around 1685, when the captain of a ship sailing from Madagascar anchored in Charleston Harbor and gave a bag of rice to a prominent local resident named Henry Woodward. Woodward propagated the rice with some success, and by the late eighteenth century, it had become the region's most important crop and a source of great wealth for the planters of Charleston and its vicinity. By 1820, there were more than 100,000 acres (about 40,000 hectares) of it, in the Carolinas and beyond, and it was being exported all over the world. Acreage declined during the Civil War and during Reconstruction, due to labor shortages and the breakup of many of the old plantations. During the Depression, as other, cheaper rice varieties became available, the once-thriving Lowcountry rice fields were abandoned altogether, and by the middle of the twentieth century, Carolina Gold had become a mere memory.

In the 1980s, an ophthalmologist named Richard Schulze obtained Carolina Gold seed rice from a United States Department of Agriculture (USDA) seed bank and planted it on his farm near Charleston. Today, there are about 150 acres (60 hectares) of it cultivated in the area. In 1997, Campbell Coxe planted 20 acres (8 hectares) of the grain on his family's historic Plumfield Plantation near Darlington, about 100 miles (160 kilometers) north of Charleston. He sells it under the Carolina Plantation label. Carolina Gold is a nicely chewy and particularly flavorful rice, with a character that is both nutty and slightly floral. Its former popularity is easy to understand.

WILD RICE

Wild rice isn't rice at all, but a kind of grass or cereal grain (*Zizania palustris*) growing in shallow lakes and streams around the Great Lakes and in other parts of southeast-central Canada and the northeast-central United States. (Related species are found in some Atlantic and Gulf coastal regions and in parts of China.) French explorers in the seventeenth century thought it looked not like rice but like another grain, and called it *folles avoines*, "crazy oats." For centuries, Native Americans in what are now Michigan, Wisconsin, and Minnesota have harvested the grain, knocking it off the plants with clubs, straight into their canoes. It is then dried, hulled, cleaned, and packaged for sale. It keeps well, and is an extremely nutritious grain, high in protein and full of vitamins and minerals and the essential amino acid called lysine.

The tricky part about wild rice is finding the real thing. Wild rice became popular in America as a "gourmet" food in the 1950s and 1960s, and the supply of this wild-growing, hand-harvested treat couldn't keep up with the demand. Scientists developed a hybrid version of the plant that could be cultivated in diked paddies and mechanically harvested. The result is a less flavorful grain, shiny, black, and smooth—in contrast to the wild version, which is duller, a little rough in texture, and irregular in color, ranging from black to brown to gray. Commercial wild rice, while cheaper and more plentiful, bears about the same relationship on the palate to its wild-harvested counterpart that farmed salmon does to the wild-caught kind.

Charlie Worrath is one of Minnesota's top fishing guides, but he and his wife, Terri, also run Moose Lake Wild Rice in Deer River, Minnesota, founded by Terri's father in 1973. The Worraths aren't purists (they do sell cultivated wild rice, clearly labeled as such), but their certified whole-grain wild-harvested version, only about $1.50 (£1) more expensive per pound (half-kilogram), is what you want. It has a pleasant texture when properly cooked, alternately soft and a little crunchy, as well as a grassy, nutty flavor much more intense than that of white rice, and pretty addictive.

DESSERTS & CONFECTIONS

ALMOND TOFFEE

In 1919, when he was seventeen, Chester K. "Chet" Enstrom went to work in an ice cream factory in Colorado Springs, Colorado. There was a candy factory across the street, and he would sometimes go in and help when he had finished his ice cream shift. In 1929, with partner Harry Jones, Enstrom launched the Jones-Enstrom Ice Cream Company. Enstrom continued making candy on the side, almost as a hobby, and developed a special knack for almond toffee. Toffee is made by caramelizing sugar with butter until the mixture grows firm and glossy. Particularly buttery toffee with nuts added is sometimes known as English toffee, and it is for those toffees that Enstrom became famous.

By 1960, his hobbyist toffee had earned enough of a reputation around town that he started a second company, Enstrom Candies. He envisioned it as a small-scale mom-and-pop operation—his business model, he used to say, was "We're just making a little almond toffee for a few of our friends"—but demand quickly grew too great and he geared up production, selling the business to his son and daughter-in-law when he was ready to retire. Today, Enstrom's grandchildren and their spouses run the business, and members of a fourth generation have recently joined.

Enstrom's toffee comes covered in both milk and dark chocolate. Made with California almonds, sweet butter, and cane sugar, with a crushed almond coating over the chocolate, it has a rich caramel flavor and a melt-in-your-mouth consistency nicely offset by the exterior almond dust. Call it an artisanal Heath Bar.

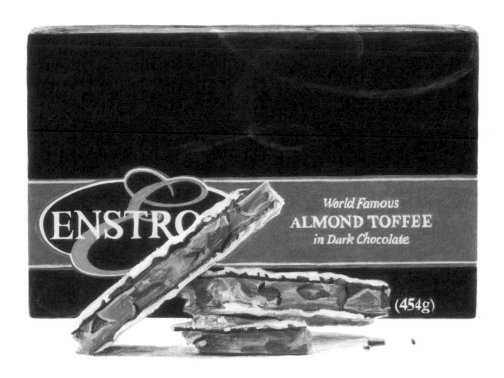

APPLE & APRICOT CANDY

It would be an understatement to say that we didn't eat a lot of exotic food at my house when I was growing up, but I have since become aware that occasionally we enjoyed things that were perhaps more exotic than we realized. A good example is the box of confections we always seemed to have in the house around the year-end holidays, labeled "Aplets and Cotlets." These were highly unusual, compared to the commercial candy bars and hard candies that otherwise helped us satisfy our sweet teeth. They were like little blocks of solidified jelly, with pieces of walnut inside and a dusting of powdered sugar outside. I thought they were wonderful. What I didn't realize was that they were basically an ancient Middle Eastern specialty called lokum, or Turkish delight.

Lokum is a starchy flavored gelatin, made from various varieties of fruit (dates are popular) and flavored with rose water, lemon juice, or other essences. Legend has it that lokum was invented by a prisoner of the Sultan of the Ottoman Empire, who presented it to the ruler as a gift. The sultan had chipped a tooth on hard candy, so he appreciated the lokum's softness and freed the prisoner, naming him official confectioner of the realm. The truth is that it was the creation of a real confectioner, Bekir Effendi, at his Istanbul shop in the late eighteenth century. Around the mid-nineteenth century, an enterprising British visitor to the city bought large quantities of lokum and shipped it home, renaming it "Turkish delight."

Aplets and Cotlets (they may be purchased separately, but we always had mixed selections of them, so I can't help thinking of them that way) were in turn devised by two Armenian immigrants to central Washington State, who arrived in the delightfully named town of Cashmere in 1918 and bought an apple farm, which they christened Liberty Orchards. After growing apples for several years, they sought to expand their product range, and one of them had the idea of trying to make a version of lokum using their own apples and locally grown walnuts. It was a success, and a version based on Washington apricots soon followed. Today, the company produces a large range of variations based on many other fruits and nuts, as well as a line of chocolates, but Aplets and Cotlets remain their best seller. Someone once proposed that Aplets and Cotlets be named Washington's official state candy. Regrettably, this did not come to pass.

BENNE WAFERS

Sesame seeds are eaten pretty much throughout Asia, the Middle East, and Africa, and in parts of North and South America. The sesame plant seems to have originated in sub-Saharan Africa, spreading along trade routes around the Eastern Hemisphere; slaves almost certainly brought sesame to the Caribbean and the American South.

Though sesame seeds produce a highly flavored oil and are used in soups and stews in Africa and ground into paste in the Middle East, they are most often associated with baking, both sweet and savory, appearing as a flavoring or topping for everything from bagels to dim sum and an assortment of Indian confections. In South Carolina and parts of neighboring states, sesame seeds go under their Wolof (African) name, *benne*, and are said to bring good luck. In this area, they are commonly made into cookie-like wafers.

Benne wafers are most strongly associated with Charleston, South Carolina, but the best ones I've found come from a bit farther south, in Savannah, Georgia. Byrd Cookie Company was founded there in 1924, and added benne wafers to its repertoire after World War II. These are small bet-you-can't-eat-just-one treats, buttery and crisp, packed with sesame seeds and sweetened with a blend of maple sugar and brown sugar. They crunch in the mouth and leave a pleasantly haunting flavor behind. Byrd's, a fourth-generation family-run concern, also makes addictive little savory rounds that it calls benne bits. These are like miniature crumbly biscuits that are made with toasted sesame seeds, aged Cheddar, and various spices, probably including cayenne. If you prefer salty to sweet, you'll like these even better than the more traditional sugary wafers.

BUTTER MINTS

Since ancient times, mint has been used as a medicinal element, meant to aid digestion and have a calming effect, and the earliest mint candies were probably lozenges sold more for salutary purposes than as mere candy. Nevertheless, mint excels as a candy ingredient, especially when combined with chocolate, as it often is (see page 223), but even in more or less unadorned form.

In 1932, Katharine Beecher, who a few years earlier had started a small candy company in Manchester, Pennsylvania, invented what was to become one of the most popular, irresistible mint confections in America: butter mints. These are little pillows of sugar, butter, and cream, with a nice but not overpowering minty flavor, which melt delightfully in the mouth, coating the palate with richness. There was always a bowl of butter mints put out at our house when company was coming, back in the 1950s and 1960s, and I remember going to grown-up dinner parties as a youngster at which they would be passed around with the coffee. Because they're rich, they're filling, but that never discouraged me and my contemporaries from loading up on them. They were very hard to stop eating.

Beecher ran her candy company, selling butter mints and other items, until her death in 1952 (a street in Manchester called Buttermint Alley honors her achievements). Her son, Henry, kept the business going until 1974, when he sold it to Pennsylvania Dutch Candies, based near Manchester in Camp Hill. Pennsylvania Dutch has itself been a family-run company, under the Warrells, since 1965. Under current CEO Lincoln Warrell, they specialize in old-style candies like sanded candy drops, peanut brittle, and of course Beecher's Butter Mints.

CANDY BAR

Snickers, a slab of nougat with peanuts and caramel, cloaked in chocolate, is not just a classic American candy bar—it's a cultural icon, a symbol of dietary excess, a popular pick-me-up, and an advertising-world powerhouse, associated through sponsorship with NASCAR and the Super Bowl, and with such personalities as Mr. T, Betty White, Aretha Franklin, Roseanne Barr, and Don Rickles, all of whom have done commercials for it. It is also a recognizable enough "flavor" to be incorporated into a host of other products, including ice cream bars, cookies, energy bars, cheesecake (created by the Cheesecake Factory chain), peanut butter, and chocolate spread.

The man ultimately responsible for this essential component of our nation's sweet life was Franklin Clarence Mars, a Minnesota-born candy merchant who tried unsuccessfully to manufacture candy in Tacoma, Washington, before establishing his first successful company—which became Mars, Inc.—in Minneapolis in 1920. The firm's first big candy bar was the Milky Way, which resembles a broader Snickers without the peanuts. Mars moved the company to Chicago in 1929, and a year later introduced the Snickers bar, which he named after his favorite horse. (The Mars bar itself was first produced by a company plant in the United Kingdom in 1932.) Still a family company, Mars—which bought the Wrigley chewing gum company in 2008—now owns such brands as Uncle Ben's rice, and markets not only Snickers and Milky Way but M&Ms, Skittles, and Twix.

CANDY CORN

Emil Brach didn't invent candy corn, but he helped make it the most popular Hallowe'en candy of all. (The National Confectioners Association estimates that 20,000,000 pounds of it—some 9,000,000 kilograms—are sold annually!) This unique confection is mostly sugar and (appropriately enough) corn syrup, with enough wax to give it a waxy, toothsome texture. In shape, it more or less resembles kernels of corn—a particularly elongated variety of kernel—but it's bigger than corn and in color it's not much like anything in nature, with its bands of bright yellow, orange, and white.

Candy corn was first made in the 1880s by confectioner George Renninger, an employee of the Wunderle Candy Company in Philadelphia. It caught on, and in 1900, the Herman Goelitz Candy Company of Oakland, California—later to become famous as the manufacturer of Jelly Belly (see page 219)—began making it for wide distribution. Emil Brach went into the candy business in Chicago in 1904, opening Brach's Palace of Sweets, where he specialized in caramels. Soon he, too, was making candy corn. His company grew, and candy corn became an increasingly important part of his business.

Since 1968, when Brach's was bought by American Home Products, it has had four owners, but its commitment to candy corn has never flagged, and Brach's is by far the best-selling brand. It is said that the firm makes enough each year to encircle the earth four-and-a-quarter times if the kernels are laid end to end. I can't imagine any cosmic worker having the discipline to actually arrange them in that manner, though, without popping a good many into his or her mouth along the way.

CARAMEL CORN

There is one sweet snack food brand that almost everybody knows, and whose name almost everybody gets slightly wrong—both facts thanks to the 1908-vintage pop song "Take Me Out to the Ball Game," which contains a line that people often sing as "Buy me some peanuts and Cracker Jacks." In fact, the song refers to Cracker Jack, singular, the correct name of this turn-of-the century elaboration of caramel corn. The product is said to have gotten that name when the Rueckheim brothers, Frederick and Louis, gave a sample to a friend back in 1896, and he exclaimed, "That's crackerjack!"—period slang meaning it was top-notch.

The first version of Cracker Jack, called simply "Candied Popcorn and Peanuts," had been introduced three years earlier by the Rueckheims at the World's Columbian Exposition, better known as the Chicago World's Fair. Frederick kept refining the recipe until he developed a way to keep the peanuts and popcorn separate in their bath of caramelized sugar and molasses. In 1912, he added a tiny toy to every package (I remember getting a little whistle once).

The company making Cracker Jack was bought by Borden in 1964, and they in turn sold it to Frito-Lay in 1997. I used to love getting Cracker Jack at the movie theater or at Gilmore Field, where my dad took me to see the L.A. Angels when they were still a Pacific Coast League team, and I have a pretty good memory of the way it tasted. I sampled some recently and it still had that dark, deep, caramelized sugar flavor—with an overtone of something almost smoky that I remember from back in the days when Steve Bilko was still knocking them over the fence.

CARAMELS

Caramelization occurs when water is removed from sugar (the word "caramel" apparently derives from the Medieval Latin term *cannamellis*, sugar cane), a process that rearranges molecular structure to yield the characteristic brown color and lightly burnt flavor. Caramel candy, also called simply caramels, is made by combining caramelized sugar, and sometimes corn syrup, with boiled milk or cream, butter, salt, and vanilla flavoring. The result is a chewy, buttery candy with an appealing concentrated sweetness.

The Knudsen family of Red Wing, Minnesota, in the southeast corner of the state, just across the Mississippi River from Wisconsin, started selling homemade cheesecake in the early 1980s. By the end of that decade, they had added caramels, made in the old home candy-making style, which soon became the focus of their business. Today, Peggy and Ron Knudsen and their sons, Josh and Noah, have automated production and taken over the 1875-vintage Kappel Wagon Works (which manufactured buggies) as their factory. They produce as much as 700 pounds (about 320 kilograms) of the candies daily.

Knudsen caramels are as chewy as caramels should be, but also soft enough not to stick to the teeth. The flavor suggests brown sugar (which is in fact an ingredient) and, faintly, roasted almonds, with a buttery gloss. (The Knudsens proudly use top-quality butter from Minnesota dairies.) Cut into rectangles—Peggy Knudsen says that they're "two-bite size"—and wrapped in filament paper with twisted ends, like old-fashioned penny candy, the caramels are packed into plastic bags, boxes and old-fashioned glass jars. Knudsen says she tries to keep a flavor in the candies that will remind people of their grandmother's recipe. She must have had a wonderful grandmother.

CHOCOLATE BAR

Let's make this clear right here at the beginning: The Hershey's Bar is not the best chocolate in America. Not even close. It's a very widely distributed, mass-produced product, substantially less expensive than (for instance) artisanal dark chocolate, and it has none of that chocolate's exotic complexity and bittersweet appeal. What the Hershey's Bar is is an American icon, an instantly recognizable object, a symbol of creativity-turned-commerce, a flavor of our childhoods. (Huge quantities were sent to our troops during World War II.) It doesn't put on airs, pretending to be something that it's not. It is to the best chocolate of Scharffenberger, Patric, or Armano what Coors is to your favorite microbrew—just simply on a different level, but perfectly enjoyable under some circumstances. In fact, there's something about the Hershey's Bar's milk chocolate (in which cacao actually plays a pretty small role) that is very appealing— something smooth and creamy, with a flavor of caramelized milk and a lingering mouth-coating sweetness.

The Hershey's Bar is also a symbol of Yankee stick-to-it-iveness. It wouldn't be here if Milton Snavely Hershey hadn't persevered. Born in Derry Township, Pennsylvania, he apprenticed as a young man at a small candy factory in nearby Lancaster. In 1876, when he was eighteen, he started his own confectionery business in Philadelphia. He lasted six years, then had to close. Undeterred, he tried to manufacture candy in New York. When that effort failed, too, he moved west, to Denver, where he went to work for a candymaker who taught him how to make milk caramel. In 1886, returning to Pennsylvania, he founded the Lancaster Caramel Company, which was finally a success. On a visit to the World's Columbian Exposition in Chicago in 1893, he met a chocolatier and saw demonstrations of some German-made chocolate-making equipment. He bought it on the spot and shipped it home to produce chocolate coverings for his caramels. Around this time, he made the first version of what was to become the Hershey's Bar.

In 1896, Hershey bought a milk processing plant to supply the milk chocolate he had developed. In 1899, he came up with a new method of making milk chocolate more cheaply and consistently than it had been made before, the particulars of which are still a trade secret. The next year, Hershey sold his caramel company for the then-astounding sum of $1 million (about $26.6 million or £16.6 million, today), and a few years after that, he began construction on a chocolate plant in his hometown of Derry Township, in what came to be known as Hershey, Pennsylvania. The company subsequently rolled out many other varieties of chocolate, and today owns a number of famous candy brands, including Reese's and Kit Kat—but the Hershey's Bar remains, as one advertising slogan put it, "America's Candy Bar."

CHOCOLATE CLUSTER

As unlikely as it might seem today, the Goo Goo Cluster—a tooth-numbing Tennessee-born free-form sprawl of caramel, marshmallow nougat, and chocolate, generously studded with peanuts—was once sold under the slogan "A Nourishing Lunch for a Nickel." (Another Tennessee confection, the MoonPie, see page 212, was also once eaten for lunch.) The candy was created in 1912 by the Standard Candy Company of Nashville, and the company claims that the Goo Goo Cluster was the world's first combination candy bar—that is, previous ones had been made exclusively of one ingredient, whether chocolate or nougat or caramel, and this was the first to meld together several elements.

The recipe was developed by Standard's boss, Howell Campbell, Sr., with the help of a plant supervisor named Porter Moore. (According to company lore, Campbell blended chocolate the way a master distiller blends whiskey.) At first Campbell didn't know what to call his creation, and nobody is quite sure exactly how the candy finally got its name. Howell Campbell, Jr., however, once said that his father used to talk about it on the streetcar that he rode to and from work every day. One morning, he also started talking about his newborn son, who'd say "goo goo." A schoolteacher riding with him suggested that he give that name to the candy, since it was so good that people would ask for it from birth. Could have happened, I suppose. Standard Candy is still in business, turning out up to 20,000 Goo Goo Clusters an hour according to what is said to be the original recipe.

CHOCOLATE MARSHMALLOW COOKIE

Marshmallow creme, also known under the trade name Marshmallow Fluff, is a spreadable paste that resembles the softened interior of marshmallows. It was apparently originally used around the turn of the nineteenth century as a cake filling. The first commercially produced version of the substance appeared in 1917, and before long it had found a role as one of the principal constituents of MoonPie—the trademark for which was registered on January 1, 1919, in Chattanooga, Tennessee.

The specialty apparently had its origins in the eating habits of local coal miners. There are two versions of the story floating around, both involving a salesman for the Chattanooga Bakery named Earl Mitchell, Sr. According to one version, Mitchell noticed that miners at the shops along his route were dipping graham crackers (see page 33)—one of his firm's big sellers—in marshmallow creme and letting it harden into frosting. He relayed this information to one M. P. Shauf, the bakery foreman, and Shauf experimented until he had developed a large pie made of graham crackers and marshmallow creme. His young grandson, visiting the bakery, thought the popped bubbles in the creme looked like the craters of the moon.

The official MoonPie Web site's version has it that Mitchell visited a mine company store and some miners asked him to make them something big and filling. "About how big?" Mitchell inquired. "A miner held out his hands, framing the moon, and said, 'About that big!'" *Then*, says this iteration of the tale, Mitchell noticed the miners applying marshmallow creme to their graham crackers. The bakery took the idea and ran with it, making a sandwich out of the crackers and creme and coating the whole thing with chocolate.

However it came to be, by the 1930s, the MoonPie had evolved into a Southern tradition, and as an oversize snack, it had become a popular quick lunch for miners and other manual laborers—often washed down with an RC Cola. The country singer "Big Bill" Lister, who toured for several years as the opening act for Hank Williams, even had a hit in 1951 with a song called "Gimme an RC Cola and a Moon Pie." The specialty's Tennessee origins aside, Alabama has embraced the MoonPie, with an annual MoonPie eating contest in Bessemer and a lighted reproduction of one, 12 feet (about 3.5 meters) high, raised each New Year's Eve in Mobile. MoonPies are also thrown from carnival floats during Mobile's large and frenetic Mardi Gras parade every year.

What does a MoonPie taste like? It's sort of like a fossilized s'more. Imagine the wheat-and-honey flavor of graham crackers combined with sweet, gooey cream and slightly waxy chocolate of no particular distinction—not exactly, in other words, an epicurean treat, but undeniably a real American tradition.

CHOCOLATE MICE

These little creatures, handcrafted by L. A. Burdick, are almost too cute to eat: tiny, benevolent-looking rodents, short and plump, with upturned noses, chocolate-coated almond ears, candy dots for eyes, and long silk ribbon tails in different hues. But they're also far too good *not* to eat. They come in three flavors: white chocolate with a cinnamon-flavored interior, milk chocolate with mocha inside, and (my favorite) dark chocolate cloaking an intense orange center. Larry Burdick, who runs L. A. Burdick with his wife, Paula, got the idea for the mice when he was studying chocolate-making in Switzerland. One chocolate shop he worked at, in Bern, had the tradition of forming leftover chocolate scraps into inexpensive candies for children, and somebody had the idea of shaping these into mice with scraps of knitting yarn pasted on (with chocolate) as tails.

Back in the U.S., in the mid-1980s, Burdick started making artisanal chocolates of his own for restaurants and caterers in New York City, and he remembered the mice and began fashioning them. They scampered on to become something of a trademark for him. His business slowly grew, and he moved his chocolate factory and his family to Walpole, a small town in southwestern New Hampshire. Today, in addition to the factory and a high-volume mail-order business, Burdick runs three café-chocolate shop combinations (in Walpole, as well as Cambridge, Massachusetts, and New York City), and a French restaurant in Walpole.

All Burdick chocolates are made in small batches. No molds are used: the chocolates are all piped and formed by hand. He uses rich, high-quality *couverture* chocolate (containing extra cocoa butter, at least 32 percent) from Switzerland, France, and Venezuela, made primarily from Caribbean and South and Central American cocoa beans. In addition to the mice, Burdick produces chocolate penguins, Easter bunnies, Thanksgiving turkeys, even ghosts in coffins for Hallowe'en— as well as a range of bonbons in more conventional form. There's something about those mice, though …

CHOCOLATE TRUFFLES

My wife doesn't eat dessert, and doesn't have much interest in cookies or candy. But when we dine at Sea Salt, an excellent restaurant in Naples, Florida, she always ends her meal with a sweet from the selection of chocolates offered—specifically the Tahitian Caramel, made with vanilla-scented caramel coated in milk chocolate. There must be hundreds and hundreds of makers of artisanal chocolates in America, but the array produced by Norman Love Confections, based not far from Naples in Fort Myers, are something special enough to tempt even a savory-tooth like that of my wife. *Consumer Reports* agrees, rating Love one of the top three chocolate companies in America.

Love learned pastry-making and confectionery in France, worked for the Beverly Hills Hotel, and then began an association with the Ritz-Carlton hotel chain as corporate executive pastry chef, opening thirty pastry kitchens for them, everywhere from Boston to Bali. In 2001, he left Ritz-Carlton and he and his wife, Mary, went into

the chocolate business. Today, he sells his wares out of shops in Fort Myers and Naples as well as from his Web site. He also does a line of specialty chocolates for Godiva's "G" Collection. An innovator in chocolate-making techniques, Love has developed a technology for shell-molded chocolates that is widely used across the industry.

His chocolates are often vividly colored and always vivid on the palate. The flavorings are intense and pure, whether they're made with nothing but chocolate, like those from his single-origin Black collection (his remarkable Venezuela chocolate tastes like licorice and black tea and prune, without any of those things actually added), or enhanced with jalapeño pepper, passion fruit, ginger lime, or Florida orange. Love's truffles are particularly good. I don't know if I've ever had a better example than his dark chocolate cream, which is buttery and bittersweet. It's the kind of truffle you want to devour, but force yourself to savor slowly, just to make it last.

DULCE DE LECHE ICE CREAM

Literally "sweet from milk," dulce de leche is a dense sauce of caramelized sugar and condensed or boiled-down milk, popular throughout Central and South America under various names (and in Mexico, where it is called *cajeta*, and is usually based on goat's milk). It is a constituent element of many traditional cookies, cakes, and other confections, and is sometimes simply spread on toast like jam, or spooned over ice cream like some indulgent fudgy version of butterscotch topping.

It was probably inevitable that sooner or later somebody would have the idea of making it *into* ice cream. The first company to do so, in 1997, was apparently Häagen-Dazs, the popular worldwide brand with the faux-Scandinavian name, founded in the Bronx in 1961. (Häagen-Dazs products are made by Dreyer's, a subsidiary of Nestlé, who licenses the brand from General Mills, and operates the business separately in the U.S. and North America.)

The Häagen-Dazs Web site says that its dulce de leche ice cream is "inspired by Latin America's treasured dessert," and is flavored with caramel and sweet cream, then swirled with caramel ribbons. Whether or not that's really dulce de leche may be argued, and of course Häagen-Dazs is a mass-produced brand. But its offerings in general are probably as "natural" as something made on this scale can be, and this particular ice cream has a true caramelized flavor, nutty and brown-sugary—if perhaps not as relentlessly dense and sticky as actual dulce de leche—with an agreeable, silky mouth-feel. I have the feeling that a pint of this would go down all too easily for an ice cream aficionado without good self-control.

GOOEY BUTTER CAKE

St. Louis has a number of food traditions not well known outside the area, among them toasted ravioli (which is just what it sounds like), the St. Paul sandwich (egg foo yong on white bread), the prosperity sandwich (ham, turkey, and bacon, open-face, with melted cheese and cream sauce), the concrete (frozen custard mixed with various fruits or candies, earning its name because it's so thick that it won't pour out if a cup of it is held upside down), and the dense confection known as gooey butter cake. This is a firm, low-rise yellow cake rich with butter, eggs, and cream cheese, and dusted with powdered sugar. (It's vaguely reminiscent of the French cake known as *gâteau basque*, though that's made with almond flour.)

Gooey butter cake comes with a side of culinary lore—the usual accidental invention story, in this case involving a baker who inadvertently reversed the quantities of sugar and flour when making regular cake batter (or, according to another version, one who used a sugary butter meant as a between-layer adhesive in the batter instead of plain butter), but then went ahead and baked the cake anyway. More likely, someone who knew exactly what he or she was doing simply decided to make a richer, sweeter, gooier version of conventional yellow cake.

Kirk and Debbie Stieferman set up their gooey butter cake business, Gooey Louie, in 2006, using a recipe "from a St. Louis family" that is said to be four generations old. They first sold their cake in limited quantities at the Missouri Botanical Garden's annual Best of Missouri market, and the response was so good that they turned their baking into a full-time job. Their version of the cake is as rich and sweet and gooey as any, with a bright dairy flavor and a tinge of vanilla. It is regularly named as the best example of this St. Louis classic, and it's not difficult to see (or rather to taste) why.

HONEYCOMB

Honeycomb is a geometrical wonder, a complex of hexagonal wax cells created by honeybees as a home for their larvae and for honey and pollen. Bees build their rows of comb exactly three-eighths of an inch (about a centimeter) apart, and it is said that the individual cells are strong enough to support twenty-five times their own weight. Beekeepers often remove honeycomb from the hives to harvest the honey—a process called "robbing the bees"—and then return it for future use, but it is also a delicious and satisfying form of raw (waxy) honey in itself.

Ted Dennard of the Savannah Bee Company, in the Georgia city of that name, learned the beekeeper's art as a teenager from an elderly practitioner he met on his father's property in coastal Georgia. The old man asked permission to leave his hives on the land, and in return, he educated young Ted in the beekeeping process. Ted has kept bees ever since, even teaching beekeeping to farmers in Central America while in the Peace Corps, and traveling the world from Jamaica to Vietnam

to sample local honeys. His bees remained a hobby, though, at least partially because he never thought he could turn honey and related products into a viable business. In 1998, however, he started selling his tupelo honey, along with a honey-based lip balm, in stores around Savannah. He found so many customers that, in 2002, he set up the Savannah Bee Company, moving his honey-bottling operation out of his garage and into an abandoned classroom on the Oatland Island Wildlife Preserve. He paid his rent in honey.

Today, Dennard has a 40,000-square-foot (about 3,700-square-meter) warehouse on Wilmington Island, across the bridge from Savannah, as well as three retail stores in Savannah and one in Charleston, South Carolina. He sells a range of bee-related skin-care products and at least ten varieties of honey, as well as honeycomb in both round and square form. It is intense stuff, fun to chew and easy to spread, with a vivid floral flavor accented by a note of citrus that recalls Meyer lemons (see page 168).

HOT FUDGE SAUCE

One of my most vivid childhood food memories is of going to C. C. Brown's. This was an old-style ice cream parlor in Hollywood, just down the street from Grauman's Chinese Theater—a long, narrow room, as I remember it, with lots of brown wood paneling and plenty of ample pink-upholstered booths along one side. I'm sure there must have been an array of ice creams in assorted flavors, but we went there, as did almost everybody else, for one thing: the hot fudge sundaes. These were dishes full of eggy French vanilla ice cream topped with toasted almonds and real whipped cream and served with little brown pitchers of molten fudge on the side; pouring the chocolate over the ice cream solidified part but not all of it, and a big spoonful of the combination was a marvel of contrasting flavors, textures (the fudge was slightly grainy), and temperatures.

This institution's founder, Clarence Clifton Brown, claimed to have not just perfected but actually invented the hot fudge sundae. This is said to have taken place at his original ice cream parlor in downtown Los Angeles in 1906. In 1929, Brown's son, Cliff, moved the establishment to Hollywood Boulevard, where he started attracting an A-list clientele. Joan Crawford is said to have once signed autographs outside the parlor, and Marlon Brando, Bob Hope, Marilyn Monroe, and Kirk Douglas were among the regulars.

In 1963, Cliff sold the business to John A. Schumacher, who ran it with his family until 1996. By that time, Hollywood Boulevard had become tacky and unsafe, and business was down. The Lawry's chain bought the rights to the C. C. Brown trademark (and presumably the recipe), and still sells excellent fudge for sundae purposes under the name.

SINCE 1906

cc.Brown's

of HOLLYWOOD

THE ORIGINAL
HOT FUDGE SAUCE

NET WT: 10.5 oz (298 g)

JELLY BEANS

The brightly colored, variously flavored little candies known as jelly beans—a name that accurately describes both their shape and the nature of their interior—were first made some time in the mid-1800s, somewhere in America, but nobody is sure exactly when, where, or by whom. So-called penny candy, sold loose, in bulk, became popular in confectionery shops around the country in the late nineteenth century, and jelly beans—originally fruit-flavored jelly encased in a soft sugar coating—were one popular expression of the genre. They cost a lot less than a penny apiece, though; an advertisement in the *Chicago Daily News*, published in 1905, offered them in wholesale quantities for nine cents a pound ($2.22 or £1.45, per pound, or half-kilogram, today). Around that same time, the term "jelly bean" came into slang usage to mean a dandy or a gigolo, presumably a reference to the candy's vivid hues and smooth surface.

The Herman Goelitz Candy Company in Oakland, California, which had helped popularize candy corn (see page 207) in the early twentieth century, began to specialize in jelly beans in the 1960s, adding them to a product line that included, in addition to candy corn, the first American-made gummi bears. One early fan of Goelitz jelly beans was Ronald Reagan, who apparently discovered them shortly after he became governor of California in 1967, and later took them to the White House (and onto Air Force One, which never left home without them). He is said to have taken to them as an aid to give up pipe-smoking.

In 1976, a Los Angeles confectioner named David Klein had an idea for a mini-jelly bean made with natural flavorings, which he called the Jelly Belly. He approached the Goelitz company with the notion, and a partnership was formed. Goelitz later bought Klein out, and renamed the company Jelly Belly.

The days of a few simple fruit flavors are long gone, of course. Jelly Belly maintains a rotating roster of at least fifty varieties, including such flavors as Root Beer, Bubble Gum, Buttered Popcorn, Margarita, and Caramel Corn. (Discontinued flavors include Baked Bean, Buttered Toast, Peanut Butter Pumpkin Pie, and Roasted Garlic.) You either like jelly beans or you don't, but if you're a fan, Jelly Bellies are the gold standard.

KEY LIME PIE

The key lime is a sorry-looking specimen, small and often pale in color compared to its more robust, bright green cousin the Persian lime. Key limes, named for Key West, Florida, in whose environs they thrive (and also called Mexican or West Indian limes), have seeds, too. But their juice is sharper, more aromatic, and more flavorful than that of the Persian. Key limes make excellent margaritas and other cocktails—and they are the, er, key ingredient for the wonderful, uniquely American confection known as key lime pie.

Legend has it that key lime pie was invented by a cook working for William Curry, the nineteenth-century Bahamian-born marine salvager who became Florida's first millionaire. A frozen variation, said to have been favored by a vacationing Harry S. Truman, was later developed by one Fern Butters, who ran Fern Inn on Upper Matecumbe Key in Islamorada. The most famous key lime pie around today, though, is one made under the direction of a transplanted Yankee named Randy Essig.

Essig grew up in North Syracuse, New York, practically living in the luncheonette that his parents owned. At the age of fifteen, he was frying fish at a local seafood house, and loving the restaurant world. He went on to work in the nightclub business, and might have stayed in the Northeast if he and his wife hadn't taken a vacation to Florida in 1978 after a particularly harsh winter back home. Not long afterwards, they moved to the upscale Gulfside community of Naples, south of Fort Myers.

In 1989, Essig bought into a local produce market, and helped expand it into a fish market and restaurant. In 2003, after his partnership had unraveled, he opened his own place in Naples, Randy's Fishmarket and Restaurant. He'd first tasted key lime pie in the late 1970s, after moving to Florida, and, loving it, tried every example he could find. He claims to have discovered the perfect one in 1990, and he managed to obtain the recipe.

At first, Essig just offered the pie as dessert at the restaurant—but he remembered, he says, that the restaurant he'd worked for in Syracuse made good money selling its coleslaw and mac and cheese to go, and when customers started asking if they could take home one of his pies, he began packaging them for retail sale. He now sells as many as 50,000 a year, and once moved 1,620 pies in eight minutes on the QVC shopping channel.

It's a simple, attractively straightforward pie made with real key lime juice, condensed milk, and sugar poured into a graham cracker crust and frozen. The interaction of the milk and the lime's acid sets the pie, so it doesn't need to be baked. It's bright and sweet in flavor with plenty of lime showing through. Essig has recently developed chocolate-covered key lime pie on a stick—in effect frozen bars of this specialty. Is America a great country, or what?

MAPLE SUGAR CANDY

My mother's family came from New Hampshire and Vermont, and every Christmastime when I was young, they'd send off—to us out in the snowless wilderness of West Los Angeles— a large tin container filled with maple sugar molded into maple leaves, Christmas trees, even mini-Santa Clauses. I remember the tins because they were imprinted with scenes of white-cloaked streets and clapboard houses and forests frosted with rime, scenes that gave me my first and lasting impressions of what New England looked like. And I remember so well the way the candy tasted: grainy, tooth-achingly sweet, and slightly piney. I couldn't get enough.

The process of making maple sugar was originally developed, not surprisingly, by Native peoples in the "maple belt" of eastern Canada and the northeastern United States. It is made by boiling maple sap long past the point needed to produce syrup, indeed until the sap's water content is virtually gone. The resulting sugar is twice as sweet as the ordinary granulated white stuff. I haven't seen the kinds of large assortments of maple sugar that we used to get from Mom's folks in a long time, but every once in a while I treat myself to a good-sized maple sugar maple leaf made by Coombs Family Farms in Brattleboro, in southern Vermont.

The Coombs family first started farming here in the mid-1800s, and current proprietor Arnold Coombs is a seventh-generation maple man. (It is said that he first entered the family sugarhouse when his father, while bringing the newborn home from the hospital, stopped there to check on the sap he was boiling down—and that he was tapping trees himself by the age of eight.) Today, Coombs sources maple sap from about 2,000 small farms, in addition to his own property, and produces syrup, maple sugar, and maple candy on site, using all natural ingredients. The syrup is excellent, and the candy is every bit as sweet and irresistible as the candy that came out of those New England-themed tins so long ago.

MARSHMALLOWS

It takes real imagination to envision a connection between the tangle of long, skinny roots of the plant known botanically as *Althaea officinalis* and the soft, puffy confection we call marshmallows, but a connection there is: This plant is the original marshmallow—that's its common name. It wasn't a confection, however; it was medicine, prescribed in China, the Middle East, and Europe alike, particularly as a decongestant and a treatment for ulcers. The ancient Egyptians mixed the sap of the plant with honey to make a remedy for sore throats, and the medieval French refined the idea by adding egg whites to what they called *pâté de guimauve*, or marshmallow paste. By the late 1800s, French confectioners had figured out a way to mimic the flavor and consistency of this paste using gelatin and cornstarch, leaving out the marshmallow altogether.

The modern recipe, innocent of anything medicinal, is made primarily with gelatin, sugar, and corn syrup, which are whipped into the familiar sticky but airy consistency. In that form, marshmallows are eaten right out of the bag, roasted on skewers or sticks for "s'mores" (the campfire "sandwich" of blackened marshmallows and chocolate between two graham crackers, said to have been invented by a Girl Scout in 1927), floated in hot chocolate, melted over mashed sweet potatoes at Thanksgiving, and utilized in such commercial concoctions as MoonPies (see page 212).

The Doumak company started making marshmallows in Los Angeles in 1921. In 1954, Alex Doumakes, son of the firm's Greek immigrant founder, developed a process for extruding marshmallows in the form of long cylinders, which could be easily cut into pieces. This innovation is considered to have revolutionized the marshmallow business. Doumak, Inc. moved to Bensenville, Illinois, in 1961, and today sells marshmallows under the Campfire name—an obvious reference to s'mores—and various private labels.

More interesting are the numerous "artisanal" handmade marshmallows now on the market. Some of the best are sold under the 240Sweet brand out of Columbus, Indiana, a company run by two former caterers, Alexa Lemley and Samantha Aulick. Their marshmallows are completely organic, without preservatives or stabilizers. It should be said, however, that the company doesn't sell a plain white marshmallow; the closest thing to that is its Tahitian vanilla-flavored offering. They're more famous, though, for their scores of more imaginative possibilities—among them carrot and gingersnap, red bean and sesame, and even turkey with sage dressing. One wonders what the Egyptians would have made of that.

The Taste of America

MINT CHOCOLATE

We were great movie-goers, my grade school buddies and me, showing up every Saturday afternoon at the Bruin or the Village or the Picwood in West Los Angeles to sit through the latest double feature. From cowboy epics to monster flicks, all were inevitably accompanied not by popcorn but by candy—frozen Mars Bars, chewy little gumdrop-like Jujubes, and most of all Junior Mints.

Junior Mints—simply gooey mint cream cloaked in dark chocolate—were a gift to the American schoolchild from the James O. Welch candy company of Cambridge, Massachusetts, the same firm that gave us Sugar Daddies, Sugar Mamas, and of course Sugar Babies. (Trivia: Welch's brother and business partner,

Robert Welch, founded the militantly anti-Communist John Birch Society.) Junior Mints are said to have been named in punning reference to a popular Broadway show called *Junior Miss*, based on a series of *New Yorker* short stories by Sally Benson (whose best-known work was *Meet Me in St. Louis*). *Junior Miss* was reputedly one of James Welch's favorite plays. Although the play closed in 1943 *Junior Miss* also became a weekly series on CBS Radio at the time Junior Mints were launched in 1949.

Welch's company, Junior Mints included, was bought by the National Biscuit Company (which became Nabisco) in 1963. Today the brand is owned by Tootsie Rolls.

NEW YORK CHEESECAKE

Cheesecake—a confection based on various kinds of soft, fresh cheese, including ricotta, cheese curd, or cream cheese—is made in various forms all over Europe and in parts of South America. Some are "refrigerator cakes," meaning that they are set in the refrigerator but not baked; some include gelatin, and many are flavored with chocolate, vanilla, fruit, or other additions. Though there are many regional variations in America, most with a crust of crumbs made from graham crackers (see page 33), there seem to be two main kinds sold in bakeries and featuring on restaurant dessert menus: a comparatively low-slung, creamy variety, and a taller kind with a slightly granular texture. The latter version is known as New York cheesecake, and to connoisseurs of such things, principally New Yorkers, there is no finer cheesecake in all the world.

Because cheesecake is in itself a simple dessert, it invites adornment, and New Yorkers fool with it as much as anybody. The classic interpretation, though, is made with just cream cheese, heavy cream, sugar, eggs, and vanilla, with a crust that is more a formality than a noticeable attribute. The celebrated Junior's restaurant, originally from Brooklyn but now with branches in Manhattan and at the Foxwoods Casino in upstate Connecticut, developed a famous version of cheesecake in 1950, and it is still widely appreciated today. Many smaller enterprises make superior versions, though, and one of the best is a small, old-fashioned-looking bakery on Manhattan's Upper East Side called Two Little Red Hens. The cheesecake here is towering, with a perfect brown crust of baked cheese on the exterior and a creamy, rich, very faintly tart filling. It defines the genre.

PEANUT BRITTLE

According to one tall tale told about Tony Beaver, a fictional lumberjack out of West Virginia folklore, peanut brittle was invented when this so-called Paul Bunyan of Appalachia saved a riverfront town from flooding by filling breaches in the levee with peanuts and molasses. In reality, nuts have been preserved in sugar in various forms for centuries, and the almond-based pralines of France and their pecan-studded New Orleans cousins (see page 227) are close relatives of this treat.

Peanuts first became popular in the American South during the Civil War, and the first peanut brittle recipes appeared in regional cookbooks around that time. Brittle is nothing more than hard candy, traditionally made with corn syrup, generously studded with peanuts and broken into shards.

The Vincent family settled in southern Virginia, near the North Carolina border, in the early eighteenth century, and started farming the land. Peanuts arrived in the area around 1830, and they added them to their crops. Peanuts did very well in Virginia (they are now a multi-million-dollar business there), and they soon became the focus of the Vincents' efforts. Today, Lindsey and Scott Vincent operate the Good Earth Peanut Company in the same region, in the town of Skippers. They started the business in 1989, originally boiling peanuts in their home kitchen and selling them mostly to family and friends. Gradually, the company grew and they were able to buy an old Vincent family warehouse and expand their product line to include other nut varieties and an assortment of butters, sauces, and preserves. And they started making peanut brittle using an old family recipe. It's sweet and crunchy and has a very intense flavor of peanuts; a chocolate-dipped version is even better. .

PEPPERMINT STICK ICE CREAM

The most famous savory culinary specialty of the Midwestern metropolis of Cincinnati is goetta, a kind of oatmeal-bound sausage (see page 132); the most famous sweet culinary specialty is Graeter's ice cream. The company produces more than twenty flavors of frozen confections, from chocolate and vanilla to coconut chip and cookie dough. Its Buckeye Blitz ice cream (named after the "Buckeye State" of Ohio, the buckeye being a kind of tree) combines chocolate with peanut butter, peanut butter cookie dough, and chocolate chips. Arguably its most definitive variety, however—and, at least in some quarters, its best loved—is peppermint stick.

The Graeter family came to Cincinnati from Bavaria in the mid-1800s, and young scion Louis Charles "Charlie" Graeter started making ice cream, with a hand-cranked machine that froze the ingredients with rock salt and ice. After marrying, he and his wife, Regina, expanded the operation, producing ice cream and chocolate candy in the back room of their house in the Walnut Hills neighborhood of the city. Charlie died in a streetcar accident in 1919, but Regina carried on, expanding the business and opening several stores around Cincinnati. Her great-grandchildren run the business to this day, operating more than a dozen ice cream parlors in Cincinnati and elsewhere in Ohio and in northern Kentucky.

Graeter's ice cream is astonishingly dense. It is made with French pot freezers, which fold the chilling custard mixture back on itself continuously, forcing out most of the air. The result is that a pint of the finished product weighs almost a pound, or half a kilogram (most commercial pints weigh about 8 ounces, or a quarter-kilogram). Peppermint stick ice cream is a purely American invention. Graeter's makes it only around Christmastime each year, using natural peppermint oil and big shards of handmade peppermint candy. For legions of Cincinnatians, and for anyone else who has been lucky enough to encounter it, Graeter's peppermint stick ice cream virtually symbolizes the holiday season.

PRALINES

The nut-and-sugar confections called pralines take their name from that of Maréchal du Plessis-Praslin (born César, duc de Choiseul), the French diplomat whose cook supposedly invented the recipe as a digestive aid for his master—though the term isn't recorded in print until half a century after the maréchal's death. French pralines are made with almonds and caramelized sugar. Their American counterparts, native to New Orleans, are based on pecans, and have cream added to the sugar to produce something more like fudge than candy. They have been a favorite sweet in this part of the world since at least the mid-1800s, when entrepreneurial black women started selling homemade pralines on the street.

Pierre and Diane Bagur, second-generation French Creoles, opened a shop in the French Quarter of New Orleans in the early 1930s. They wanted to sell the kinds of souvenir, edible and otherwise, that visitors to the city would take home as representative of its culture. Pralines were an obvious candidate for their shelves, and they developed a recipe and started making them in the back of the shop, caramelizing the sugar in a copper pot and pouring out the pralines onto marble slabs. Their grandchildren and great-grandchildren run the business, now known as Aunt Sally's Pralines, to this day. The company produces variations on the theme, including chocolate-covered pralines and a "lite" version with 85 percent less sugar than the classics. It's those classics you want, though—buttery, sugary, and intensely pecan-flavored.

RED VELVET CAKE

A real American cake, the red velvet is related to the rich chocolate-on-chocolate specialty known as devil's food, but with a less chocolatey crumb (though it is flavored with cocoa) and a white frosting. Red velvet cake is so named, in fact, because it is red in hue—anything from dark brownish-red to a bright strawberryish shade. The color came about originally because the cocoa powder it includes contains anthocyanin pigments, responsible for lending numerous fruits and vegetables a red cast; the red color is accentuated when the cocoa is mixed with buttermilk or other acidic ingredients. The hue was particularly vivid before so-called Dutch-process cocoa, which contains an alkaline that lowers acidity, came into common use. Some recipes from the mid-twentieth century call for intensifying the red color with beet juice, and today many recipes include red food coloring.

Red velvet cake is commonly considered to be a Southern specialty, but there doesn't seem to be any firm proof of its origins. It was popular at the Waldorf-Astoria Hotel in New York City, in fact, in the 1920s, long before a lot of Southerners had ever heard of it. It was also well-known in the restaurants at the Eaton's department stores in Canada in the 1940s and 1950s. Some trace the cake's Southern reputation to the 1989 comedy-drama *Steel Magnolias*, set in Natchitoches, Louisiana, which featured an armadillo-shaped version as a groom's cake. (Texas-born singer and actress Jessica Simpson later had a red velvet wedding cake.)

At its best, red velvet cake is moist and dense but not overly sugary, with a subtle glow of chocolate; some versions frost the cake with buttercream icing, but the more traditional—and, I think, better—interpretations use a rich cream cheese icing instead. One of the best, most consistently satisfying red velvet cakes made anywhere is by Very Vera's in Augusta, Georgia. The company is owned by Vera Stewart, a onetime teacher who learned the art of baking cakes from her grandmother. After her two sons were born and she decided to be a stay-at-home mom, she started baking seriously herself, and in 1984 she started a small catering business. This grew into a full-scale commercial operation, turning out both savory dishes and a wide range of cakes and cookies. In my opinion, Very Vera's red velvet cake is her greatest triumph. I especially like that she has made it her own by customizing it with a Georgia touch: toasted pecans scattered over the frosting.

SALT WATER TAFFY

Salt water taffy is not made with salt water. Invented on the Boardwalk in Atlantic City, New Jersey, it is said to have earned its sobriquet after a flood tide inundated a candy shop near the beach, though this sounds suspiciously like folk etymology. Most likely, it was dubbed "salt water" simply because it was sold at the shore. In any case, the name first appears in 1886, shortly after a former glassblower and fishmonger named Joseph Fralinger had taken over a Boardwalk candy shop and perfected a recipe for the chewy, molasses-based candy (the word "taffy" may come from ratafia, an alcohol distilled from molasses). Another candy merchant, Enoch James, refined the recipe and first wrapped it in bite-size pieces in waxy paper. Fralinger, meanwhile, expanded his shop to additional locations, and had the bright idea of selling his taffy, packaged in one-pound (half-kilogram) boxes, as a souvenir of Atlantic City.

Both Fralinger's and James's candy stores, now under one ownership, are still in business, in multiple locations in Atlantic City and elsewhere in New Jersey. Both make a good product, but many taffy-lovers prefer the version made about 10 miles (16 kilometers) down the coast in Ocean City, in the back of Shriver's candy store. Founded by William Shriver in 1898 and owned since 1959 by the Dairy Maid Confectionery Company of Philadelphia (Ocean City was a traditional summer destination for Philadelphians), Shriver's is known for making some of the best chocolate fudge in the region. But its salt water taffy is remarkable: soft and not excessively sweet, with a full range of flavors that don't taste anywhere near as artificial as they obviously are—among them chocolate, vanilla, peanut butter, licorice, molasses, cinnamon, peppermint, and lime. There are seasonal flavours too, including piña colada.

"TURKEY" CANDY

This unique candy from upstate New York—sometimes jokingly called "the world's only legal joint"—has nothing to do with turkey. Turkey Joints are a regional confection in the old-fashioned style, made by a single candy manufacturer, Nora's Candy Shop. They are a cult favorite in Rome, New York, and far beyond, inspiring enthusiastic paeans galore.

Nora's was opened in 1919 by Tasos and Nora Haritatos, and their signature candy appeared soon afterwards. Exactly how Turkey Joints were invented is unclear, but their name comes from the fact that they resemble a bird's bone—sort of. Usually about 3 or 4 inches (7.5–10 centimeters) long, with an irregular, shiny surface, Turkey Joints consist of a thin layer of hard candy, almost iridescent, enclosing a "marrow" filling made of creamy chocolate nougat made with bits of Brazil nuts. Some of these nutty bits poke through the exterior glazing a little, making the bones slightly knobbly in places. The contrast of crisp, easily shattered exterior and soft (though nut-strewn) interior is delightful, and the nuts ennoble the rather ordinary chocolate inside.

Turkey Joints are made by hand and packed, standing vertically, in glass jars. They are traditionally a holiday treat, the holidays in this case meaning both Christmas and Easter, and are shipped from Rome from October through May. A more recent variation on the candy glazes the exterior with chocolate. Purists aren't interested.

WHOOPIE PIE

Picture an overgrown, soft and spongy Oreo cookie, or maybe two cupcakes placed frosting-to-frosting and smooshed together. That's a whoopie pie.

The whoopie pie is a regional American confection. The trouble is, there's controversy over just which region it belongs to. In Lancaster County, Pennsylvania, the Amish claim it as a Pennsylvania Dutch invention, developed out of local baking traditions. No, say the people of Maine—it was created in the Pine Tree State, and has been a staple at Labadie's Bakery in Lewiston, north of Portland, since 1925. In fact, in 2011 the Maine state legislature named the whoopie pie the Official State Treat—not to be confused with the Official State Dessert, which is wild Maine blueberry pie. (There is also a contingent that claims the Boston community of Roxbury as the specialty's birthplace, but let's not get into that.) In response, the Pennsylvania Dutch Convention and Visitors Bureau launched a "Save Our Whoopie," complete with an online petition against Maine's "confectionery larceny."

Just where the name "whoopie pie" came from is another matter for debate, though it seems reasonable to assume that it might derive simply from the joyous reaction of a whoopie-pie-lover when confronted with a whoopie pie.

There is no single canonical recipe for the thing, but any interpretation worthy of the name boasts a high frosting-to-cake ratio (the pie has been described as "a frosting delivery vehicle"). The classic version seems to involve chocolate on the outside and a cream filling within. Some outer layers are the texture of cake or brownies, while others more closely resemble cookie dough.

The Friars' Bakehouse in Bangor, Maine (actually run by two local Franciscan friars) makes excellent whoopie pies. If you prefer Pennsylvania, the versions produced by Coco Love Homemade in Philadelphia are excellent. Back in Maine, Cranberry Island Kitchen in Portland has been praised for its whoopie pies, but they are atypical versions, in the shape of scallop shells, mussel shells, and hearts, among other things.

CONDIMENTS

BARBECUE SAUCE

I love barbecue sauce, but not on barbecue. I'm a purist when it comes to pit-smoked meats, that is. I like Texas brisket seasoned with nothing more than salt and smoke; I like North Carolina pulled pork glistening with apple cider vinegar and dusted with black pepper. That's about it. By "barbecue sauce," I mean a mixture of sweet, acidic, and spicy ingredients, typically including (in various ratios and combinations) ketchup, vinegar, sugar and/or molasses, garlic, mustard, black

pepper, chile powder or flakes, cayenne, and various other spices, sometimes with a little fruit blended in just for fun. I think of it as a tasty condiment for burgers, roast chicken, and a few other things (and I like it as a flavoring; see page 12), but I don't like it messing with the smoke.

Supermarket brands of barbecue sauce are just fine with me. The first of these went on the market back in the early 1900s, under the Georgia Barbecue Sauce Company label. Heinz entered the competition in 1940. My go-to standard, KC Masterpiece, was initially concocted in 1978 by a Kansas City physician and amateur barbecue pitmaster named Rich Davis. (The brand was later spun off into a chain of restaurants, now closed, and has been owned for some years by a division of the Clorox Company.)

The commercial barbecue sauce I like the best right now, however, is Pine Ridge BBQ and Dipping Sauce, made by Herbadashery—a "retirement project" started in 1991 by Barb and Eli Dicklich in Casper, Wyoming, that now includes a catering operation and lines of yard decorations, plants, and garden supplies as well as Pine Ridge products. The story is that a woman named Melissa Armstrong, living on the 28,500-acre (11,500-hectare) Pine Ridge Ranch in Kaycee, about 60 miles (96 kilometers) north of Casper, ran out of the brand-name barbecue sauce her family liked when she was preparing dinner one evening, so she improvised her own. They liked it even better, and she started making it for sale. In 2006, she sold the recipe and name to the Dicklichs, and I'm happy to say that it is now available outside the immediate area. It's not a goopy, ketchup-texture sauce. It flows nicely, isn't overly sweet, has a nice chile bite, and is lively enough to perk up anything it touches. I've even let a few drops fall on raw oysters.

BEACH PLUM JELLY

The beach plum, *Prunus maritima*, grows in sand dunes and salty coastal soil from Maine to Maryland. First identified in 1785, it is considered an almost heraldic New England fruit, evocative of summer cottages and seaside strolls. Both Plum Island, Massachusetts, and Plum Island, New York, are named after it.

Cold-resistant and hardy, the beach plum can be successfully cultivated, but in its wild form, it is being crowded out of its natural habitat by development in many areas. I used to buy beach plums occasionally in August and September at farmstands in eastern Long Island and on Cape Cod, but have seen them less and less in recent years, and they are all but unknown in supermarkets. Residents of and regular summer visitors to portions of Long Island and the New England coast sometimes know where to find beach plums growing, but they tend to be as protective of their secret source spots as any mushroom hunter or trout fisherman is of his or hers.

Beach plums, small and purplish-blue, aren't unpleasant to eat right off the bush—they taste much like so-called Italian prune plums, with a more pronounced tartness—but they're better in the form of jam or jelly. Beach plum jelly, in fact, has long been a staple of home canning in coastal New England, and there are a number of small-scale commercial brands available. (In the early twentieth century, when the fruit was still abundant in the wild, Ocean Spray, the big cranberry packers, used to produce it.) A number of shops on the Massachusetts coast and elsewhere in the region sell beach plum jelly, much of it produced by the same manufacturer. Cold Hollow Cider Mill in Waterbury, Vermont, a hundred miles or more from the nearest ocean beach—a well-known cider producer owned by descendants of Thomas Chittenden, the state's first governor—makes their own excellent example from scratch in a jelly room near their property's original nineteenth-century barn.

A very simple product, beach plum jelly contains nothing more than juice of the fruit, pectin, and sugar. If it's well made, it has a smooth, cohesive texture, with neither flecks of fruit nor liquid pooling in the jar, and is intensely fruity, with a pleasant, puckery bite. Spread on toast with a little unsalted butter, it tastes like summer at the shore.

BOILED CIDER

When Willis Wood's ancestors set up Wood's Cider Mill between Weathersfield and Springfield, in southeastern Vermont, back in 1882, on land the Woods had first settled in 1798, their twin-screw cider press was powered by a water mill. Today, it's run by hand and electricity—but it's the same old-fashioned, indestructible press, capable of turning out about 200 gallons (a little more than 750 liters) of cider at a run. Willis Wood's father grew up on the farm, but left to study engineering and to work in Boston, where Willis was brought

up. As a child and young man, though, he continued to visit the family farm, and learned how to make apple cider, maple syrup, and other traditional products. In the 1980s, he and his wife, Tina, bought the property from a cousin of Willis's great-grandfather, and have operated it ever since, installing their ancient press in a new sugarhouse and cider mill in 2003.

They make excellent cider (including an unpasteurized version which, by law, can be sold only on the farm) and maple syrup, cider jelly, and a once common but now rare old-style condiment called boiled cider. Like cider jelly, boiled cider is a product that has been made and enjoyed in New England since colonial times. Both fell out of fashion as tastes changed, and their production pretty much died out in the twentieth century. Wood's has never stopped making either one. Because both are completely natural, with no added ingredients, they are starting to become popular again with customers who appreciate authentic artisanal products.

Boiled cider starts with apples, primarily McIntosh, some grown on the Woods' farm and some purchased from neighbors, that are pressed into juice. Then they're reduced to a thick syrup in a wood-fired stainless steel evaporator. The result is not overly sweet, but is so intensely apple-like in flavor that it tastes like the soul of the fruit. Boiled cider, which was also once known as "apple molasses," was a great favorite of Shaker cooks, known for their straightforward food traditions. They used it in pies and to add extra flavor to applesauce. It also makes a good glaze for pork or chicken, and can be poured onto ice cream or pancakes to nice effect.

BREAD AND BUTTER PICKLES

Bread and butter pickles are similar to dill pickles—cucumbers pickled in brine—but sweeter in flavor (the brine has sugar added to it). They are also usually sliced before pickling, which can lend them a more intense flavor. While dill pickles, usually brined whole, are a classic garnish for deli sandwiches and other goods, these are the ones that usually get put inside the sandwiches or chopped up in potato salad, tuna salad, and similar deli-case specialties. All the big national pickle-makers have a version of these, but the best are quite possibly those labeled as Hunn's Private Stock Bread & Butter Chips, produced in Garland, Texas, just outside Dallas.

Pat Hunn spent his career in the condiment business, packaging pickles and similar items under the Hunn's Private Stock label. In 2006, his association with the packing plant that

he'd been using ended and he started looking around for someone else to take over the work. He approached another Dallas-area firm, the Goldin Pickle Company, established in 1923, which had become one of the country's leading manufacturers of pickle relish for institutional catering. At first, he was simply going to contract Goldin to pack his pickles, but then the two enterprises discussed a merger. Hunn ultimately purchased Goldin, and renamed it First Place Foods, which is now the parent company of the Hunn's Private Stock brand.

In addition to their sweetness, and to the crisp texture and vinegary tang you'd expect from pickles, Hunn's "chips" have an attractive aromatic flavor—garlic, cloves, mustard seed—that perks up sandwiches, and anything else to which they're added, superbly.

CAESAR DRESSING

Caesar salad is by far the most famous "Italian" salad of our era. Found at almost every Italian restaurant in America and even now some in Italy, it is a staple at American eateries on every level and even a "flavor" to be applied to things that have nothing to do with salad (such as pita chips, almonds, and chicken wings). The amusing thing, of course, is that this "Italian" salad was in fact invented in what I like to call the little Italian hill town of Tijuana, Mexico.

The story has been told a million times. Cesare (or Caesar) Cardini, born near Lago Maggiore in Italy's Lombardy region, immigrated to America in the 1910s. His brothers had earlier left Italy and ended up in Mexico City, where they ran restaurants, and Caesar followed them into the trade, running his own establishments first in Sacramento and then in San Diego. With the advent of Prohibition in 1920, he moved across the border to Tijuana, where alcohol (and so much else) was legal. There, he got married, had a daughter named Rosa Maria, and ran first a restaurant and then, in 1927, a hotel. And invented—probably—what was first called Caesar's salad.

Rosa always said that the salad was improvised at her father's first Tijuana restaurant on July 4, 1924, when an unexpected rush of customers caught Cardini by surprise and he ran out of food for some of his standard dishes. He supposedly quickly improvised the hearty salad, which he tossed tableside, possibly as a distraction to make up for the lack of other menu choices. The exact recipe has been endlessly debated, but it certainly included whole leaves of romaine lettuce—Rosa later said that it was meant to be eaten by hand (maybe Cardini had run out of forks, too?)— tossed with a coddled egg, olive oil, garlic, Worcestershire sauce, grated Parmesan (some sources say Romano), freshly made croutons, and ... Almost everybody says lemon juice, but my Tijuana-born friend Carolynn Carreño, whose father ran a well-regarded restaurant in the city in the 1950s and 1960s and tossed many a Caesar, is adamant that what should be used is lime juice, pointing out that lemons are seldom used in Mexico and that the word *limón* can be applied to either fruit.

In 1948, after Caesar salad had started to become famous, Caesar and Rosa started Caesar Cardini Foods, selling bottled versions of the dressing. The company is now owned by Marzetti, a division of the Ohio-based Lancaster Colony Corporation, which makes specialty food items, glassware, and candles. There are fifteen regular and light dressings in Marzetti's extension of the Cardini line, some of which—raspberry pomegranate vinaigrette, roasted Asian sesame, aged Parmesan ranch— the Cardinis would likely never have imagined. The Original Caesar Dressing is pretty good, as bottled dressings go: thick but not goopy, with a nice level of acidity and garlic. (For a taste of the real thing, visit the revivified Hotel Caesar's, on Tijuana's Avenida Revolución. It was taken over in 2010 by the Plascencia family, who are Tijuana's restaurant royalty, and an absolutely classic Caesar salad is again made there tableside—with lime juice, *gracias*.)

CASHEW BUTTER

One of my favorite places to go when I was a kid in Los Angeles in the 1950s was the Farmers Market, at the corner of Fairfax Avenue and Third Street. This wasn't at all what we think of when we hear that term today. It was a sprawling permanent structure, open-air in some places, filled with food shops (bakeries, butchers, an ice cream shop, a spice merchant, a small all-purpose grocery) and prepared food stands, offering everything from Mexican to barbecue to burgers; a branch of the emblematic Southern California coffee shop chain Du-par's anchored one corner. It was always a lively place, full of color and good smells and interesting things to see. One of the latter was the immense nut-butter-stirring mechanism in permanent operation, visible through a large window, at Magee's House of Nuts. Huge, thick sheets of golden-brown nut butter were stretched and stirred in continuous motion in a big tub by big paddles, a bit like taffy being pulled, but somehow softer and more sensuous. I was fascinated by the sight. My parents usually had to tear me away.

The Farmers Market originally *was* a farmers' market. In 1934, back when much of Los Angeles County was still agricultural, a group of local produce growers started bringing their trucks to what was then a large, vacant plot of land just north of the Wilshire District. Temporary structures were built, then a permanent covered marketplace. The first non-farm business to set up shop there was Magee's. Roy and Blanche Magee had started selling nuts at the Grand Central Market, in downtown L.A., in 1917. Learning of the success of the new farmers' market some miles to the west, they moved their operation there. Since all the original farmers are long gone, Magee's is the Market's oldest tenant.

Magee's peanut butter is superlative, and they also make good macadamia and almond butter. My favorite, though, is their cashew butter, made from top-quality Brazilian cashews. Company publicity points out that cashews are high in proteins and low in saturated fats; a good source of calcium, magnesium, iron, the B vitamins, and zinc; and reportedly good for cardiac health. That's all very well and good, but the best thing about Magee's cashew butter is its flavor: faintly reminiscent of peanuts, but somehow "nuttier," a little sweeter, just salty enough, and positively opulent.

CONSERVES

Anyone who wants to establish definitively the difference between preserves, jam, and conserves will have to consult both culinary manuals and lexicons of regional usage. All involve fruit (or sometimes vegetables), stewed, then canned or otherwise "put up," often with sugar and/or pectin (a gelling agent) added. For preserves, the fruit is often puréed or finely chopped; jam may include larger pieces; conserves are typically made with the fruit more or less intact. But any of these terms may be used to describe any of these styles, in one part of the country or another.

The June Taylor Company in Berkeley, California—no relation to the June Taylor Dancers who were a staple of television variety shows in the 1950s and 1960s—produces conserves, marmalades, fruit butters, and syrups, among other products. The conserves are particularly seductive. Organic, sustainably grown fruit—including heirloom varieties—is sourced from family farms around the San Francisco Bay Area. The fruit is cut into large pieces by hand, then cooked in small batches with only minute quantities of sugar (organic

sugar, need we specify?) added, sometimes along with complementary herbs. Instead of adding pectin, the company extracts natural pectin from the fruit's own seeds and membranes. Conserves are hand-poured into jars and letterpress labels are applied by hand. The package looks very "artisanal."

You won't find standard flavors here. June Taylor conserves include tayberry (a Scottish cultivar not unlike our loganberry, though sweeter); Triple Crown blackberry and lemon thyme; blackberry with lemon verbena; strawberry with rose geranium; strawberry with Provençal lavender; Summer Sweet peach with Greek bay leaf; and Rose Diamond nectarine with white sage blossom, among many others. (The particulars change according to season, and from year to year.) Maybe best of all, though, is Burbank plum, Meyer lemon and Altar rose geranium, combining a sweet, luscious, *plummy* plum with an aromatic acidity that keeps the conserve this side of cloying. Taste this, or one of its cousins, and you'll never want another brand again.

CREAMED HONEY

Since medieval times, Catholic monasteries and convents around the world have been making food and drink products to sell for self-support—everything from cookies and candies to wines and liqueurs. One traditional monastery specialty has always been honey, and for whatever reasons (I've been unable to find an explanation), American monasteries from one coast to the other seem to be particularly interested in making one specific form of this ancient sweetener: creamed, or whipped, honey.

Conventional honey contains large crystals of glucose, which over time will clump and solidify. (If you've ever dipped into a jar of honey that's been around for a while, you'll know what I'm talking about.) In 1928, a Canadian-born master beekeeper named Elton J. Dyce (who later became director of Cornell University's honeybee program)

developed a method of whipping and pasteurizing honey to reduce the size of the crystals. The smaller crystals then prevent the reformation of larger ones so that the honey turns opaque and remains soft and spreadable, not dissimilar to a thickened version of creamed butter.

Excellent creamed honey is produced by the Cistercian nuns at Redwoods Monastery, founded in 1962 by four sisters from Belgium in the remote Northern California community of Whitethorn, near Eureka. (For its isolation, the area is known as the Lost Coast.) The nuns use Grade A clover honey, and package it both plain and with the addition of organic flavorings and essences (orange, lemon, ginger, almond, and cinnamon). The plain variety has flavor enough for me—a floral, grassy character that spreads across the palate as easily as the honey spreads on to toast.

HONEY

Honey is an emblem of sweetness (and in the Anglo-Saxon world, at least, of endearment), so it is perhaps indelicate to mention that honey is basically nectar regurgitated by bees. There is considerable variation from one honey to the next precisely because it *is* nectar, which carries floral characteristics unique to the plant that produced it. Orange blossom honey really does taste a little like how orange blossoms smell; chestnut honey really does have some of the meaty bitterness of chestnuts. Most commercial honey doesn't possess much recognizable flavor because it is usually blended from several sources. So-called monofloral honey, however, made with the help of bees who have visited only one kind of plant, can evoke the savors and aromas of the subject fields and orchards vividly.

Rick and JoAnn Wallenstein have left little doubt as to what their specialty is: their property in Petaluma, in California's Sonoma County, is called the Lavender Bee Farm. Here, the couple grows three varieties of lavender, to be dried and sold commercially: English, Provençal, and lavender grosso. For the past decade or so, they have also tended about eighty beehives, stocked with more than three million wild-caught bees, producing about 100 pounds (45 kilograms) of honey in a single year.

The Wallenstein bees aren't fed artificially: only 40 percent of the honey is removed from the hives at a time, leaving them plenty with which to nourish themselves. And the honey that is extracted from the honeycombs is done so without heat, commonly used in larger operations, so the honey retains a fresher flavor. It really does have a haunting scent of lavender, too, and finishes clean, with a lingering echo of perfume.

HOT SAUCE

I have a friend who carries a bottle of Tabasco in a custom-made leather case, slightly smaller than something you'd keep your sunglasses in, every time he goes out to eat. In his opinion, there are very few foods, regardless of cuisine, that do not benefit from being anointed with this vinegary, pleasantly spicy condiment. The world is full of hot sauces, but there is probably no other that inspires passion and loyalty across a broad spectrum of fans as much as this one: Tabasco has long been included in U.S. military rations; American astronauts demand it in space—apparently they begin to lose their sense of taste after a few days out of the earth's atmosphere, and crave Tabasco's fire and acidity; and an Australian aficionado went on TV and drank two bottles of it in thirty seconds, securing a place in the *Guinness Book of World Records*.

Tabasco was created by Edmund McIlhenny, a Maryland-born banker who prospered in New Orleans until the Civil War, fled to Texas with the Confederate Army, and ended up after the conflict living on Avery Island, Louisiana, just southwest of New Iberia—a salt dome surrounded by bayous and marshland, owned by the Avery family, McIlhenny's in-laws. McIlhenny tended the family garden on the island, growing tabasco chiles, among other fruits and vegetables, and at some point in the late 1860s he concocted what he eventually called Tabasco Brand Pepper Sauce. He went on to patent it in 1870. McIlhenny himself, who died in 1890, apparently didn't realize how large a market there might be for his invention, but his sons did. They built a large business that remains family-owned to this day, producing not only Tabasco sauce but six other hot sauces under the Tabasco label, including ones flavored with chipotle, jalapeño, and habanero chiles.

Until the 1960s, all the chiles used in Tabasco were grown on Avery Island. Some still are, but most are produced under contract on farms throughout Central America, using seeds propagated on the island. Tabascos, like most chiles, ripen from green to red, and the workers who hand-harvest them for the company carry a small red stick with them; chiles ripe enough for harvest match the stick's color. The chiles are ground and salted—mines on Avery Island supplied salt to the Confederates and still provide at least a portion of what is used for Tabasco—and the mash is aged in old oak whiskey barrels for three years in island warehouses. Finally, it is mixed with vinegar, aged another month, and bottled.

Classic Tabasco sauce is not particularly spicy, measuring no more than 5,000 Scoville units (the cult favorite Dave's Insanity Sauce clocks in at 180,000 units, by comparison), but it has a good flavor and imparts a mild burn to the palate, nicely outlined by acidity. It makes a great secret ingredient to stews and sauces, perks up grilled meats, and is an indispensable ingredient in any good Bloody Mary.

JALAPEÑO JELLY

Spicy foods often work well with a counter-point of sweetness added; an excellent example of this blending of sensations can be found in jelly made from the juice of jalapeño chiles. This is a popular condiment in Texas and other Southern states, served alongside meats, on crackers with cream cheese as an hors d'oeuvre, and even simply spread on toast.

The definitive commercial version of this sugar-and-fire specialty is Braswell's, made not in Texas but by the A. M. Braswell Jr. Food Co. in Statesboro, in eastern Georgia. The firm got its start just after World War II, when Albert Braswell returned home to Georgia from the service with a GI Bill but no job. His mother made excellent pear preserves, and he thought there might be a local market for them. He

borrowed her recipe, bought fruit from local growers, hired a local couple to help him peel, slice, and cook the fruit, then canned the preserves and sold them out of the back of his truck. His business grew from there, and today Braswell's has about a hundred employees, producing almost a million cases of preserves, jellies, and other condiments out of a 100,000-square-foot (9,290-square-meter) facility. Braswell's son, Al Jr., took over the company after his father's death. Today the business is run by a four-man team, which includes Al Jr.'s stepson, Frank Farr, and Braswell's produces a wide range of condiments, many based on Georgia-grown products (Vidalia onion preserves are a specialty).

Braswell's Hot Jalapeno Jelly has a vaguely fanatical following, for good reason. Unlike some chile-based jellies, it has some real heat, and the sweetness isn't cloying. It tastes like good jalapeños lightly glazed with sugar, then turned soft—a very pleasant sensation. The folks at Braswell's, in fact, like to say that the product is "out of this world." Indeed, the astronaut Jeffrey Williams, though he's a Wisconsin boy with no particular Southern connection, was so enamored of the Hot Jalapeno Jelly that he requested, on three separate occasions, that it be stocked in the pantry for his visits to the International Space Station.

KETCHUP

In 1981, as a federal cost-cutting measure, John Rusling Block, the Secretary of Agriculture in the Reagan administration, proposed classifying pickle relish and ketchup as vegetables in the national school lunch program. The outcry against this proposal was quick and loud, and the measure was never implemented—although my daughters seemed to regard ketchup as a vegetable until they reached high school, and I suspect ours was not the only household in which this was true.

Until it was surpassed, in the early 1990s, by salsa (see page 256), the seasoned, barely pourable tomato-based sauce called ketchup was undeniably the all-American condiment. The Germans and the English ate mustard, the Asians ate soy sauce, and we ate ketchup. I doubt that most of us realized (or realize still), though, that ketchup has Asian origins, and for centuries had nothing to do with tomatoes at all. The word itself may derive from the Chinese *kôe-chiap*, meaning a sauce of brined fish. Sauces of this type, with similar names, migrated to other Asian destinations, and became particularly popular in Malaysia, Indonesia, and neighboring countries, where they were known as *kicap* or *kecap* (pronounced "kichap"), a direct ancestor of the word "ketchup." British soldiers discovered the sauces there and brought them home, and by the late eighteenth century, they had become a staple in England. There were versions still made with seafood, including anchovies and oysters, but also variations based on pickled mushrooms, walnuts, cucumber, and other

foodstuffs. The earliest tomato-based ketchup dates from around 1800.

Colonists brought ketchup to America, where the tomato version became popular enough that by the late 1830s, it was being sold commercially. Henry Heinz, the son of German immigrants to Pennsylvania's Allegheny River Valley, was relentlessly ambitious as a youngster, hawking vegetables door to door at the age of eight and selling hand-filled bottles of horseradish sauce that he'd made according to his mother's recipe when he was nine. He continued selling produce and sauce after graduating from college and going to work at his father's brick factory, and in 1869, established his first company, with that horseradish sauce as its focus. The company went bankrupt, but Heinz started again in 1876, this time adding a tomato ketchup to his product line. His enterprise thrived, and of course it is still going strong today.

Though the H. J. Heinz company currently sells—never mind "57 Varieties"—hundreds if not thousands of products, under its own and other labels, it remains best known for that ketchup, moving more than 650 million bottles a year worldwide. Heinz may or may not be the best ketchup on the market, but it is the one to which all the rest are inevitably compared. It's sweet, with an acidic overtone and a faint suggestion of cloves, and it has a vivid ripe-tomato taste. Even the federal government can't make it a vegetable, but, for better or for worse, it will probably always be a definitive part of the American diet.

MAPLE SYRUP

Pancakes, waffles, and French toast were often seen on our family breakfast table when I was a boy, and on the table with them were also big golden-yellow ingots of Adohr butter and oblong aluminum cans of Log Cabin maple syrup, cans actually shaped and imprinted with faux-timbers to resemble miniature log cabins. It was labeled "pure maple syrup," if I remember correctly, though I have lately read that it was apparently never quite that (the maple syrup it contained seems to have been mixed with cane syrup). All I knew was that it was wonderfully viscous and sweet and tasted like something intense and genuine. It remains one of the most vivid flavor memories of my childhood.

Maple syrup is the boiled and filtered sap of the black, sugar, or red maple tree, tapped straight from the source for a month or two in late winter and early spring each year throughout the Northeast and in parts of the Midwest. Vermont and New Hampshire are particularly known for their maple syrup. The process of extracting the sap and turning it into a foodstuff was developed by Native Americans many centuries ago. The lore was passed on to early European settlers, and the syrup became a staple of the colonial household.

Today, maple syrup is graded A or B, with the former subdivided into three classifications: light amber, medium amber, and dark amber. (Vermont uses a slightly different grading system.) As you might expect, grade B syrup is less expensive than grade A, but it's often the most flavorful and, if you will, "maple-y" kind. Owners Don and Dorrie Upton—who have devoted their retirement (Don was an agricultural cooperative manager) to making what *Yankee Magazine* called "the best syrup in New England" a few years back—don't produce grade B syrup at their Monadnock Sugar House at the base of Mount Monadnock, near Jaffrey, New Hampshire. But their dark amber A is pure maple joy, evocative of snowy woods and forest smells, and family breakfast on the table.

MAYHAW JELLY

All but unknown outside a handful of Southern states, the mayhaw—the berry that grows on trees of the genus *Crataegus*—is a small red or yellow fruit with yellow flesh that tastes rather like a very tart apple. Call it the cranberry of the South, if you will, because like that northern fruit, it grows in wetlands (though on trees rather than low bushes) and is too acerbic to be eaten plain. Like the cranberry, though, it yields juice that is delicious with a little sugar added (it is also sometimes fermented into wine), and makes a bright-hued, bright-flavored jelly that was once much appreciated in traditional households, particularly in East Texas, Louisiana, and Georgia. It is a spring fruit—a mayhaw grower in Texas once told me, "They ought to call them aprilhaws, because they're mostly gone by May"—and several Southern communities celebrate its annual appearance.

Miller County, in southwestern Georgia, is the heart of that state's mayhaw country, and there, in the town of Colquitt, a company called The Mayhaw Tree, founded in 1983 by social worker Joy Jinks and three other local women to bring employment to this impoverished region, produces a textbook-perfect example of mayhaw jelly. In some parts of the South, mayhaws have been grafted onto hawthorn trees, to which they are related, and grow on dry land. The Mayhaw Tree, though, harvests wild mayhaws growing in marshy land, either picking them by hand or scooping fallen ones out of the water with fishnets. Based on a recipe dating from the Civil War, the fruit is boiled and pressed to produce a coral-colored juice, then mixed with sugar and pectin to produce a jelly that deftly balances tart and sweet. As it says on the lable, this is definitely "a Southern tradition."

MAYONNAISE

It's impossible to imagine many classic American sandwiches—the BLT, the club, tuna salad, egg salad, the lobster roll, and so on—without the simple condiment called mayonnaise. Likewise such staple side dishes as coleslaw and potato salad. (It's also an unlikely "secret ingredient" in some cake recipes.) In its simplest form, mayonnaise is an emulsion of olive oil and eggs, with salt and a little vinegar and/or lemon juice added. Theories of its origin and the etymology of its name abound, but it was probably invented in the mid-eighteenth century by a French chef, his identity long since forgotten, in the port of Mahon, on the Spanish island of Menorca—a town whose name in the local language is Maó, thus "mayonnaise."

The English, who had occupied Menorca throughout the eighteenth century when it was not temporarily in French and/or Spanish hands, were eating mayonnaise, and calling it that, by the 1820s, if not earlier, and it was known in America by the late nineteenth century. The first commercial mayonnaise sold in the now familiar glass jars was Mrs. Schlorer's brand, which appeared in Philadelphia in 1907. In 1912, a Manhattan deli owner from Germany, Richard Hellmann, began selling a version, made according to his wife's recipe, under the Hellmann's label. Another well-known mayonnaise is Best Foods, originally produced by a company that, in the words of one financial Web site, traces its origins to "a number of nineteenth-century flaxseed, cottonseed, and flour-milling businesses." Best Foods made a mayonnaise that was particularly popular west of the Rockies. In 1932, it bought the Hellmann's

brand, but because Hellmann's was well established in the eastern portion of the country, the decision was made to continue marketing it there under that name. Thus, what is basically the same mayonnaise is sold in many states as Hellmann's and in many others as Best Foods. (Some tasters have maintained that there is a slight difference between the two products, with Hellmann's being a touch sweeter and Best Foods a little more tart or acidic.)

The best of the commercial mayos, however, may well be a regional contender, Duke's, from Richmond, Virginia. This one originated in 1917, when Eugenia Duke, a housewife in Greenville, South Carolina, began assembling sandwiches with her homemade mayonnaise for soldiers stationed at nearby Fort Sevier. The doughboys started asking for her mayo recipe, and a local drugstore asked if they could sell her sandwiches ready-made. Soon, a Greenville grocery store was selling bottles of her mayonnaise. As her business grew, Duke expanded from her kitchen to a larger building, and, according to company lore, on the day she assembled her eleven thousandth sandwich, she invested in a delivery truck. Soon, she gave up sandwich-making and concentrated on bottling the mayo. In 1929, Duke sold her operation to the Richmond-based C. F. Sauer Company, which hired her as its chief salesperson and which continues to manufacture the mayonnaise according to her recipe (whose ingredients include soybean oil and cider vinegar) to this day. Duke's is a bright-flavored mayonnaise, not at all sweet, with a pleasant tang. I think it's the next best thing to homemade.

MISO

Miso is produced by fermenting soybeans, barley, and/or rice with salt and a variety of mold called *kōji* (*Aspergillus oryzae*), also used in the production of sake and soy sauce. With the help of the miso soup served in every Japanese restaurant and of Nobu Matsuhisa's famous black cod with miso, imitated all over America in restaurants Japanese and otherwise, miso has become a familiar condiment in this country. It is also a staple of the macrobiotic diet, popularized for Americans by Michio Kushi in the 1950s. In a sense, Kushi and his wife, Aveline, are the godparents of the best miso made in America—Three-Year Barley Miso from South River Farm in Conway, Massachusetts, in the Berkshire foothills.

South River's proprietors, Christian and Gaella Elwell, met while studying at Kushi's macrobiotic institute in Brookline, Massachusetts, in 1976 (the institution is now in Becket, in the same state). There, they ate miso soup every morning for breakfast, and liked both its flavor and its apparent health-giving properties. Since the only miso available in the U.S. at that time was imported from Japan, they began wondering whether they could produce it themselves. They heard about Asunaro, a "school of Oriental medicine and fermented foods" founded by Naburo Muramoto in Glen Ellen, California, and went there to learn how miso was made. Back in Massachusetts, they bought 60 acres (24 hectares) of farmland on the South River, planted an assortment of cereal crops and legumes, and began producing miso of their own. As it happened, another American with a miso-making bent, Thom Leonard, whom the couple had met at Asunaro, started his own small miso production facility in Ohio in 1979. When he was unable to make a go of it, he sold his equipment to the Elwells, and this allowed them to go into business on a full-scale commercial basis.

Today, using centuries-old Japanese farmhouse traditions, the Elwells produce more than 60 tons (54 metric tons) of miso annually, in a number of varieties—including, besides Three-Year Barley, such examples as Hearty Brown Rice, Chickpea, Azuki Bean, and Golden Millet. Three-Year Barley, made with well water, organic barley, soybeans, sea vegetables, sun-dried sea salt, and *kōji* culture, is aged over three summers. Dark brown in color, it is a particularly substantial miso, with a complex flavor that is lightly earthy, faintly vegetal, and just salty enough. It is remarkably versatile in the kitchen, making a great glaze or marinade for meat, fowl, and seafood; an essential ingredient for many Asian noodle dishes (and a great "secret ingredient" for Italian ones); a nice addition to baked beans and other vegetable dishes; and of course the heart of a classic Japanese soup—the dish that started the Elwells on their path in the first place.

MUSTARD

There must be hundreds of "artisanal" mustards made in America, not to mention the many mainstream brands (French's, Gulden's, Grey Poupon, and so on). They come flavored with Napa Valley wines, craft beer, balsamic vinegar, and every variety of fruit you can imagine. A lot of them seem to come from New England, for some reason. I'm not a great mustard-lover myself, but I tend to think that if you're going to eat mustard, it should taste like mustard and not like Chardonnay or kiwi fruit, and I also tend to think that it should be good and hot. That's why I'm partial to the hot mustard sold by Philippe's in Los Angeles.

As any student of American vernacular eating probably knows, Philippe's is (as they proudly bill themselves) the "home of the original French dip sandwich." It is also one of the oldest restaurants in L.A., dating from 1908 (though it did move once, in 1951, to make room for a freeway). Philippe's—the pronunciation of the name is a matter of some disagreement, but as an old L.A. boy, I've known for decades that it's "fil-IPP-eez"—was established as a neighborhood sandwich shop, downtown, by a French immigrant named Philippe Mathieu. The story is that he was making a roast beef sandwich for a cop one day when he accidentally dropped the French roll he was using into the pan juices from the recently roasted meat. The cop wanted it anyway, and the next day came back with friends, all wanting their sandwiches "dipped." (They're called "French" either because of the roll or in reference to Mathieu's nationality; nobody remembers.) In 1927, the restaurant was bought by Harry, Dave, and Frank Martin, three brothers who ran a livery stable nearby. Their family still runs it today.

Philippe's is self-service. There are ten lines, each manned by a "carver" who makes the sandwich or serves up other food, such as salads, soups, breakfast dishes, chili, beef stew, and desserts. Everything is on paper plates. There are long communal tables, ceiling fans, and sawdust on the floor. Coffee is 45 cents (about 27 pence).

The restaurant prepares about 40 gallons (150 liters) of hot mustard twice a week. A lot of this gets slathered on the sandwiches, but it is also available for sale at Philippe's and by mail order. It is straightforward, medium-dense, very mustardy, and, as mustard goes, very spicy. Some observers have maintained that there's horseradish in it, and others that it's just Colman's powdered mustard mixed with something hot. The ingredient list, though, reads simply, water, mustard seed, vinegar, salt, spices, xanthan gum. That seems about right to me.

OLIVE OIL

The first olive trees in the New World were brought to Mexico by the Spanish in 1524, but they didn't travel north, into what was then called Alta California, until Franciscan friars brought them along in the late eighteenth century, planting them at nineteen of the twenty-one missions they established along the California coastline. The Franciscans made oil, but it was the olives themselves, frequently canned, that became most important as cultivation spread around California and grew into a commercial concern. (The state is by far the largest producer of olives in America.) It wasn't until the 1980s that entrepreneurs with an artisanal bent began to try to make extra-virgin oil that could compete with the best of Italy or Spain in California.

They haven't really succeeded. As one California-based olive oil expert puts it, "The producers keep following the directions in the recipe, but the oils keep coming out just so-so." An exception, I'd say, is McEvoy Ranch olive oil, which is pretty terrific. So is the story behind it. Proprietor Nan McEvoy is San Francisco Bay Area nobility, the granddaughter of Michael De Young, who founded the *San Francisco Chronicle* in 1865 and for whom the city's De Young Museum is named. McEvoy joined the newspaper staff as a young woman, and worked her way up to chairwoman of the board in 1981, a position she held until her retirement in 1995.

McEvoy had bought a 550-acre (about 220-hectare) ranch in Petaluma, in Sonoma County, in 1991, and after reading a book on olive oil, she met with a Tuscan oil expert, Maurizio Castelli, and began importing olive seedlings from Tuscany. Today, the ranch grows about 18,000 trees in 82 acres (33 hectares) of groves, yielding about 4,000 gallons (15,000 liters) or so of oil annually, making McEvoy the largest certified organic oil producer in California. The oil is pressed on the property, in a state-of-the-art Rapanelli mill (the ranch also custom-presses for smaller growers). McEvoy's signature Traditional blend comprises six Italian varieties (Frantoio, Leccino, Pendolino, Maurino, Leccio del Corno, and Coratina), the first two of those accounting for about 85 percent of the oil. It comes out greenish-yellow in color, rich, peppery, and nutty, without too much bite—and it's a whole lot better than so-so.

ORANGE MARMALADE

The history of orange marmalade begins in Ancient Greece, with another kind of fruit entirely: quince. Greek cooks discovered that the long, slow process of boiling quince pulp with honey would yield a dense, solidified jelly. This was thanks to the fruit's high concentration of pectin, the gelling agent in jams and jellies, though they didn't know that then. The technique spread throughout the Mediterranean, and quince paste became a popular accompaniment to cheese. The Spanish word for quince is *membrillo*, and the same term describes the paste, which remains popular to this day. The Portuguese word for the fruit is *marmelo*, and they call their paste *marmelada*—hence "marmalade" for any thick fruit preserve.

When we think of marmalade, of course, we think of bitter oranges. That's thanks to an eighteenth-century Scottish confectioner from Dundee named James Keiller. According to the lore, Keiller had ordered a shipment of sweet Valencia oranges from Spain, but the bitter Seville variety arrived instead. His wife supposedly had the brilliant idea of turning them into preserves, with sugar added to moderate their sharpness. (Like quince, bitter oranges have a high pectin content.) This tale has been pretty much discredited—among other things, there are written references to orange marmalade about 120 years before Keiller set up shop—but the Dundee merchant did indeed popularize this bittersweet condiment, and it is still sold, in decorative crocks, under the James Keiller & Sons label.

Darrell Corti is a legendary Sacramento, California grocer—the kind of grocer who speaks four or five languages and knows as much as anyone in America about subjects as diverse as Chinese tea, Iberian fortified wines, Italian pastry, and French digéstifs. In fact, there seems to be very little about food and drink that he doesn't know; his colleagues admiringly call him "the professor."

Corti has great respect for tradition in the production of alcoholic beverages and foodstuffs alike, and often has items made according to his specifications, to be sold bearing the Corti Brothers private label. One example is Corti Brothers Capital Vintage Marmalade, which he first produced in 1980. Its name, he explains, is a pun on the word "Capital, since Sacramento is California's capital," but also in the British English sense of top-quality or first-rate. The marmalade is made according to a recipe from the 1860s that Corti found in the celebrated *Mrs Beeton's Book of Household Management*, perhaps the most famous of British cookbooks. The Corti version is made with Seville oranges—picked from trees in the streets of Sacramento—with sugar and water added, nothing more. It is "vintage" because it is aged for about a year in its jars before sale.

Corti's marmalade is thick, chunky, and dark; its hue is far from the sunny yellow-orange of most commercial marmalade. It has a bitter-orange flavor that is undeniably intense, but not acrid; the aging mellows it superbly.

PEANUT BUTTER

We once did a blind tasting of peanut butters at *Saveur* magazine, including all the popular supermarket brands plus some of the newer, supposedly more "natural" ones. About a dozen editors and other staff members took part. Usually when we had tastings of this kind, there was some kind of consensus, but in this case, there was widespread and dramatic disagreement. When the samples were unmasked, we realized that almost everybody had given top honors to whichever brand he or she had grown up with. Peanut butter, we decided, quite possibly more than any other food, really was the taste of home for anybody growing up in America.

Indeed, peanut butter can claim America as its home. There were antecedents: the Aztecs ground peanuts into a kind of paste, and a Canadian confectioner named Marcellus Gilmore Edson was granted a U.S. patent in 1884 for a commercial version, to be used in the manufacture of candy. But peanut butter to be eaten in much the same form we eat it today was patented in 1895 by Dr. John Harvey Kellogg, the physician and nutritionist who went on to inspire the famous cereal empire that bears his name (see pages 190 and 194). A vegetarian who preached the meatless gospel to his patients, he promoted what his patent described as "a pasty adhesive substance that is for convenience of distinction termed nut butter" as a meat substitute.

Peanut butter just for fun was introduced to a general audience at the Louisiana Purchase Exposition, a World's Fair in St. Louis, in 1904. Local manufacturers went on to sell it in Ohio and California. In the latter state, the peanut butter market was established by one Joseph Rosefield, who developed a process for homogenizing it so that the oil didn't separate. His creation later became Peter Pan peanut butter, and another company he started morphed into Skippy. A true peanut butter pioneer, Rosefield also made the first crunchy version, adding crushed peanuts back into his homogenized product. The popular Jif brand, owned by Procter & Gamble, dates from 1958.

By that time, the Philadelphia-born, California-based entrepreneur Laura Scudder (see page 12) was already making peanut butter of her own—and incidentally the product that I liked best at the *Saveur* tasting was one sold under her label. I enjoy smooth peanut butter, but prefer the crunchy variety, and in that regard, I'm still a Laura Scudder loyalist. The brand's organic "nutty" peanut butter contains nothing but organic roasted peanuts and a little salt—other brands include palm oil and sugar, among other ingredients—and I think it's good enough to eat right out of the jar.

PICKLED GHOST PEPPERS

Brooklyn is something of a pickle capital, with artisanal producers such as the Brooklyn Brine Company, a small-batch-pickle outpost of McClure's of Detroit, and local branches of The Pickle Guys and Guss' Pickles joining old-school producers like Clinton Hill Pickles, Mr. Pickle, and Ba-Tampte. Newcomers Chris Forbes and Evelyn Evers only started their Brooklyn-based business, Sour Puss Pickles, in 2009, but have already made a name for themselves not just with traditional-style dill and bread-and-butter pickles (see page 237) but with a range of pickled vegetables, including garlic scapes, lemon cucumbers, and ramps (see page 176). They also preserve several varieties of chiles, including the legendary ghost pepper, or *bhut jolokia,* mainly cultivated in northeastern India and Bangladesh, which was briefly touted a few years back as being the hottest chile in the world. (Though they have been measured at just over one million on the Scoville scale, these chiles have since been surpassed in firepower by varieties including the Infinity, the Trinidad Moruga Scorpion, and the Naga Viper.)

Forbes and Evers buy the chiles from Eckerton Hill Farm in Lobachsville, Pennsylvania, just northeast of Reading. This enterprise was started in 1995 by management consultant and writer Tim Stark, who grows an estimated one hundred kinds of tomato and at least forty varieties of chile, and has written a book about his adventures called *Heirloom: Notes from an Accidental Tomato Farmer.* The chiles, packed in 16-ounce (about 450-gram) jars, are then pickled in apple cider vinegar diluted with filtered water and seasoned with sea salt, sugar, cardamom, cloves, black peppercorns, and various other spices. The pickling process doesn't exactly ameliorate the fire of the chiles, but it puts the spiciness into perspective, and makes the ghosts much more palatable than they are on their own—trust me.

The Taste of America

RANCH DRESSING

In the mid-twentieth century, there were four salad dressings commonly encountered in restaurants: vinaigrette, or oil and vinegar; French (an orange-hued, sweet tomato-spiked glop unknown in the land of Molière and Bardot); Roquefort (dense and chunky and often made with a cheaper blue cheese than its name would suggest); and Thousand Island (basically Russian dressing with more "stuff" chopped up in it). Prime rib joints and steak houses sometimes added Green Goddess— a kind of herbed mayonnaise invented in San Francisco in the 1920s—to the mix, and that was about it. Then, in the early 1970s, seemingly out of nowhere, something called ranch dressing started flowing onto our salads. This was a creamy, sourish blend of mayonnaise and buttermilk seasoned with various herbs and spices, garlic definitely among them. By the middle of the following decade, it had become ubiquitous, found on every menu, in every salad bar. It pretty much sent French and Thousand Island packing. It even ended up becoming an official "flavor," applied to corn chips, potato chips, sunflower seeds, actual mayonnaise—even, believe it or not, dental floss.

Where did this phenomenon come from? From the Hidden Valley Guest Ranch in the hills behind Santa Barbara. This was the property of Steve and Gayle Henson, a colorful couple who came to California from Alaska, where Steve had made good money in the plumbing business. The ranch was famous for its steak dinners, and one day Steve improvised a salad dressing out of ingredients at hand to go with the accompanying greens. His guests loved it, so he started selling the flavoring mixture in foil packets, for them to mix with buttermilk and mayonnaise at home. The ranch faltered financially, but in 1972, the Clorox Company approached the Hensons and bought the recipe and the Hidden Valley name, reportedly for $8 million ($44 million or £27 million, in today's money). The company reworked the formula, among other things substituting buttermilk flavoring for the real thing, and hit the market with it in a big way.

There are a number of commercial brands of ranch dressing available today (Clorox owns "Hidden Valley" but not, obviously, "ranch"), and Hidden Valley alone offers numerous variations on the theme. I can't honestly say that I notice a great deal of difference between the various brands available, and I don't eat ranch dressing often, but when I do, I like to pay tribute to the dressing's origins and buy the Hidden Valley foil packets, still available, that allow you to mix your own, preferably with the best buttermilk and mayonnaise (see page 248) available.

SALSA

The big news in the condiment world back in 1991 was that sales of salsa had overtaken those of ketchup in dollar volume in America, and it hasn't looked back since. Exactly how you define "salsa," of course, is open to question; the word simply means "sauce" in Spanish. But the term is generally used in this country today to describe some combination of chopped raw vegetables and sometimes fruit, the quintessential salsa being some variation on what is known in Texas and parts of Mexico as *pico de gallo* (rooster's beak) or *salsa fresca* (fresh sauce)—the traditional ingredients of which are onions, chiles, and tomatoes. This salsa goes wonderfully with all kinds of food, not only tacos, enchiladas, quesadillas, and other *antojitos* (street snacks), but simply cooked meat, fish, and fowl as well.

There isn't much reason for anybody living any place where fresh produce is available to buy pre-made *pico de gallo*, but if you have to reach for a supermarket brand, the one I've found that comes closest to homemade is sold under the Santa Barbara label. This was originally made by Craig Bigelow, a colorful character in that eponymous Southern

California seaside town. In the 1970s, Bigelow ran a local restaurant called the Head of the Wolf, which became a kind of literary salon, frequented by such folk as Raymond Carver, Kenneth Rexroth, and Thomas Sanchez. He later expanded the place and renamed it Gallagher's. He also ran a clothing store, Bigelow and Santry.

In 1984, Bigelow decided to make and package his own *pico de gallo*. He did all the work himself at first, and gradually built the product into a successful California supermarket brand. In 1998, Bigelow—who died in 2006—sold the business to California Creative Foods. Today the brand belongs to the Sabra Dipping Company, better known for its hummus and other Mediterranean products.

Bigelow always said that he could make better salsa in California than others could in other places because he had year-round access to great produce. I'm not sure where all the ingredients in Santa Barbara Pico De Gallo come from today, but I know that even in the winter months, it's full of fresh-tasting vegetables, with just enough heat to make it interesting.

SEA SALT

The waters off Downeast Maine, the south-eastern corner of the state, from Penobscot Bay up to the New Brunswick border—and especially the portion closest to the Bay of Fundy—were once one of the richest fishing grounds in North America. In the days before refrigeration, much of the fish landed there was preserved in salt, and accordingly, saltworks flourished in the area, capturing and evaporating seawater to produce mineral-rich sodium chloride. In the twentieth century, with the advent of ever faster and more efficient methods of packing and shipping seafood, and the corresponding depletion of Atlantic fisheries, the saltworks closed one by one.

Sea salt has become an essential condiment on American tables today, of course. We buy pricey gray *fleur de sel* from France, flaky Maldon from England, and exotic colored salts from every other corner of the world. Sea salt is rarely refined as table salt is—some people say that the comparison between the two products is like that between whole wheat and white bread—and so it typically contains traces of many minerals (iron, calcium, zinc, and magnesium among them) and tends to have a bright, complex flavor. In its purest form, it is indisputably a natural, organic product.

It's little wonder, then, that American entrepreneurs are now beginning to produce sea salt. Stephen C. Cook's family was in the lobstering business, and in the 1950s opened the still-thriving Cook's Restaurant (now Cook's Lobster House) in Garrison Cove, on Bailey Island, Maine. He became a lobsterman himself, but in 1998, observing the rising popularity of sea salt and knowing something of its past in Maine, he decided to try producing it himself. He studied the art of salt extraction, formed the Maine Sea Salt Company—the state's first new saltworks in two centuries—and released a trial product, which he called "salt for cooking lobster." It sold well, so he expanded his range. His natural sea salt, now made in solar salt houses in Marshfield, is a so-called Celtic-style salt, gray and clumpy like *fleur de sel*, and absolutely alive with the bite of the sea.

SEASONING MIX

I wonder whether the classic Baltimore seasoning mix, Old Bay, would have become as enduringly popular if it were still being marketed under its original name, Delicious Brand Shrimp and Crab Seasoning. The herb and spice blend was invented by a German immigrant to Maryland named Gustav Brunn, sometime in the 1940s, and while of course the recipe is "secret," it has long since been revealed that it includes mustard, paprika, black pepper, red pepper, cloves, cinnamon, allspice, nutmeg, cardamom, mace, ginger, celery seed, and bay leaf, plus salt. Brunn wasn't exactly a pioneer; crab was so plentiful and cheap around the Chesapeake Bay in those days that bars offered it to patrons for free, and several local companies had already formulated seasoning blends with which to boil them by the time Brunn came along with his recipe.

Brunn's version became particularly successful, however, especially after he renamed it "Old Bay" after the Old Bay Line of passenger ships that sailed between Baltimore and Norfolk, Virginia, in the early twentieth century. In 1990, the McCormick & Co. spice company bought the brand, and continues to sell it in the original yellow canister, with the mix's flavor unchanged, as far as I can tell. In Baltimore and vicinity, Old Bay is still widely considered essential for a crab boil, but it has many other uses as well. Folks sprinkle it on popcorn, French fries, and corn on the cob; it gets mixed into the flour to coat fried chicken; and Pennsylvania-based Herr's Snacks uses it to season their excellent Old Bay potato chips.

SORGHUM SYRUP

On back roads around the South and parts of the Midwest, you'll sometimes pass little makeshift stands selling mason jars full of a dark amber substance—"Sorghum," according to the signs propped up against the jars. What on earth is sorghum? I wondered this the first time I saw one of these purveyors. Silly me.

So-called grain sorghum is a relative of millet, native to Africa but now grown not just throughout that continent but also in Asia, the Middle East, Europe, and the Americas. It is the third most important cereal crop in the United States in quantity (after corn and wheat), and the fifth most important in the world. Believed to have been introduced to U.S. soil by Benjamin Franklin, grain sorghum is a hardy crop, flourishing in poor soil and requiring a minimum of care. Though it is a staple part of the diet in many parts of Africa, in America it is grown mostly as a forage crop for farm animals or used by the ethanol industry for conversion into biofuel (it thrives in drier, hotter regions where corn doesn't do very well). The variety called sweet sorghum, however, which (not surprisingly) has a particularly high sugar content, is sometimes made into a dense molasses-like syrup, and that's what is in those roadside jars. The syrup is sometimes sold as molasses, in fact, though molasses is technically made from sugarcane (or sometimes sugar beets).

Sorghum syrup—used on pancakes, biscuits, or grits (see page 195), or in baking—isn't sold exclusively on back roads. Some of it is available through specialty food shops and mail-order sources. One that's comparatively easy to find, and very good, comes from the Barry Family Farm east of Cridersville, Ohio. The Barrys bought a plot of exhausted farmland in 1994, nourished the soil and banned the use of chemicals from the property, and began growing a variety of fruits and vegetables. In 2000, they opened an on-site cannery to produce jams and preserves, and began making sorghum syrup from a small planting of the grain they'd grown. The syrup's flavor recalls that of molasses, with a hint of honey-like floral character, but it lacks the bitterness molasses can have. If maple syrup (see page 246) is, as it is often described, a taste of New England, sorghum syrup is the flavor of rural America slightly to the south and west.

SPIEDIE MARINADE

Spiedies consist of meat that's cut into pieces, marinated, skewered, grilled (preferably over charcoal), and then served on a long, soft Italian roll. (The traditional method of removing the meat from the skewer is by using the split roll as a kind of glove, grasping the meat with it and then pulling out the skewer with the other hand.) Extra marinade is typically added as a sauce. Though they pop up here and there around the country, spiedies are basically a regional specialty of Binghamton, New York, south of Syracuse, near the Pennsylvania border, and the surrounding territory.

The name is a corruption of *spiedo*, Italian for spit or skewer, and the original spiedie was lamb marinated in olive oil, vinegar, garlic, lemon juice, and mint, threaded on a skewer, and then grilled. The first spiedies were probably served by an Abruzzese immigrant named Camillo Iacovelli, at a restaurant called the Parkview Terrace in Endicott (the so-called "birthplace of IBM"), a few miles west of Binghamton, in the 1930s. Camillo's brother, Agostino—"Augie"—opened his own place, Augie's, in the same town in 1939, and ended up getting a lot more publicity for spiedies than his brother had received. Another local restaurateur, a Ukrainian immigrant named Peter Sharak, also served spiedies at his Sharkey's Bar & Grill (still operating) in Binghamton itself, though apparently not until some years after Augie's introduced the specialty. (Sharkey's nonetheless calls itself the "home of the spiedie.")

Today, meats other than lamb are commonly found in spiedies, chicken most of all, but also sometimes beef, pork, even venison; other variations on the theme are on display annually at the Spiedie Fest and Balloon Rally in Binghamton. Of course, every spiedie-maker, amateur and professional, has his or her own marinade/sauce recipe, which invariably is "secret."

The first person to bottle the marinade was Rob Salamida, who started making spiedies at the New York State Fair in Syracuse in 1963. In 1975, after a tornado swept through the fair and came close to destroying his stand, he gave up spiedie-making to concentrate on selling his sauce, originally bottling it at home on his parents' pool table (which he thoughtfully covered with plywood). Today, his State Fair Spiedie Sauce, made in a 15,000-square-foot (about 1,400-square-meter) plant, is the best seller in the category. A sharp, peppery condiment with plenty of garlic and a nice edge of vinegar coming through, it works well on just about any kind of poultry, meat, or seafood.

SRIRACHA SAUCE

You find it on restaurant tables—Vietnamese, Thai, and otherwise—all over America: a distinctive, stocky, green-topped bottle, its brilliant red contents showing through, and its exterior bearing a depiction of a rooster, text in four languages (Chinese, Vietnamese, Spanish, and English), and the legend "Sriracha HOT Chili Sauce"—presumably to ensure that you don't get the wrong idea. What you may not realize, as you generously apply this medium-hot, slightly sharp, faintly garlicky, and salty-sweet condiment to your food, is that it was formulated and is produced not in some distant land but in Rosemead, California, just east of Los Angeles.

Sriracha seems to borrow its name from Si Racha, a coastal town in central Thailand, where hot sauces of a similar nature are popular. This one, however, got its start in 1980, when an ethnic Chinese immigrant from Vietnam named David Tran, who had been a farmer near Saigon, took $50,000 in family savings (about $140,000, or £86,000 today), and opened a small shop to manufacture a sauce according to his own tastes. He originally made it with serrano chiles, but he decided that he preferred the sweetness and intensity of red jalapeños—that is, those that have been allowed to ripen on the vine, developing a fuller flavor and a little more heat than green ones typically have. He dubbed his enterprise Huy Fong Foods, after the Taiwanese freighter that had taken him from Vietnam to Hong Kong on the first step of his journey to America. The bird on the label signifies that he was born in the Year of the Rooster, according to the Chinese zodiac.

Chiles for the sauce are harvested in the fall, when they have grown glowingly red, at farms both north and south of Los Angeles. The chiles are mashed and processed with machinery modified by Tran. Today, with a new 23-acre (9-hectare) factory in Irwindale, just northeast of Rosemead, and with Tran's son, William, handling day-to-day operations, Huy Fong turns out about twenty million bottles of sauce a year.

DRINKS

APPLE CIDER

Kansas, it must be said, does not immediately come to mind as an apple-growing state. Washington is by far the largest producer of the fruit, with New York and then Michigan as rather distant runners-up, while the United States Department of Agriculture (USDA)'s statistical breakdown of apple production hasn't even listed Kansas since 2005. But of course in food, as in so many other things, quantity and quality don't always go hand in hand, and Kansas apples can be as crisp and aromatically delicious as anyone's, whether eaten as nature yields them, cooked in a pie, or pressed into cider. And the cider that comes out of the Louisburg Cider Mill, near the Missouri border just south of Kansas City, is about as good as it gets.

Cider in America, it must be noted, isn't like cider in Europe. We use the term more or less interchangeably with "apple juice." Some states do make a legal distinction for labeling purposes, specifying that juice is filtered and pasteurized while cider is cloudy and pretty much as it comes out of the press—but there is no consistency in such definitions, so some cider may be perfectly clear. Louisburg's isn't. It's dense, almost murky in appearance, though in flavor it's crystal clear: It tastes like really good apples, period.

The Louisburg folks don't grow apples, but they source them from commercial orchards, primarily from along the Missouri River north of Kansas City. The cider is made by traditional methods in a 120-plus-year-old barn that was restored and converted into a cider mill in 1977. Arriving in 1,000-pound (450-kilogram) crates, the apples are washed, and then fed into a hammermill, which shreds them into a pulpy substance called "pomace." This is layered between large cloth mesh sheets, then squeezed in a hydraulic press at 3,500 pounds of pressure per square inch (about 24,000 kilopascals). The juice is next pumped into cooling tanks, rested for a few days, and then bottled. Chilled (not too much), and poured into a glass, it seems the very soul of apples.

BIRCH BEER

Though far less common than its cousin, root beer (see page 270), birch beer is similarly a carbonated soft drink or soda flavored with various roots and herbs. The main difference is that birch bark oil, which is highly aromatic, is the overriding flavor. Though there are a dozen or more brands available around the northeastern United States (about the only place where people drink much of it), the birch beer market is pretty much owned by the Boylan Bottling Company of Teterboro, New Jersey. This is as it should be, because it was a New Jersey pharmacist named William Boylan who first concocted it, back in 1891, as a patent medicine that he christened Boylan's Birch.

In 1900, as soft drinks were becoming popular in America, Boylan launched a bottling company. The onset of Prohibition in 1920 was good for business, and Boylan sold vast quantities of what he called Boylan's Draught Birch Beer. After repeal, the Boylan family switched their attentions to the distribution of real beer and spirits, and sold their recipes and customer list to Frank Fiorina, who had worked as a delivery driver for the firm. Fiorina focused on the birch beer, selling it all over Passaic County, New Jersey, but not much farther afield. His grandsons inherited the company in the mid-1970s, and expanded the business to include a full line of fountain syrups. Throughout the 1990s, they successfully rolled out one new soft drink after another, but the company's Birch Beer—made, like all Boylan sodas, with cane sugar, not corn syrup—remains at the heart of the firm's success. It is serious stuff, with a forthright herbaceous heft, a slight medicinal tinge, and a ghost of mint.

CELERY TONIC

The legendary columnist Walter Winchell once dubbed Dr. Brown's Celery Tonic "Jewish champagne." Supposedly created by a physician named Brown in the Williamsburg section of Brooklyn in the 1860s, the sugary, carbonated tonic—like so many other soft drinks of the time—was a kind of transitional beverage between patent medicine and soda pop. The oil of celery seeds was an ingredient of some early elixirs (scientists have demonstrated that it might actually have some value in lowering blood pressure) and Dr. Brown's formula used it liberally. It has been suggested that the eponymous doctor originally created his tonic for immigrant children on Manhattan's Lower East Side, recognizing that their diet was probably not very healthy. However, it ended up finding its greatest popularity among adults in the Jewish delis of New York as early as 1869. Some connoisseurs found it the ideal accompaniment to a pastrami sandwich (see page 136); many still do.

Dr. Brown's Celery Tonic was first sold in bottles, filled by the local Scholz Bottling Company, in 1886. It was successful enough to encourage imitations, and for a time there were numerous celery tonics on the market. Only Dr. Brown's, however, survived the turn of the nineteenth century. In the early 1900s, the Food and Drug Administration asked Dr. Brown's to stop using the term "tonic" for its celery soda. It was promptly renamed Cel-Ray. The New York American Beverage Company bought Scholz in the 1920s and continued to bottle Dr. Brown's until 1967. The brand was later bought by the Canada Dry Bottling Company of New York. (There are other soft drinks in the Dr. Brown's line, including a good cream soda.) Dr. Brown's Cel-Ray is an acquired taste, to say the least. It really does have the flavor of celery, with a peppery heat that suggests a sort of vegetal ginger ale and a light, almost citrusy finish.

COFFEE

Hawaii used to be the only U.S. state where coffee trees grew; now an exotic fruit orchardist in Santa Barbara, California, has had limited success with them. But Hawaii remains America's coffee-growing capital. There were early plantings of coffee on Oahu as early as 1813, and it was later cultivated around Hilo on the "big island" of Hawaii, but it flourished in neither location. In 1828, though, a missionary named Samuel Ruggles transplanted some cuttings from Hilo to the volcanic slopes of the Kona district on the opposite side of the island, and here the trees found a home.

Kona coffee is medium in body and intensely aromatic, with a recognizable flavor that is faintly chocolately but clean and almost angular. It is one of the most expensive coffees in the world, both because the production is small and because it is perceived as being particularly elegant. The persistence of its character may be seen from the fact that a great deal of "Kona blend" coffee is sold, in which the Hawaiian beans are cut with lesser, usually Central American varieties; something of the Kona personality always shines through.

Founded in 1997 by Marin and Cathy Artukovich on the slopes of Mauna Loa, the Koa Coffee Plantation is one of almost 800 coffee farms on the island of Hawaii (there are now some successful growers on Kauai and Molokai as well). The trees grow at an elevation of around 2,700 feet (about 820 meters), considered ideal for coffee, and the site's cloudy afternoons and frequent rainfall retard maturation—which is a good thing, because the beans develop more flavor the longer they remain unpicked.

The Koa Coffee Plantation is known for its rare Peaberry Kona. Most coffee cherries (as the unprocessed fruits containing the beans are called) contain two face-to-face flat beans; about one in twenty, or even less, contain a single oval-shaped bean, called a peaberry. These have a more intense flavor than the other beans, and coffee made

exclusively from them has been called "the champagne of Kona." The farm does so well with its peaberry coffee, in fact, that it even buys in single berries from other growers. A freshly (and properly) brewed cup of Koa Peaberry Kona is a marvel of subtlety and flavor; rather than the champagne of Kona, I'd call it the grand cru Burgundy.

COLA

What can be said about Coca-Cola? That it is by far the most popular soft drink in the world? That Coca-Cola has been called the most valuable *brand* in the world? That it is the most prominent symbol of American cultural imperialism, advertised and consumed in corners of the world where even McDonald's fears to tread? That it has a unique flavor, instantly identifiable, and is as much a part of life in these United States as our language or our flag?

Well, there is more to be said, of course. Here are a few things: First, Coke (that most eminent of nicknames) was invented in about 1865 by a Georgia pharmacist named John Stith Pemberton, originally in the form of an alcohol- and coca-laced kola-nut-flavored patent medicine that he hoped would help him kick the morphine habit he had acquired as a wounded Confederate veteran. Second, the formula evolved over the years, losing first its alcohol, then, in progressive stages, its coca—though the recipe still includes coca leaves with the cocaine extracted. Third, Coca-Cola was originally distributed only as a syrup, and individual soda fountains added their own carbonation, but in 1891, a candymaker in Vicksburg, Mississippi named Joseph Biedenharn became the first-ever Coke bottler. Fourth, the secret formula for Coca-Cola was held in the vault at the main branch of SunTrust Bank in Atlanta for eighty-six years, but now resides at the World of Coca-Cola museum in the company's Atlanta head-quarters. Finally, the New Coke, introduced in 1985, was a very bad idea.

GINGER ALE

Carbonated ginger-flavored beverages date back at least to the early nineteenth century in Europe, and by the 1860s, ginger ale had become a popular beverage in the United States. Sidney Lee, a wholesale grocer in Birmingham, Alabama, developed his own variation on the drink in 1901. Working with a chemist named Ashby Coleman, Lee originally marketed it as a ginger tonic to cure stomach ailments. It became popular locally not just as a curative but as a soft drink. Lee gave it the fanciful name Buffalo Rock, and it became his principal product.

Though the distinction is rarely made on labels these days, there are two styles of modern ginger ale: golden and dry. The latter is most common, a comparatively light, refreshing substance with a noticeable but somewhat subdued tang of ginger. While it's a pleasant soft drink, it also makes a good mixer for vodka, gin, and other alcohol. Golden ginger ale is darker in color, a bit sweeter, and considerably more pungent— more "gingery"—very much like ginger beer. Buffalo Rock's ginger ale is golden (though they apply the term only sporadically)— serious, full of flavor, and in general better for drinking straight than for mixing (though it does make a splendid float, with a big scoop of good vanilla ice cream).

Today, Buffalo Rock is still run by the Lee family, and in addition to producing their definitive ginger ale, the company is one of the country's largest privately owned bottlers of Pepsi-Cola and other soft drinks considerably more popular, though arguably with less character, than their namesake product.

ROOT BEER

Root beer, along with variations on the theme like birch beer (see page 265) and sarsaparilla, can trace its history back to the colonial era, when roots and herbs and barks of various kinds were boiled in water as a way of making it safe to drink. The resulting brews were frequently fermented into low-alcohol beer, the alcohol having a further purifying effect. Not surprisingly, it was a temperance advocate who created a non-alcoholic version. He was a Philadelphia pharmacist named Charles Hires, who supposedly had the idea for root beer in something approximating the modern sense when he was served "root tea" on his honeymoon in New Jersey. He mixed up his own formula in dry form and sold it to soda fountains, where water, sugar, and yeast were added.

It sold slowly until he served a liquid version of what he had decided to call root beer at the U.S. Centennial Exposition in Philadelphia in 1876. Encouraged by his friends in the anti-alcohol movement, he described it as "The Temperance Drink"—and bottled root beer did end up becoming enormously popular as a beer substitute during Prohibition.

The Hires brand of root beer is still sold, now under the ownership of the Dr Pepper Snapple Group, but it has a fairly generic flavor. There are a number of other national brands—among the best known are Dad's, A&W, and Barq's—and a surprising number of small regional bottlings. I've counted more than seventy-five different root beer labels myself, and I'm sure I'm missing some. Root beer recipes tend to be fairly complex, including things like sassafras, licorice, spruce, balsam, burdock, wintergreen, hoja santa, hops, fennel, nutmeg, even sometimes chocolate—among many other things. In a good root beer, no one flavor predominates, though suggestions of licorice, mint, and something indefinably medicinal are common.

Among regional brands, I'm partial to Frostop root beer, which I discovered years ago in a convenience store in Detroit on a hot August evening when I was looking for something cool and flavorful to slake my thirst. Having grown up with Dad's, I remember being surprised at how rich and mysterious the Frostop variety tasted—not too sweet, but with a lot going on, including what I thought of as a rather oaky taste. Frostop, I later learned, was developed by one L. S. Harvey, who opened a root beer stand called Frostop, in Springfield, Onio, in 1926. That stand grew into a national chain of drive-ins, some of which still exist, though they are now individually owned. It's worth watching for one, or looking for Frostop in convenience store coolers.

SOFT DRINK

Dr Pepper has never become a mega-brand (or a symbol of Yankee commercial hegemony) on the order of its slightly younger counterpart, Coca-Cola (see page 268), but it's an American original, born about 1885 at a drugstore soda fountain in Waco, Texas, and now enjoyed by soft-drink lovers all over the country and beyond. Dr Pepper doesn't taste like anything else; it's not a cola or a root beer; there are suggestions of fruit in its savor (I've always thought I detected a soupçon of prune juice)— but it's a long way from being a fruit drink. It's just a mellow, complex, very satisfying draught with a faint hint of spices (cinnamon?) and a modest caffeine kick. (Dr Pepper's famous, cryptic advertising slogan "10 2 4," was inspired by research undertaken at Columbia University in the 1920s, which found that the body's blood sugar tended to drop, sapping energy, at 10:30 a.m., 2:30 p.m., and 4:30 p.m. every day, and that a jolt of sugar taken half an hour before those times could obviate the symptoms.)

Like many other soft drinks, the original Dr Pepper was strictly a fountain drink, concocted to order with syrup and seltzer water. The first bottling plant was opened not quite 100 miles (160 kilometers) northwest of Waco, in the Texas town of Dublin, in 1891. It's still going strong—though as of early 2012, it no longer produces the soft drink. In the 1980s, when other Dr Pepper bottlers started sweetening it with high-fructose corn syrup instead of cane sugar, the Dublin plant decided to keep using cane sugar, and their version of the drink, proudly labeled Dublin Dr Pepper, became a cult favorite. Too much of a cult favorite for Dr Pepper Snapple Group, the main Texas bottler, apparently; they took the Dubliners to court and won a suit forcing them to stop producing Dr Pepper. That has left a bad taste in the mouths, as it were, of Dr Pepper lovers, whether they were used to drinking the Dublin version or not.

SPARKLING CIDER

In Europe, cider sparkles because it is fermented; the interaction of sugars in the apple juice with yeast produces alcohol and carbon dioxide, the latter of which animates the apple juice with bubbles. (The same thing happens with champagne.) In America, where cider is mostly non-alcoholic, sparkling cider is made by artificially carbonating the juice, no alcohol involved. Though there are some smaller brands of sparkling cider—including Belfast, first made in San Francisco by Irish immigrants, and now, mysteriously, very popular with the city's Chinese community—the most famous and most popular sparkling cider is Martinelli's, from the California apple capital of Watsonville, in Santa Cruz County.

When the company's founder, Stephen G. Martinelli, who had come to the region from Ticino, Italian-speaking Switzerland, in 1859, started producing cider in 1868 from locally grown apples, it was in the European tradition, alcohol most definitely included, and was described as "champagne type." (Cider with alcohol is known generically in the U.S. as hard cider.) In 1890, the cider won a gold medal at the California State Fair, and ever since then the brand has been known as "Martinelli's Gold Medal" (it has received more than fifty at various competitions since then). Martinelli's son, Stephen Jr., developed a method for making non-alcoholic sparkling cider, and the product became popular during Prohibition. The business is still family-owned today.

Martinelli now bottles a range of still ciders and juices, combining apple with other fruits. They have considerable competition in the juice business, but their sparkling cider—clean, clear, sweet but not cloying, and genuinely bright with apple flavor—virtually owns the bubbly segment of the market. Perhaps for that reason, company spokesmen say that, despite renewed interest in hard cider in America, they have no plans to re-enter that arena.

TEA

Americans are better known for dumping tea into Boston Harbor (and, more recently, for forming a rag-tag political party whose name commemorates that dumping) than for drinking the stuff. We do consume tea, of course, and it was an American tea merchant named Thomas Sullivan who invented, for better or for worse, the tea bag, but we drink far more coffee than we do tea; we use about three-quarters of a pound of tea (about a third of a kilogram) per capita each year and just over 9 pounds (4 kilograms) of coffee. Anyway, most people realize that this country produces coffee, in Hawaii (see page 267), while we don't grow tea. Or do we?

Well, yes, we do. Tea plants were first brought to these shores as early as 1722, when they were cultivated in coastal Georgia; they reportedly grew well, but were neglected and died out. In 1799, a French botanist installed more tea plants near Charleston, South Carolina, where they likewise did well—but nobody successfully cultivated them on a commercial basis until 1888, when Dr. Charles Shepard started growing them on his Pinehurst Tea Plantation in Summerville. In the early 1900s, the Pinehurst tea bushes were transplanted to a property in Rantowles, just west of Charleston.

The plants survived well into the twentieth century, albeit becoming a little overgrown, and when the Thomas J. Lipton tea company set up a research station on Wadmalaw Island, just to the south, they were transplanted there, along with more bushes from the original Pinehurst plantings. The tea plants flourished under Lipton's care until 1987, when a Lipton manager, Mack Fleming, and a third-generation, British-trained tea taster named William Barclay Hall took over the 127-acre (51-hectare) property, renamed it Charleston Tea Plantation, and branded a signature product they called American Classic Tea. The partnership dissolved in 2003, but the R. C. Bigelow company, the massive Connecticut-based tea producer that produces the popular Constant Comment, bought it and formed a new partnership with Hall.

Charleston Tea Plantation is one of only two commercial tea plantations in America, and though it has added flavored teas to its line, including one called Governor Gray (as opposed to Earl Grey), American Classic Tea remains its claim to fame. A rich black tea, well balanced and medium-dark, it has a light floral sweetness and finishes with a mild astringent bite. This is not one to toss overboard.

DIRECTORY OF PRODUCERS

SNACKS

Barbecue Potato Chips
Diamond Foods, Inc.
503-364-0399
www.kettlebrand.com

Black Walnuts
Hammons Products Company
888-429-6887
www.hammonsproducts.com

Boiled Peanuts
The Lee Bros. Boiled
Peanuts Catalogue
843-720-8890
www.boiledpeanuts.com

Cheese Crackers
The Center
800-939-3720
www.gingersnapsetc.org

Cheese Straws
McEntyre's Bakery, Inc.
1184 Concord Road Southeast
Smyrna, GA 30080
770-434-3115
www.mcentyresbakery.com

Corn Chips
PepsiCo, Inc.
800-352-4477
www.fritos.com

Cracklings
Kim's Processing Plant, Inc.
417 Third Street
Clarksdale, MS 38614
662-627-2389

Macadamia Nuts
The Hershey Company
808-966-8616
www.maunaloa.com

Olives
Graber Olive House
315 East Fourth Street
Ontario, CA 91764
800-996-5483
www.graberolives.com

Pecans
Oren's Kitchen
510-847-6265
www.orenskitchen.com

Pearson Farm
888-423-7374
www.pearsonfarm.com

Pistachios
Fiddyment Farms
563 Second Street
Lincoln, CA 95648
916-645-7244
www.fiddymentfarms.com

Popcorn
Pinnacle Foods Inc.
888-310-3747
www.timschips.com

BAKED GOODS

Bialys
Kossar's Bialys
367 Grand Street
New York City, NY 10002
212-253-2138
www.kossarsbialys.com

Biscuits
Callie's Charleston Biscuits
1895 Avenue F
North Charleston, SC 29405
843-577-1198
www.calliesbiscuits.com

Common Crackers
Vermont Common Foods, LLC
802-775-4111
www.vermontcommonfoods.com

Corn Tortillas
Luna's Tortillas, Inc.
214-747-2661
www.lunastortillas.com

Doughnuts
Congdon's Doughnuts Family
Restaurant & Bakery
1090 Post Road, Route 1
Wells, ME 04090
207-646-4219
www.congdons.com

Flour Tortillas
La Abuela Mexican Foods, Inc.
800-229-0140
www.la-abuela.com

Fry Bread
Red Corn Native Foods
918-287-3899
www.redcorn.com

Graham Crackers
Potters Fine Foods, LLC
608-663-5005
www.potterscrackers.com

Kolaches
Weikel's Store & Bakery
2247 West State Highway 71
La Grange, TX 78945
979-968-9413
www.weikels.com

Matzo
Aron Streit, Inc.
212-475-7000
www.streitsmatzos.com

Meat Pie
Runza National, Inc.
800-929-2394
www.runza.com

New Orleans Beignets
Café du Monde
800 Decatur Street
New Orleans, LA 70116
504-525-4544
www.cafedumonde.com

Pasties
Pasty Central, LLC
877-727-8911
www.pasty.com

Potato Knishes
Yonah Schimmel Knish Bakery
137 East Houston Street
New York City, NY 10002
212-477-2858
www.knishery.com

Pretzels
Martin's Pretzel Bakery
1229 Diamond Street
Akron, PA 17501
717-859-1272
www.martinspretzelspa.com

Saltines
Mondelēz International, Inc.
www.nabiscoworld.com

San Francisco Sourdough Bread
The Acme Bread Company
1601 San Pablo Avenue
Berkeley, CA 94702
510-524-1327
www.acmebread.com

Savory Palmiers
La Tulipe Desserts
455 Lexington Avenue
Mount Kisco, NY 10549
914-242-4555
www.latulipedesserts.com

Schnecken
Busken Bakery, Inc.
2675 Madison Road
Cincinnati, OH 45208
513-871-2114
www.busken.com

DAIRY PRODUCTS

Ash-Coated Soft-Ripened Cheese
Andante Dairy
www.andantedairy.com

Bandage-Wrapped Firm Cheese
Fiscalini Cheese Company
7231 Covert Road
Modesto, CA 95358
209-545-5495
www.fiscalinicheese.com

Bread Cheese
Carr Valley Cheese Company, Inc.
S3797 County G
La Valle, WI 53941
608-986-2781
www.carrvalleycheese.com

Butter
Five Star Butter Co.
702-987-0113
www.fivestarbutter.com

Canned Cheese
Washington State University
509-335-4014
www.cougarcheese.wsu.edu

Cheese Curds
Ellsworth Cooperative Creamery
232 North Wallace Street
Ellsworth, WI 54011
715-273-4311
www.ellsworthcheesecurds.com

Cream Cheese
Mondelēz International, Inc.
www.kraftbrands.com/philly

Crème Fraîche
Kendall Farms
805-466-7252
www.kendallfarmscremefraiche.com

Creole Cream Cheese
Mauthe's Progress Milk Barn
601-542-3471
mauthefarms.blogspot.co.uk

Double-Cream Soft-Ripened Cheese
Sweet Grass Dairy
19635 US Highway 19 North
Thomasville, GA 31792
229-227-0752
www.sweetgrassdairy.com

Extra-Aged Firm Cheese
Uplands Cheese Company, Inc.
888-935-5558
www.uplandscheese.com

Fresh Cheese
Mozzarella Company
2944 Elm Street
Dallas, TX 75226
214-741-4072
www.mozzco.com

Mild Blue Cheese
Berkshire Cheese, LLC
413-842-5128
www.berkshirecheese.com

Mild Firm Cheese
Matos Cheese Factory
3669 Llano Road
Santa Rosa, CA 95407
707-584-5283

Mild Goat Cheese
Emmi Corporation
707-825-1100
www.cypressgrovechevre.com

Mild Semi-Firm Cheese
Meadow Creek Dairy
6380 Meadow Creek Road
Galax, VA 24333
276-236-2776
www.meadowcreekdairy.com

Mild Semi-Soft Cheese
Mid-Coast Cheese Company
209-826-6259
www.franklinscheese.com

Pimento Cheese
Blackberry Farm
1471 West Millers Cove Road
Walland, Tennessee 37886
800-557-2203
www.blackberryfarm.com

Sheep's Milk Yogurt
Old Chatham Sheepherding Company
155 Shaker Museum Road
Old Chatham, NY 12136
888-743-3760
www.blacksheepcheese.com

Strong Blue Cheese
Maytag Dairy Farms
641-792-1133
www.maytagdairyfarms.com

Strong Firm Cheese
Beecher's
1600 Pike Place Market
Seattle, WA 98101
206-956-1964
www.beechershandmadecheese.com

Strong Sheep's Cheese
Beaver Brook Farm
139 Beaver Brook Road
Lyme, CT 06371
860-434-2843
www.beaverbrookfarm.com

Strong Goat Cheese
Rians
707-996-4477
www.laurachenel.com

Strong Semi-Soft Cheese
DCI Cheese Company
262-677-3407
www.dcicheeseco.com/liederkranz

Strong Soft-Ripened Cheese
Rians
7500 Red Hill Road
Petaluma CA, 94952
800-292-6001
www.marinfrenchcheese.com

Triple-Cream Soft-Ripened Cheese
Cowgirl Creamery
Tomales Bay Foods
80 4th Street
Point Reyes Station, CA 94956
866-433-7834
www.cowgirlcreamery.com

FISH & SHELLFISH

Abalone
Catalina Offshore Products, Inc
5202 Lovelock Street
San Diego, CA 92110
619-704-3639
www.catalinaop.com

Blue Point Oysters
Blue Island Oyster Company
631-563-1330
www.blueislandoyster.com

California Lobster

Catalina Offshore Products
5202 Lovelock Street
San Diego, CA 92110
619-704-3639
www.catalinaop.com

Anderson Seafoods
714-777-7100
www.andersonseafoods.com

California Spot Prawns
Farm-2-Market
800-477-2967
www.farm-2-market.com

Canned Tuna
Katy's Smokehouse
740 Edwards Street
Trinidad, CA 95570
707-677-0151
www.katyssmokehouse.com

Caviar
TNC Holding Comapany
415-543-3007
www.tsarnicoulai.com

Copper River Salmon
Seattle Fish Company
4435 California Avenue SW
Seattle, WA 98116-4108
206-938-7576
www.seattlefishcompany.com

Crab Cakes
Chris' Marketplace
301-565-1681

Dungeness Crab
i love blue sea
415-300-0940
www.ilovebluesea.com

Finnan Haddie
Stonington Seafood
536 Sunshine Road
Deer Isle, Maine 04627
207-348-2730
www.stoningtonseafood.com

Florida Stone Crabs
Joe's Stone Crab
11 Washington Avenue
Miami Beach, FL 33139
305-673-0365
www.joesstonecrab.com

Geoduck
Taylor Shellfish Farms
Seattle Melrose Market
1521 Melrose Avenue
Seattle, WA 98122
206-501-4321
www.taylorshellfishfarms.com

Hot Smoked Trout
Sunburst Trout Farms, LLC
128 Raceway Place
Canton, NC 28716
828-648-3010
www.sunbursttrout.com

Lobster Stew
Hancock Gourmet Lobster Company
207-725-1855
www.hancockgourmetlobster.com

Maine Lobster
Lucky Catch Lobster Company
207-773-4103
www.luckycatchlobster.com

Maine Shrimp
Wild Edibles, Inc.
Grand Central Market
Lexington Avenue at 43rd Street
New York City, NY 10017
212-687-4255
www.wildedibles.com

Olympia Oysters
Taylor Shellfish Farms
Seattle Melrose Market
1521 Melrose Avenue
Seattle, WA 98122
206-501-4321
www.taylorshellfishfarms.com

Quahogs
The Lobster Guy
Ferry Wharf Fish Market
296 Great Island Road
Narragansett, RI 02882
866-788-0004
www.thelobsterguy.com

Rainbow Trout
Pure Food Fish Market
Pike Place Market
1531 Western Avenue
Seattle, WA 98101
206-622-5765
www.pikeplacemarket.org
www.freshseafood.com

Rock Shrimp
Wild Ocean Seafood Market
688 South Park Avenue
Titusville, Florida 32796
321-269-1116
www.wildoceanmarket.com

Shad Roe
Captain Marden's Seafoods
279 Linden Street
Wellesley, MA 02482
781-235-0860
www.captainmardens.com

She-Crab Soup
Bost Distributing Co., Inc.
919-775-5931
www.bostdistributingcompany.com

Smoked Catfish Paté
Taste of Gourmet
The Crown
112 Front Street
Indianola MS 38751
662-887-4522
www.tasteofgourmet.com

Smoked Mullet Spread
Walt's Fish Market
and Restaurant
4144 South Tamiami Trail
Sarasota, FL 34231
941-921-4605
www.waltsfish.com

Smoked Salmon
Acme Smoked Fish Corporation
30-56 Gem Street
Brooklyn, NY 11222
718-383-8585
www.acmesmokedfish.com

Smoked Salmon Jerky
SeaBear Company
360-293-4661
www.seabear.com

Smoked Weathervane Scallops
SeaBear Company
800-858-0449
www.gdseafoods.com

Soft-Shell Crab
Harbour House Crabs
1170 Eisenhower Boulevard
Harrisburg, PA 17111
717-939-2008
www.ilovecrabs.com

Walleye
Red Lake Nation Foods, Inc.
19050 Highway 1 East
Redby, MN 56670
218-679-3513
www.redlakewalleye.com

Wild Catfish
Wild Ocean Seafood Market
688 South Park Avenue
Titusville, Florida 32796
321-269-1116
www.wildoceanmarket.com

Yellowfin Tuna
Honolulu Fish Company
808-833-1123
www.honolulufish.com

POULTRY

Free-Range Chicken
Pitman Farms
www.maryschickens.com

Guinea Hen
D'Artagnan, Inc.
800-327-8246
www.dartagnan.com

Quail
Diamond H Ranch
1598 Highland Drive
Bandera, TX 78003
830-796-4540
www.diamondhquail.com

Rock Cornish Game Hen
Eberly Poultry, Inc.
717-336-6440
www.eberlypoultry.com

Smoked Turkey
Greenberg Smoked Turkeys, Inc.
903-595-0725
www.gobblegobble.com

Turducken
Hebert's Specialty Meats
2101 East 71st Street
Tulsa, OK 74136
866-298-8400
www.hebertsmeats.com

Turkey
STAR Farm
270-528-1758
www.bourbonredturkey.com

Wild Turkey
D'Artagnan, Inc.
800-327-8246
www.dartagnan.com

MEAT

Alligator
Gatorama
863-675-0623
www.gatorama.com

Andouille
Jacob's World Famous Andouille
505 West Airline Highway
LaPlace, LA 70068
877-215-7589
www.cajunsausage.com

Bacon
Nueske's Applewood
Smoked Meats
203 North Genesee Street
Wittenberg, WI 54499
800-392-2266
www.nueskes.com

Beef Bacon
Menefee Ranches, LLC
www.popsgrassfedbeef.org

Beef Jerky
Woody's Smokehouse
903-536-9663
www.woodys-smokehouse.com

Bison
Wild Idea Buffalo Company
866-658-6137
www.wildideabuffalo.com

Boudin
Rabideaux's Sausage Kitchen, Inc.
105 Highway 165
Iowa, LA 70647
337-513-4442
www.rabideauxssausagekitchen.com

Bratwurst
Dewig Bros. Packing Co., Inc.
100 Maple Street
Haubstadt, IN 47639
812-768-6208
www.dewigmeats.com

Breakfast Sausage
Jones Dairy Farm
920-563-2432
www.jonesdairyfarm.com

Chorizo
El Popular
219-397-3728
www.elpopularchorizo.com

Cincinnati Chili
Skyline Chili, Inc.
www.skylinechili.com

Country Ham
Benton's Smoky Mountain
Country Hams
2603 Highway 411 North
Madisonville, TN 37354
423-442-5003
www.bentonscountryhams2.com

Goetta
Glier's Goetta Company
859-291-1800
www.goetta.com

Grass-Fed Beef
Hearst Corporation
866-547-2624
www.hearstranch.com

Hot Dogs
Liehs & Steigerwald
1857 Grant Boulevard
Syracuse, NY 13208
315-474-2171
www.liehsandsteigerwald.com

Liverwurst
Weeping Radish Farm Brewery
6810 Caratoke Highway
Grandy, NC 27947
252-491-5205
www.weepingradish.com

Pastrami
Greenblatt's Deli–Restaurant
8017 Sunset Boulevard
Hollywood, CA 90046
323-656-0606
www.greenblattsdeli.com

Pepperoni
Vermont Smoke and Cure
802-482-4666
www.vtsmokeandcure.com

Ponce
Poché's Market and Restaurant
3015 Main Highway
Breaux Bridge, LA 70517
337-332-2108
www.poches.com

Rabbit
The Rare Hare Barn, LLC
316-259-4262
www.rareharebarn.com

Smoked Beef Tongue
Café Rouge
1782 Fourth Street
Berkeley, CA 94710
510-525-1440
www.caferouge.net

Summer Sausage
Nodine's Smokehouse
Route 53, 39 North Street
Gochen, CT 06756
860-491-4009
www.nodinesmokehouse.com

Surryano Ham
S. Wallace Edwards &
Sons, Inc.
888-901-4267
www.surryfarms.com

Tasso
Manda Fine Meats
225-344-7636
www.mandafinemeats.com

Texas Chili
ConAgra Foods, Inc.
www.wolfbrandchili.com

Texas Hot Links
Kreuz Market
619 North Colorado Street
Lockhart, TX 78644
512-398-2361
www.kreuzmarket.com

Smitty's Market
208 South Commerce
Lockhart, Texas 78644
512-398-9344
www.smittysmarket.com

Venison
Broken Arrow Ranch, Inc.
800-962-4263
www.brokenarrowranch.com

Wagyu Beef
Morgan Ranch, Inc.
308-346-4394
www.morganranchinc.com

FRUITS & VEGETABLES

Asparagus
Arnett Enterprises, LLC
209-677-7327
www.misterspear.com

Avocado
Aguajitos Ranch, Inc.
805-968-2772
www.aguajitosinc.com

Beefsteak Tomatoes (seeds)
W. Atlee Burpee & Co.
800-888-1447
www.burpee.com

Canned Tomatoes
Muir Glen
800-624-4123
www.muirglen.com

Cherries
Orchard View Farms, Inc.
4055 Skyline Road
The Dalles, OR 97058
541-298-4496
www.orchardviewfarms.com

Chimayo Chiles
El Potrero Trading Post
17A Santuario Road
Chimayo, NM 87522
505-351-4112
www.potrerotradingpost.com

Chipotles
Tierra Vegetables
651 Airport Boulevard
Santa Rosa, CA 95407
707-837-8366
www.tierravegetables.com

Collard Greens
McCall Farms, Inc.
www.gloryfoods.com

Cowpeas
Plumfield Plantation, Inc.
843-395-8058
www.carolinaplantationrice.com

Cranberries
Willows Cranberries
508-295-9990
www.willowscranberries.com

Dates
Brown Date Garden
760-397-4309
www.browndategarden.com

Fiddlehead Ferns
Earthy Delights
517-668-2402
www.earthy.com

Golden Russet Apples
North Star Orchard
www.northstarorchard.com

Hatch Chiles
Hatch Chile Express
575-267-3226
www.hatch-chile.com

Heirloom Potatoes
Wood Prairie Farm
800-829-9765
www.woodprairie.com

Lima Beans
The Pictsweet Company
731-663-7600
www.pictsweet.com

Mangoes
Erickson Farm, Inc.
561-924-7714
www.ericksonfarm.com

Marionberries
Oregon Hill Farms
32861 Pittsburg Road
St. Helens, Oregon 97051
503-397-2791
www.oregonhill.com

Meyer Lemons
Snow's Citrus Court
916-663-1884
www.snowscitrus.com

Okra Pickles
Talk o' Texas Brands, Inc.
800-749-6572
www.talkotexas.com

Pawpaws
Edible Landscaping
361 Spirit Ridge Lane
Afton, VA 22920
434-361-9134
www.ediblelandscaping.com

Peaches
Frog Hollow Farm
925-634-2845
www.froghollow.com

Persimmons
Seeds and Such, Inc.
1105 R Street
Bedford, IN 47421
888-321-9445
www.persimmonpleasures.com

Pinquito Beans
Susie Q's Brand
805-937-2402
www.susieqbrand.com

Pixie Tangerines
Ojai Pixie Tangerines
www.ojaipixies.com

Prunes
Bowyer Farms
503-868-7526
www.bowyerfarms.com

Ramps
Ramp Farm Specialties
304-846-4235
www.rampfarm.com

Ruby Red Grapefruit
Red Cooper
800-825-8531
www.redcooper.com

Smoke-dried Tomatoes
Boggy Creek Farm
512-926-4650
www.boggycreekfarm.com

Softneck Garlic
Gourmet Garlic Gardens
325-348-3049
www.gourmetgarlicgardens.com

Sun Gold Tomatoes (seeds)
W. Atlee Burpee & Co.
800-888-1447
www.burpee.com

Sweet Onions
Locati Farms, Inc.
509-525-0286
www.locatifarms.com

Tangelos
Svrlinga Groves
863-670-6963
www.florida-citrus.com

Taro
Maui Direct
808-661-1457
www.mauidirect.com

Watermelon
Victory Seeds Company
503-829-3126
www.victoryseeds.com

White Asparagus
Metzger Specialty Brands, Inc.
866-972-6879
www.tillenfarms.com

White Nectarines
Blossom Bluff Orchards
www.shop.blossombluff.com

White Truffles
Earthy Delights
517-668-2402
www.earthy.com

CEREALS, GRAINS, & POWDERS

Breakfast Cereal
Post Holdings, Inc.
www.postfoods.com

Dried Corn
Hanover Foods Corp.
717-632-6000
www.johncopes.com

Filé Powder
Uncle Bill's Spices
225-937-8527
www.unclebillspice.com

Flour
Stafford County Flour Mills Co.
800-530-5640
www.hudsoncream.com

Granola
CC Made
www.cafefanny.com

Kellogg Company
866-374-4442
www.bearnaked.com

Grits
Anson Mills
803-467-4122
www.ansonmills.com

Hominy
Rancho Gordo, Inc.
707-259-1935
www.ranchogordo.com

Mississippi Tamales
Fat Mama's Tamales
303 South Canal Street
Natchez, MS 39120
601-442-4548
www.fatmamastamales.com

Rice
Plumfield Plantation, Inc.
843-395-8058
www.carolinaplantationrice.com

Wild Rice
Moose Lake Wild Rice
218-246-2159
www.mooselakewildrice.com

DESSERTS & CONFECTIONS

Almond Toffee
Enstrom Candies, Inc.
701 Colorado Avenue
Grand Junction, CO 81501
800-367-8766
www.enstrom.com

Apple and Apricot Candies
Liberty Orchards Co., Inc.
117 Mission Avenue
Cashmere, WA 98815
509-782-2191
www.libertyorchards.com

Benne Wafers
Byrd Cookie Company
912-355-1716
www.byrdcookiecompany.com

Butter Mints
The Warrell Corporation
www.warrellcorp.com

Candy Bar
Mars, Inc.
www.snickers.com

Candy Corn
Ferrara Candy Company
www.ferrarausa.com/brachs

Caramel Corn
PepsiCo, Inc.
www.fritolay.com

Caramels
Knudsen's Caramels
219 West 3rd Street
Red Wing, MN 55066
651-385-0800

Chocolate Bar
The Hershey Company
www.hersheys.com

Chocolate Cluster
Standard Candy Co.
www.googoo.com

Chocolate Marshmallow Cookie
Chattanooga Bakery, Inc.
800-251-3404
www.moonpie.com

Chocolate Mice
L. A. Burdick Chocolate
47 Main Street
Walpole, NH 03608
603-756-2882
www.burdickchocolate.com

Chocolate Truffles
Norman Love Confections
11380 Lindbergh Boulevard
Fort Myers, FL 33913
239-561-7215
www.normanloveconfections.com

Dulce de Leche Ice Cream
General Mills, Inc.
800-767-0120
www.haagendazs.com

Gooey Butter Cake
Gooey Louie
6483 Chippewa
St. Louis, MO 63109
314-352-2253
www.gooeylouiecake.com

Honeycomb
Savannah Bee Company
104 West Broughton Street
Savannah, GA 31401
912-233-7873
www.savannahbee.com

Hot Fudge Sauce
Lawry's Foods, LLC
100 North La Cienega Boulevard
Beverly Hills, CA 90211
866-529-7971
www.ccbrowns.com

Jelly Beans
Jelly Belly Candy Company
800-522-3267
www.jellybelly.com

Key Lime Pie
Randy's Fishmarket Restaurant, Inc.
10395 Tamiami Trail North
Naples, FL 34108
239-593-5555
www.randysfishmarketrestaurant.com

Maple Sugar Candy
Coombs Family Farms
888-266-6271
www.coombsfamilyfarms.com

Marshmallows
Lemleys' Catering
812-372-9898
www.240sweet.com

Mint Chocolate
Tootsie Roll Industries, Inc.
773-838-3400
www.tootsie.com

New York Cheesecake
Two Little Red Hens Bakery
1652 Second Avenue
New York City, NY 10028
212-452-0476
www.twolittleredhens.com

Peanut Brittle
Good Earth Peanut Company
5334 Skippers Road
Skippers, VA 23879
800-643-1695
www.goodearthpeanuts.com

Peppermint Stick Ice Cream
Graeter's, Inc.
2704 Erie Avenue
Cincinnati, OH 45208
800-721-3323
www.graeters.com

Pralines
Aunt Sally's Praline Shops, Inc.
810 Decatur Street
New Orleans, LA 70116
504-944-6090
www.auntsallys.com

Red Velvet Cake
Very Vera, Inc.
3113 Washington Road
Augusta, GA 30907
706-860-3492
www.veryvera.com

Salt Water Taffy
Dairy Maid Confectionery Company
9th and Boadwalk
Ocean City, NJ 08226
609-399-0100
www.shrivers.com

"Turkey" Candy
Nora's Candy Shop
321 North Doxtator Street
Rome, NY 13440
315-337-4530
www.turkeyjoints.com

Whoopie Pie
Coco Love Homemade, LLC
www.cocolovehomemade.com

Cranberry Island Kitchen
52 Danforth Street
Portland, ME 04101
207-774-7110
www.cranberryislandkitchen.com

The Friars' Bakehouse
21 Central Street
Bangor, ME 04401
207-947-3770

CONDIMENTS

Barbecue Sauce
Herbadashery Shoppe &
Garden, LLC
123 South Fenway
Casper, WY 82601
307-265-0036
www.herbadashery.com

Beach Plum Jelly
Cold Hollow Cider Mill
800-327-7537
www.coldhollow.com

Boiled Cider
Wood's Cider Mill
802-263-5547
www.woodscidermill.com

Bread and Butter Pickles
First Place Foods, LLC
972-272-1111
www.firstplacefoods.com

Caesar Dressing
Lancaster Colony Corporation
800-999-183
www.marzetti.com

Cashew Butter
Magee's House of Nuts
323-938-4127
www.mageesnuts.com

Conserves
June Taylor Company, LLC
510-548-2236
www.junetaylorjams.com

Creamed Honey
Redwoods Monastery
707-986-7419
www.redwoodsabbey.org

Honey
Lavender Bee Farm
764 Chapman Lane
Petaluma, CA 94952
707-789-0554
www.lavenderbeefarm.com

Hot Sauce
McIlhenny Company
www.tabasco.com

Jalapeño Jelly
A. M. Braswell Jr. Food Co.
912-764-6191
www.braswells.com

Ketchup
H. J. Heinz Company
www.heinz.com

Maple Syrup
Monadnock Sugar House
603-876-3626
www.monadnocksugarhouse.com

Mayhaw Jelly
Hillside Orchard Farms, Inc.
800-262-9429
www.mayhawtree.com

Mayonnaise
C. F. Sauer Company
800-688-5676
www.dukesmayo.com

Miso
South River Miso Company, Inc.
888 Shelburne Falls Road
Conway, MA 01341
413-369-4057
www.southrivermiso.com

Mustard
Philippe The Original
1001 North Alameda Street
Los Angeles CA, 90012
213-628-3781
www.philippes.com

Olive Oil
McEvoy Ranch
1 Ferry Building, 16
San Francisco, CA 94111
866-617-6779
www.mcevoyranch.com

Orange Marmalade
Corti Brothers, Inc.
5810 Folsom Boulevard
Sacramento, CA 95819
916-736-3800
www.cortibros.biz

Peanut Butter
The J.M. Smucker Company
www.laurascudderspeanutbutter.
com

Pickled Ghost Peppers
Sour Puss Pickles
www.sourpusspickles.com

Ranch Dressing
The Clorox Company
www.hiddenvalley.com

Salsa
Sabra Dipping Co., LLC
760-757-2622
www.sbsalsa.com

Sea Salt
Maine Sea Salt Company
207-255-3310
www.maineseasalt.com

Seasoning Mix
McCormick & Company, Inc.
www.oldbay.com

Sorghum Syrup
Barry Farm Foods
419-741-0155
www.barryfarm.com

Spiedie Marinade
Rob Salamida Co.
800-545-5072
www.spiedie.com

Sriracha Sauce
Huy Fong Foods, Inc.
626-286-8328
www.huyfong.com

DRINKS

Apple Cider
Louisburg Cider Mill
14730 K68 Highway
Louisburg, Kansas 66053
913-837-5202
www.louisburgcidermill.com

Birch Beer
Boylan Bottling Company
800-289-7978
www.boylanbottling.com

Celery Tonic
Pepsi-Cola & National Brand
Beverages, Ltd.
856-665-6200

Coffee
Koa Coffee Plantation
866-562-5282
www.koacoffee.com

Cola
The Coca-Cola Company
www.coca-cola.com

Ginger Ale
Buffalo Rock Company
www.buffalorock.com

Root Beer
C-B Beverage Corp.
614-221-3606
www.frostop.com

Soft Drink
Dr Pepper Snapple Group
www.drpepper.com

Sparkling Cider

Golden Brand Bottling Co. Inc.
415-643-9900

S. Martinelli & Company
800-662-1868
www.martinellis.com

Tea
R.C. Bigelow, Inc.
6617 Maybank Highway
Wadmalaw Island, SC 29487
843-559-0383
www.charlestonteaplantation.com

INDEX

For Joe Gracey (1950–2011)
who wanted to taste it all

Phaidon Press Limited
Regent's Wharf,
All Saints Street
London N1 9PA

Phaidon Press Inc.
180 Varick Street,
New York, NY 10014

www.phaidon.com

First published 2013
© 2013 Phaidon Press Limited

ISBN 978 0 7148 6582 9

A CIP catalogue record for this book
is available from the British Library.

Commissioning Editor: Emilia Terragni
Project Editor: Sophie Hodgkin
Production Controller: Laurence Poos

Designed by Fraser Muggeridge studio
Illustrations by Joël Penkman

The publisher would like to thank
Joël Penkman for her commitment and
enthusiasm; all of the producers for their
time and assistance; and Sarah Boris,
Julia Hasting, Cheryl Lemmens, and
Emma Robertson for their contributions
to the book.

Printed in China